Praise for *Measuring Up*

"A beautiful, clear-eyed elegy to families. How the foundation is laid, how the structure is crafted, and, eventually, how all of us have to manage its collapse. Dan Robson's memoir is about sons and fathers. More than that, it's about the hard road that leads from being one to becoming the other."

—Cathal Kelly, author of *Boy Wonders*

"Dan Robson's book is a heart-wrenching portrait of grief. Anyone who has lost a parent will recognize it, know it intimately as you roll through the stages and finally come to the realization that a parent's ultimate gift to a child is showing them how to live."

—Tanya Talaga, bestselling author of
Seven Fallen Feathers

"Dan Robson skillfully constructs a monument to the legacy of his crafts-man father. It is a testament to the unbreakable bond between every father and son. It inspires each of us to a straighter plumb, a truer square, and a higher level."

—Murray Howe, bestselling author of
Nine Lessons I Learned from My Father

"Robson's reflection on male grief and vulnerability is as generous and courageous as the father whose ghost haunts this story."

—D.W. Wilson, author of
Once You Break a Knuckle and *Ballistics*

Also by Dan Robson

CHANGE UP
How to Make the Great Game of Baseball Even Better
(with Buck Martinez)

THE CRAZY GAME
How I Survived in the Crease and Beyond
(with Clint Malarchuk)

KILLER
My Life in Hockey
(with Doug Gilmour)

QUINN
The Life of a Hockey Legend

BOWER
A Legendary Life

The Voice in my Head

Books by Dana L. Davis

Tiffany Sly Lives Here Now
The Voice in My Head

To Kaitlyn. Listen to →

The Voice in ~~my~~ YOUR Head

DANA L. DAVIS

xoxo

ink
yard
press

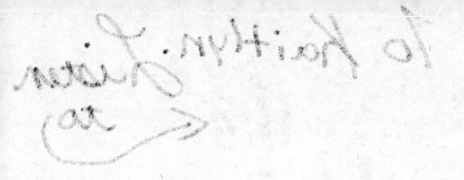

Recycling programs
for this product may
not exist in your area.

ISBN-13: 978-1-335-00849-7

The Voice in My Head

InkyardPress.com

Printed in U.S.A.

This book is all about family. So of course...I dedicate it to mine.
Mom, Dad, Shona, James, Mikey, Kiki and Cameron.
Love you guys.

And also...for Misty.

CHAPTER ONE

My hands tighten around rusted metal scaffolding as I pull myself up onto a pair of wooden planks near the rooftop of an old industrial warehouse. I pause to catch my breath, using one hand to wipe away tears turned into tiny crystals of ice, making the skin around my eyes sting. In the distance, glimmering city lights weave through streams of heavy falling rain. It's almost beautiful.

Climbing this high was the easy part. Buildings under construction always have something to grab on to. Now comes the real challenge. I take a deep breath and stand, attempting to steady my sneakers on the slippery slats of wood. I'm not wearing a hat, or gloves, or even a coat, which might seem odd considering it's December…in *Seattle*, but I don't need to be warm. At least not tonight, since tonight, I'm about to die. And people who are committing a mortal sin don't deserve to be warm.

I glance up. I'm only a couple of stories from the rooftop, but I can't climb any higher. Thin sheets of ice are forming on the wooden beams and my hands are bitterly cold. I peer over the edge and swallow. It's certainly a long way down. Perhaps this height will do.

I climb under the wobbly guardrail and reposition myself so that my feet are turned sideways and both arms are wrapped around the scaffolding. The way I'm standing isn't exactly ideal for a graceful, death-compliant leap. I'll have to jump at a slant, but once I'm airborne, I can shift my body and fall backward like a stuntwoman, screaming all the way down until...

My chest tightens at the thought. Will it hurt? Can I handle it? Should I reconsider? I heave a heavy sigh. Only, the sigh turns into a sequence of shivers that reach all the way to my internal organs, causing my heart to skip a beat.

I'm crying. Again. Now the city lights in the distance are blurring and twirling like a Van Gogh painting come to life. I'm also soaked. My thick black hair is both wet and icy and scratching my face like dead pine needles. And the wind is snapping my loose T-shirt in all imaginable directions, sending cold rain up my abdomen and chest, convincing me that if I don't die from this fall, surely I'll die tomorrow, from pneumonia. I think of my sister Violet. As if I think of anything else these days? Even though she's smarter, a little bit prettier, a whole lot nicer and in general...better, I've never been jealous. Instead, she's everything I aspire to be. She is my best friend. Or at least she was.

I squint up at the Seattle sky, covered with dense clouds,

and imagine God can see through the mass of darkness and sheets of heavy rainfall and is watching. Taking notes. Waiting for me to leap, so he can put me on the eternal naughty list and cast me away. I've often pondered: When people kill themselves, is there any part of them that wants to live? Now I know the answer. There is. At least for me. There *is* this tiny part of me that wants nothing more than to climb down this scaffolding, get my feet planted on solid ground and *live*. But then what would happen? My parents would still look through me, as if I didn't exist, the kids at school would still pity me, while simultaneously longing for Violet's return, and pain would continue to embody every part of me. Of course I want to live. But not like this.

"Help me, God..." My barely audible voice catches in my throat as a gust of wind slams into my chest, causing me to almost lose my balance. *Shit!* I attempt to stabilize, though ice has formed around the railing, burning the tips of my fingers. With each labored breath I take, I suck in cold air. It fills my lungs like a sledgehammer to the rib cage. Doesn't help that I'm full-on sobbing at this point. Perhaps it doesn't matter how I fall, just so long as it gets done. It's not like anyone cares if I die dramatically anyway. It's not like anyone cares if I live either. I am simply a sad reminder of the person who will be lost. A haunting reminder of Violet.

"Help me..." I sob. "Please, God, help me." My shoulders shake, both from the sobs and uncontrollable shivering. "I *beg* you."

I'm not exactly great at talking to God. This used to be one of Violet's strong points. We'd hold hands at night and she'd say all these eloquent prayers with words like *humbly* and *forth-with*. But when it was my turn, I'd mumble something like, *God, thanks for another day. Keep us safe. Amen.* Violet never criticized or tried to get me to be more like her. She'd only nod in full acceptance of my pitiful prayer and repeat *Amen.* This is the Violet way—one of many traits that makes it so easy to love her.

"God! If you can hear me," I cry out into the darkness. "I…beseech you!"

I don't know what that means. *Beseech?* I remember Violet said it once in prayer. Sounded a lot less like a brand of hard candies coming from her than it does from me.

"I…" I pause.

Who am I kidding? I got nothin'. Seriously *nothing* to plead to God right before I die. Besides, no matter what I say or do, tomorrow will come, and against the desperate pleas of our family, Violet will take a fatal dose of barbiturates prescribed by our very own family doctor. Ending a yearlong battle with a rare lung condition. There is no cure. The doctors try to comfort us. Reminding our family that Violet is terminal regardless. Let her go, they advise us. Though it's not as if we have a choice in the matter. Violet and I recently turned eighteen, and as a legal adult, she's decided she no longer wants to suffer. She's choosing "death with dignity." Exercising *her* right, to the right-to-die law. Well, it's my right, too. I wipe my nose with the back of my hand, puff out my aching chest and prepare to mimic my twin's bravery…die with dignity. A final moment of Earth glory. My very last fail.

I close my eyes and wipe at another frozen tear, that tiny

piece of me that wants to live gnawing at my innards, creeping to the surface, begging the question: *Why* am I up here sobbing? And why am I gripping this icy beam as if I really *don't* want to die? I suck air through my teeth as the realization settles within me. It's because I *don't* want to die. It's because I won't. Not on this night. Not when Violet still lives. It's because even though all hope is lost...I cling to it still.

"Help me," I whisper. "That's what I need, God. *Please.* Why won't you help me? Why won't you help *her*?"

And the most bizarre thing transpires. A voice pierces through the noise of the pounding rain and answers back...

"Um... Why won't *you*?"

I twist my body, terrified to think someone could be standing right beside me. But the sudden movement causes both feet to slip off the planks.

I lose my grip and fall.

CHAPTER TWO

"Indigo, can you hear me?"

"Hmm?" I mumble sleepily. "That you, Mom?" I snuggle under thin covers. "I had the craziest dream."

"Did you dream you jumped off a building?" a deeper voice, which matches my dad's, replies.

I pop one eye open to see my parents' sullen faces as they stand beside a hospital bed. Correction—*my* hospital bed? They stare at me. I stare at them. They stare at me some more.

"How are you feeling?" Dad asks with a raised eyebrow.

"Pain," I grumble, since pain *is* what I'm feeling. Like extreme physical *pain*. My head is pounding as if my skull needs to expand to make more room for my brain, and my arm feels odd. I look down. A cast? Holy hell, I broke my arm. And my legs? I can't feel them! "Am I paralyzed?" I choke.

"With stupidity."

I turn. My brother, Alfred, leans up against the wall on the other side of the room, eyes down, fiddling with his phone.

He goes on, "Paralyzed with extreme stupidity."

I wiggle my toes. Okay, I'm not paralyzed.

"Indigo, what were you thinking?" Mom wails. I know this is not a rhetorical question. Mom will literally wait, glaring at you, *daring* you not to answer one of her infamous non-rhetorical rhetorical questions.

"I'm not sure what I was thinking, Mom." But that's not the truth. I don't remember everything. But one thing *is* clear. Yesterday I wanted to die. Like Violet. *With* Violet.

"Oh, you're not sure?" Mom's silver hair is pulled into a tight bun at the back of her head, accentuating the angry veins pulsing around her hairline. "And without a *coat*? You realize you could've caught *pneumonia*!"

Surprisingly, yes. I did realize that.

Dad crosses his arms across his chest. At sixty, Dad's hair should be silvery like Mom's, but he dyes it black. What's left of it, that is. "Helen. The girl jumped off a building and you're mad because she forgot her damn coat?"

Mom ignores Dad and continues, "You had hypothermia, dislocated your shoulder, broke your arm and have a grade-two concussion. You could've died!"

"Well, duh, Mom," Alfred pipes in. "Wasn't that the point?"

Mom snaps her fingers at Alfred. "You be quiet. Nobody's even talking to you." She cocks her head to one side as she speaks. "So that's what this is about? Death was your brilliant plan?! What exactly would that have solved?"

What would death have solved? It would've leveled the playing field. Righted a wrong...

"Indigo?" Mom snaps, interrupting my thoughts. "Do you hear me talking to you?"

Another nonrhetorical rhetorical. Must. Find. Answer.

"I do hear you, Mom." Wait… I'm starting to remember more details. I snuck out of the house… I was headed to catch the train…

"Your cell phone survived the fall." Alfred's still not looking up from his own phone. "The paramedics used your thumbprint to unlock it and dialed Mom."

Alfred's sixteen years old and attends a "twice-exceptional" high school for kids who struggle in a normal school setting, but nothing's really wrong with them…and they're super smart. Or…something like that. In truth, I don't know what a twice-exceptional high school is. All I know is that twice-exceptional schools welcome kids with learning disabilities, and Mom and Dad have had Alfred diagnosed with every learning disability known to mankind. And are probably currently writing letters to the president of the United States to have new labels invented so they can have him diagnosed with those as well. ADHD, dyslexia, dyscalculia (where your brain doesn't make sense of numbers), auditory processing disorder (where your brain doesn't make sense of speech) and, my personal favorite, distractibiliphilia. I imagine that's where your brain sends signals to your hands to never put your phone down.

"I can't believe you, Indigo!" Mom cries, tears brimming to the surface. "How could you be so selfish? Were you honestly trying to kill yourself?"

I was. Though, I still can't remember much about it. Okay, I took the train and…

"Are they gonna put her on a 5150 hold?" Alfred yawns, slides his phone into his back pocket and flips his lime-green Seahawks cap forward.

"I'm not crazy," I snap, struggling to force the details to the surface. When I got off the train it was cold… I walked to the Amgen campus… I crossed a bridge…

"Indi. No offense…" Alfred starts many sentences with *no offense* followed by something intensely offensive. I wait for it. "You jumped off a building in a random, nondescript industrial zone. You're batshit."

"Watch your language, boy!" Dad bellows, as the brown skin on the bald portion of his head shines under the fluorescent lighting in the hospital room.

"I didn't jump! I fell." Technically, that's not a lie. Obviously I fell. But did I jump? Was I brave enough to actually *do* that?

"You were climbing for fun?" Mom asks.

"Helen, why on God's green Earth would she be climbing a building, in the freezing rain, at 11:00 p.m., for fun?"

Mom shrugs in response to Dad's question. "I don't know, *Isaiah*. I see people climbing buildings all the time."

Alfred chimes in, "Construction workers don't really count."

Mom frowns. "I meant on TV."

"Oh." Alfred scratches his forehead. "Like…Spider-Man?"

"It was for Vee," I blurt. "She always wanted a photo of the Amgen bridge at night, in the rain." Of course I'm lying but continue, grabbing my phone from the side table for emphasis. It's dead, so all I see is my reflection in the glass. My eyes are black-and-blue, as if I got punched in the face more than a few times. My normally flawless light brown skin has all sorts of nicks, scrapes and contusions. And my long hair is matted to my head. *Yikes.*

"The Amgen pedestrian bridge?" Mom asks.

I nod and say softly, "I thought it might help somehow. I thought it might change her mind."

Violet is a student at a Big Picture high school. I mean, I go there too, but I think they let me in only because of Violet and the whole twin thing, since I don't exactly fit the Big Picture student profile: motivated, unique and prepared for career advancement. I'm more…unmotivated, common (the perfect antonym for *unique*) and interested in career advancement only if it means I get to stay glued to Violet's side for the rest of our live-long days. Anyway, at Big Picture high schools, students have internships and work closely with career mentors. Since Violet and I are aspiring photojournalists, last semester we were with Aaron Wade, one of *National Geographic*'s *top* photojournalists. Aaron always had us hiking and climbing to get good photos. So this lie of mine, of taking a photo at 11:00 p.m. from the top of an under-construction building, across from the Amgen campus and their beautiful helix-shaped pedestrian bridge, is an awesome one.

But, awesome lie aside, Mom is crying now. Dad places a hand on her shoulder while she fishes around in her purse for a tissue. I can't stand to see my mom cry, so I turn to face Alfred, who mouths, "You dumbass."

"Could you all please…?" I want to say *leave*, but I know that will never fly with my family. Mom would go into a rage that I dare disrespect her with such insolent language. Alfred would murmur one of his signature acronyms, like *L-O-L*. His never-ending attempt at making text-speech an actual way of speaking. Dad would bellow a patronizing, *Are you the one paying for this doctor bill? No? I didn't think so. Leave that!* Instead, I ask as politely as I can, "Could you all excuse me? I need to go to the bathroom." I add, "Number two." Just to make *sure* they all get out.

Mom blinks. "Do you need help?"

"Um..." I swing my legs around the side of the bed. A movement that reminds me every muscle, joint and bone hurts like hell. And the arm that's apparently broken, and encased within this itchy cast, also rests inside a sling. Not to mention my *other* arm is hooked up to an IV. "I think I do. Yeah."

"I'll go get the nurse." Mom grabs her purse off the chair beside the bed and pulls the straps over her shoulder. "Besides, I need to talk to a nurse anyway. I can't have the hospital thinking you're suicidal. They need to know you fell, *not* jumped. Right?"

I swallow, nod and mumble, "Right."

"Okay, good. I'm not gonna be dealing with Social Services or CPS or whatever they're calling it these days. I won't have it."

"Suicide is the second leading cause of death among teens *I-R-L*, Mom," Alfred states.

"Boy, stop with the acronyms," Dad retorts. "Nobody knows what *I-R-L* means."

"In real life?" Alfred smirks as if Dad not knowing what *I-R-L* means is the ultimate fail. "Multiple attempts are common. Maybe having her assessed isn't such a bad idea. They could give us some steps to follow at home. For prevention."

In rare moments, Alfred makes a lot of sense. However, these rare moments of Alfred genius are typically followed by our parents stating something like...

"Alfred, have you lost your damn mind?" Dad barks.

Yep. Something like that.

"I have a 'step' Indigo can follow," Mom adds, rage climbing like a shuttle launching off toward outer space. "Stop scaling buildings in the middle of the damn night! Alfred, stay here with your sister in case she needs anything. Dad and I are going to find the doctor."

"Actually, Alfred?" I want to say, *Can you get the hell out, too?* Instead I ask politely, "Could you grab me a cranberry juice from the cafeteria?"

Alfred shakes his head. "Call a nurse."

"Alfred!" Dad shouts. "Get your sister something to drink from the cafeteria. What is wrong with you?"

"Geez." Alfred pushes off the wall. "I'm going. Calm yourself. *B-R-B.*"

Mom's phone chimes. "It's Michelle." Her eyes widen. "It's almost four in the morning. Why would she be calling?"

"Not sure." Dad sounds worried. "Maybe she just wants to see if it's okay to tell Violet Indigo is in the hospital."

Since I'm older than Violet by two and a half minutes, I like to think of myself as big sis. But since Michelle is older than us both by fifteen years, she's the real big sister. She's also a chief nurse practitioner who has taken a leave of absence from her position at Mercy Hospital to be Violet's in-home caretaker.

Mom only stares at her ringing phone until Dad snatches it out of her hand. He slides his finger across the screen to answer it. "What's up, hon?"

Dad's expression is hard to read. He stands, listening, barely breathing.

"What is it?" Mom almost screams, covering her mouth with her trembling hands as Alfred moves to stand at her side.

Dad holds out a hand, a signal for quiet as he continues to listen to whatever my sister Michelle is saying to make his rich brown skin look somehow drained of color. "Thank you, hon," he chokes. "We'll get there as fast as we can. We'll get the okay to bring Indigo. Discharged against medical advice? Okay. I will ask." He hangs up.

"What?" Mom asks frantically. "What's wrong?"

"Almost an entire minute." Dad's eyes well with tears. "One minute where she couldn't breathe. Longest episode yet. Violet wants to take the medication. She's in a lot of pain. She's scared. She's ready to go."

"No!" Mom wails, flinging herself into Dad's arms. "God, *no*." She weeps onto Dad's chest. "We have to stop this, Isaiah." Her voice is pained and muffled. "We can hire a lawyer. Declare her incompetent to think on her own. We have to do something!"

Dad rubs Mom's back, lays his head on top of hers and whispers, "God, please help our baby. Please *help* her."

Help her?

My bare feet slam onto the cold tile of the hospital floor

as I stand. The cord to my IV pulls at my skin. Blood rushes to my head, intensifying my headache and making the room spin as the memories flood to the forefront of my mind:

The climb.

The freezing rain.

The conversation with God.

The...voice.

I *remember*. I remember it *all*.

"Indigo Phillips, what are you doing?" Dad takes a protective step toward me.

I place a hand on my forehead, as if doing that can make the room cease to spin and give me the strength I need to unhook from all these stupid wires, get out of this room and make it to Violet. To plead with her. Beg her to reconsider. Tell her about my miracle. I heard a *voice*. That's got to mean something, right? That'll make her change her mind and choose to stay.

Only, my plan of hospital escape doesn't get me too far, because my knees buckle, and just as I feel Dad's strong arms wrap around my waist, everything goes dark.

CHAPTER THREE

I feel a light. And the light is glowing. It's a bright light. So warm. So comforting.

"God?" I moan.

"Yes, my child."

I open my eyes. A middle-aged doctor is sitting on a stool beside the bed, shining a tiny flashlight into my eyes. "Kidding." He grins. "Eyes wide for me?"

I stretch out my eyes. He points the beam directly into each of my eyeballs. I blink a few times. "Where's my family?"

He pockets the flashlight. I see him clearly now. Prominent nose, strawberry-blond hair graying at the temples, hazel eyes highlighted by the hospital room fluorescent lighting. "I'm sure they're around here somewhere. Where specifically?" He leans back and takes a peek under the bed. "I can tell you this. They're *not* hiding under the bed." He winks, pleased with his lame joke.

"Listen. I actually need to leave. I mean, I have to go. To get to my sister. It's extremely important."

"Duly noted. Hey, quick question before you take off. Do you know where you are?"

"You mean like the name of the hospital?"

"General location. Name of our planet. Galaxy."

"Seattle, Washington. Planet Earth. The Milky Way."

"Nice. Wow. Impressive." He cracks his knuckles. "Now for the tough questions. How many fingers am I holding up?"

He holds up two fingers on each hand.

"Four. Doctor, listen—"

"What's the last thing you remember?"

Hearing a voice in my head? "I slipped. I fell. I don't remember falling, though. The next thing I remember is waking up here."

"Any particular reason you were climbing a building in twenty-eight-degree weather, during a storm, without a—"

"Coat? I didn't want it getting in the way of my climb."

"Helmet. I was gonna say, without a helmet."

We're interrupted by a knock at the door; a blonde nurse peeks her head into the room. "Dr. Doheny, may I speak with you privately? It'll only take a minute."

He stands. "Be right back."

"Can I go to the bathroom?"

"Are you feeling dizzy?"

Yes, very. "No."

He removes the IV cord from the chunk of plastic protruding from my arm, freeing me from the bag of hanging saline, then quietly slips outside the door.

I stand, *slowly* this time, and shuffle toward the bathroom. Once inside, I click the door shut, careful not to make noise, as I'm suddenly aware noise intensifies the pain in my head. I step toward the sink and stare at my reflection in the mirror. I'm like a warrior returned home from battle. The skin under both of my brown eyes is purple. My bottom lip is split down the center and swollen, making it appear twice its normal size. My hair—well, it's a disaster, quite frankly. I stick a hand under the faucet, activating a stream of cold water that I graciously splash onto my face. The cool liquid seeps into the scrapes on my skin and stings. I wince.

"Hey. Remember me? I'm still here." A voice echoes in the sterile bathroom.

I back away from the mirror and slam against the door, covering my ear with my hand. Schizophrenia. That's what it's called when you hear voices in your head. Right? I don't want to add a mental illness with a name to my list of problems. I don't want this *voice*.

I glance up at the vents in the restroom. What if it's an actual person? Stalking me? "Who's there?" I turn toward the shower. Someone could be playing a terrible trick. A twisted game. They could've followed me to the building last night. Could somehow be *here* in the hospital. I reach out and yank back the curtain, revealing an empty stall.

"Hiding behind a shower curtain? How weird would that be?"

I spin around fast and stumble, yelping as I jerk the curtain off the rod. Crying out as my injured shoulder slams onto the floor of the shower stall.

"Indigo?"

Oh *no*. It's Michelle.

"Indi, are you okay?" she calls out.

No. "Yeah. I'm okay!"

I twist, struggling to put my weight on my uninjured arm so I can push myself off the floor. Only I'm wrapped in five feet of shower curtain. I hear the bathroom door creak open, followed by a loud gasp as Michelle rushes toward me, cautiously unraveling me from the cloth.

"Indigo?" She helps me to my feet. "I'm gone for a few minutes and this happens? What are you *doing*?"

"How's Violet? She didn't take the medicine yet, did she?"

"Do you really think she's that selfish? Of course she didn't take it yet! She's waiting for you!"

"She said that? She mentioned me?"

Michelle dramatically rolls her eyes and guides me out of the bathroom. I carefully crawl back into bed.

"Is she asking for me? Is she worried about what happened? Did you tell her I was okay? That I fell? That it was an accident?"

Michelle takes a seat on a chair across from my bed. Her black jeans and long-sleeved white T-shirt are wrinkled, eyes bloodshot. Her ebony shoulder-length straightened hair hangs limp and lifeless, while her face is scrubbed free of any trace of makeup. My older sister is thirty-three and married to a video game developer named Drew Delacroix. Drew's not so bad; in fact, I feel kinda sorry for the guy, what with having to put up with her on a minute-by-minute basis. My gripe is with their two terrible kids. Not to mention the future demon seed that's on the way.

"Indigo, Vee's not thinking about this madness you've created. It's your fault she can't pass right now the way she wants to."

"You act like you want her to kill herself."

"This isn't suicide. She's dying with dignity. It's the law…" She trails off, shakes her head. "Imagine trying to breathe underwater, Indi. That's what it feels like for her. She doesn't want to suffer anymore. I don't blame her."

"But God can save her. She just has to give him time."

"Sadly—" Michelle rubs her temples "—we're all outta time."

"No we're not. Violet can *live*. I promise you she can. You can help her."

I squeeze my eyes shut and lower my head, covering one ear with my hand. The stupid voice. It's *back*.

"What's with the covering of your ear? Why are you all hunkered down like a bomb's about to explode?"

"My ears are ringing, that's all."

She shrugs. "Ringing in your ears is normal. You have a concussion. *Stop*."

I look up. "Stop what?"

"Stop actin' like this! Stop being weird. Stop covering your ears. Stop jumping off buildings."

"I didn't jump. I fell."

"I don't believe you, Indigo. In fact, you know what I really think?" Her eyes narrow. "I think you climbed that building to kill your fool self. Chickened out and then fell somehow."

I blink. She's good. I can't think of a clever enough retort, so I toss out the classic, "Whatever," and shrug.

"We need to get you released so we can get back home. You're driving Mom and Dad nuts."

Michelle has a lot of nerve saying such a thing to me. If anybody's driving Mom and Dad nuts, it's her. From the constant wake-ups in the middle of the night with pointless updates about Violet's condition, to daily complaints about her soon-to-be juvenile delinquent boys, to her all-around rotten attitude and total lack of self-restraint and decorum. She's the underlying strife that keeps our family on the brink of insanity.

The door is pushed open and the doctor steps back into the room. "Sorry about that. No more interruptions." He notices Michelle. "Good morning. I'm Dr. Doheny. I'm the surgeon who operated on Indigo's arm. It was a pretty bad fracture. But she'll be good as new in no time. You're her mother?"

Michelle plasters a fake smile across her face. I'm certain it's a fake smile because Michelle *hates* when people think she's my mother. Even though, age-wise, she certainly could be. "No teenagers yet, thank *God*." She places a hand over her tiny baby bump, a strategic move meant to emphasize youth.

As a nurse practitioner, Michelle tends to despise doctors, referring to them as overpaid medical assistants. She also loathes being outranked, so any opportunity she has to throw around her nursing credentials and expertise, she takes.

"I'm the *sister*. Michelle Delacroix, NP. I imagine you've ordered an MRI?"

"She's had a CAT scan. It was normal."

"Well, I found her on the bathroom floor *and* she fainted earlier when my parents were here. I'm surprised scheduling an MRI's been overlooked. An oversight like this would never happen at the hospital I work at."

Not surprisingly, the doctor seems troubled by my sister's ice-cold persona. "I came in on my morning off specifically to check on Indigo. That being said, I didn't know about the fainting. Nor the recent fall. I can order an MRI, if you feel it's necessary."

"*I* do." Michelle raises both hands high. Like Dr. Doheny is holding a gun and she's lifting her arms in surrender. "But *you're* the doctor. So..." She leaves that *so* hanging in the air. Michelle ends a lot of sentences with *so*... It can mean many things, depending on the situation. In this case, I'm guessing it means, *Doctor, you're an incompetent fool.*

"I'll put the order in myself," he replies curtly.

"Oh wonderful," Michelle says with overexaggerated enthusiasm. "I think that's a wise move."

He scowls and grunts some unintelligible response.

"Also, we need to have Indigo discharged against medical advice. Our sister is ill and about to pass. We'd like Indigo home so our entire family can be there to say goodbye. It's somewhat urgent. She can return for the MRI."

"Very sorry to hear that." Dr. Doheny massages his chin. "But my medical advice is Indigo stay under observation for at least twenty-four hours."

Michelle smiles and replies, "That's why they call it *against* medical advice."

He scoffs. "You know, I'm surprised, what with you being

in the medical field, that you'd insist on something so incredibly dangerous."

"I'm surprised that you're surprised." Michelle places a hand on her hip and a tense moment of silence passes between the two.

"If you insist on such reckless action, may I at least finish my exam?" Without waiting for an answer, he repositions himself on the stool beside my bed. Michelle hovers, arms crossed, looking over the doctor's shoulder.

I lean my head back against the pillow. I want to say, *My bad about her. Nobody likes her except my parents.* Instead I mumble, "I was trying to take a picture of the Amgen pedestrian bridge with my phone."

"I'm sorry?" he replies.

"Before you left, you asked why was I climbing. That's why."

"I see." He drums his fingers on his knee. "Then perhaps you fell when you realized that the Amgen pedestrian bridge is east of that particular building and not visible from where you were?"

Uh-oh. I swallow. "Yeah. That's...basically what happened."

Thankfully Dr. Doheny doesn't drill in the point that I'm the world's worst liar. He moves on, unhooking my sling and carefully holding my casted arm. "Can you wiggle your fingers for me?"

I do it.

"Good. And how does that feel?"

"Fine." I'm lying again. It hurts. I rub my forehead with my free hand and feel a cut, rough under my fingertips.

"You'll be tempted not to wear the sling." He squeezes the palm of my hand. "But the nerves around your shoulder joint were badly damaged in the fall. The sling is essential." Now he's pushing my hand back. What is he, a masochist? I grind my teeth to prevent screaming out in pain. "How's that feel, Indigo?"

How do you think it feels, genius?

"No numbness or tingling?" he asks calmly. "How's the pain level?"

"Everything feels *great*." More lies. But if I admit I'm numb, tingly and hurting like I've landed in the seventh circle of hell, can I still be discharged against medicine's advocacy, or whatever Michelle said? "Since I'm feeling so amazing, that means I get to go, right?"

"Indigo, you're being released against medical advice." Michelle sighs, exasperated. "You could be howling in pain and it wouldn't matter."

I sit up. "Right. Sorry."

"Excuse me?" Dr. Doheny turns to Michelle. "Any chance you'd mind waiting in the reception area?"

I gulp. Dr. Doheny has *no* idea who he's messing with.

Michelle takes a seat on the couch. Carefully crosses her legs. "Actually, I do mind."

"Then perhaps you can keep your comments to yourself? I'm not used to being observed, assisted *or* interrupted."

Michelle shrugs innocently. "As a doctor constantly surrounded by nursing staff? I imagine you would be used to being interrupted, observed *and* assisted. In every way."

Uh-oh. Game *on*.

"As chief of staff—" Dr. Doheny places my arm back inside its sling and gently Velcros the straps in place "—I'm rarely interrupted, only observed when I ask to be and assisted only when needed."

Chief of staff? Like, the boss of the whole hospital? Dang! My gaze darts to Michelle. How do you clapback to *that*? She swallows, clears her throat and, for the first time in maybe her whole life, accepts being one-upped.

Chief of staff for the win!

Dr. Doheny stands. "I can get those AMA papers signed for you now. Sound good?"

Michelle nods without making eye contact. Dr. Doheny smiles and exits the room. The door slams shut with a reverberating thud.

"See that?" Michelle points at the door.

"See what?"

"What do you mean, see what? You saw how he talked to me. We nurses get verbally abused by doctors all the time. I'm so sorry you had to witness that, Indigo."

"I'm sorry *I* had to witness that."

Shit, shit, shit! I cover my ear with my hand again.

"Are we back to this?" Michelle stretches her eyes wide.

"Covering your ears like that is kinda odd. You should consider stopping."

My brand-new, fresh-out-of-the-box bag of insanity is

talking to me again. If I acknowledge it, will it go away? Like, *Hello, Voice? How are you today?*

"Not too shabby. Thank you for asking."

Oh my God! "Michelle, do you hear this?" I gasp. "I mean, did you just hear that?"

"Did I hear what?"

"A *voice.*"

Her eyes narrow as she slowly stands. "You're hearing voices?"

"Not voices. A voice. One *voice.*"

"Indi, are you serious? What does the voice sound like?"

I pause, thinking. "A little bit like Dave Chappelle."

"Dave Chappelle?" Michelle folds her arms across her chest. "That's why you've been covering your ears? To block out the voice of *Dave Chappelle*? First we try to kill ourselves and now we're tuned in to Comedy Central!? What's next, Indigo?"

"Michelle, it's not—"

"No, I get it. You're trying to pretend you're losin' it. This is your sad attempt to stop Violet from dying. You do realize she's dying regardless, right? Dave Chappelle in your head or not."

"It's not actually Dave Chappelle. It sounds like him. I'm not making it up! I'm hearing a voice. I swear to God!"

"You shouldn't be swearing to me. That's somewhat taboo. Uncouth. Uncivilized. Rude—"

"Shut up!" I scream. "Shut up, shut up, shut *up*!"

"Wow." Michelle shakes her head and, with what seems like overexaggerated, condescending calm, says, "Indigo. I'm going to see if the AMA papers are ready. When I return, you better be dressed and not on the bathroom floor or doing something bizarre like talking to Kevin Hart. Okay?" She snatches her purse off a chair near my bed and quickly exits.

"I like her."

I slide off the bed, feeling beads of sweat form around my hairline. "You're not real," I whisper. "This isn't real."

"What isn't real?"

"You!" I've officially gone full volume. Screaming out into an empty hospital room. "I reject you, Voice! In the name of Jesus, I reject you!"

"What does *that* mean?"

I take tiny steps backward until I find myself pressed against the wall in a corner of the room. "I guess it means like…I'm using the power of Jesus to declare the voice I'm hearing isn't real? You're not real."

"Ahhh. I get it. I mean, I don't *get* it. But I see what you're trying to say. So now it's my turn. I reject your declaration and declare instead that I *am* real. In the name of all things with a name. Including Geez luss."

"Geez luss?"

"There's this cool little second-grader dude. Lives in south Georgia. Always prays in the name of 'Geez luss.' You know…little kid accent, 'cuz he's missing about eight teeth. Has no clue what he's even talking about. I kinda like it, so I'm runnin' with it."

I frown. "I'm sorry. What is this? Why is this happening to me?"

"What do you mean, why? You asked for me. You called on me. People would kill to talk to me like

this. To hear my voice. Geez luss, Indigo! Be more grateful.”

I push myself off the wall. “Okay. Let me get this straight. Are you really trying to say that you’re God? This is the voice of *God* I’m hearing?”

“I’m not a big fan of the name. Honestly, I’m not. There are other names I tend to take more of a liking to. Like Emmanuel, the Most High, Yahweh. Lord is…eh…not my favorite either. I like Elohim. That’s got a nice ring to it. El for short. Elly.”

This is insane. I am *losing* it. That’s what’s happening here. Like the homeless man shouting on the street. That’s me. Talking in a room. To *nobody*.

“Okay, fine. I can prove I’m God so you can stop self-deprecating. Ask me anything.”

I take a seat on the edge of the bed and grab my phone from off the stand. “Ask you anything? Like…quiz God?”

“Yeah, yeah. Ask me.”

“Okay. What’s 742 times 988?”

The voice laughs. Really. It’s laughing.

“That’s what you want to know? A smorgasbord of information is now available to you and you want to know *that*?”

“You’re stalling, Voice,” I state simply. “What’s the answer?”

“Turn on your phone.”

“Why? It’s dead.”

“Jack the Ripper is dead. Your phone, on the other hand, is turned off.”

"But…" I look at my phone and press the button to power it on. Sure enough, the screen brightens as it springs to life. Why did I think it was dead? Now I'm transfixed. Staring at the screen, eager to see how many calls I've missed. How many red notifications will be waiting for me from Violet? Perhaps the thought of losing me has jolted her back to life. Reminded her of the connection we once had. The bond that, before scarring lung tissue took center stage in our lives, was unbreakable. Only there are no red icons that await me. No missed calls. No messages. I swallow away the lump starting to form in my throat.

"Hello? Is this thing on? 733,096."

"What?" I'm compelled to look at the ceiling. As if that's where this voice is currently residing.

"You asked what's 742 times 988. It's 733,096. Your phone's on now. Fact-check me on Google."

"Is that right?"

"This is *boring*. Challenge me. I'm Almighty God, for crying out loud. I can do basic math. Ask me something cool, like who built the pyramids."

"Fine." I set my cell beside me on the bed and ask, with very little enthusiasm, "Who built the pyramids?"

"The Egyptians."

I roll my eyes. "A five-year-old could tell me that. I thought you were gonna say aliens or something."

"First of all, have you talked to a five-year-old lately? Trust me. They know nothing about the pyramids. Second, what makes somebody an alien?"

"They're from outer space."

34

"This is outer space."

"You know what I mean. I'm an Earthling. Any living thing not from Earth is an alien."

"Then I shalt correct my original answer. Egyptian *Earthlings* built the pyramids."

I lean back on my uninjured arm as a thought occurs to me. "I have a better question. If you're who you say you are, if you really are God, why won't you let my sister live? She hasn't done anything to anybody. If you really are God, then you're well aware that Violet's been talking to you her whole life. Lavishing you with words like 'omnipotent' and 'Mighty King.' She literally worships you. And now she's…" I quiet for a moment, eager to compose myself. Talking to a voice is one thing. But crying to one? Not gonna happen. I exhale. "You're all-powerful. Right?"

"Tru dat. Tru dat."

"Why won't you let her live?" I whisper.

No response.

I wait. "*God?* You got nothing to say to that, do you?" I hold up my middle finger and stick out my tongue, grateful the voice-in-my-head-madness is over.

I see a duffel bag on the couch, move toward it and reach inside to find a change of clothes from home, toiletries and hair supplies. I slip out of my hospital gown and struggle into an oversize, long-sleeved T-shirt. It's tough with only one properly working arm, but I manage, though I can't stick my cast through the sleeve, so it sorta hangs limply at my left side. I step easily into my sweatpants and slip on brown Uggs, then take the brush Mom packed and awkwardly force it through my hair. I don't need to see my reflection to know I need more than a brush. I need a *hat*. I collapse onto the couch and lower my head into my hand.

"Here's the thing. She can live. But only if you help. Think you can do that?"

"Voice?" I moan. "I thought I got rid of you."

"You were about to get dressed. I wanted to give you privacy. Duh."

"God would never say *duh*, Voice."

"I invented language. I can say whatever I want. Who's gonna criticize my speech? I'm sorta unim-peachable."

I close my eyes. "What can I do to make you go *away*?"

"Help Violet and I'll leave. I promise. And I'm God. I never break a promise."

I pop open an eye. "What am I supposed to do? She's taking medicine to kill herself today. Because she's *suffering*."

"Get her to agree to travel to Coyote Buttes. If she can make the three-mile trek across the open desert to a rock formation called the Wave, she will live."

I sit up. "The Wave? In *Arizona*?"

"Mmm-hmm. That's the Wave I'm talking about."

"You mean…" I stand. Too fast, though, and I start to feel the room spinning. God, I don't wanna pass out again.

"Don't worry. You won't pass out again."

"How would you know?"

"I'm God. I know everything."

"You're not God! You're a series of synaptic misfires! Easily fixed with the proper medication."

"Care to make a wager?"

"Now you're God, gambling?" I throw up my hands. "Unbelievable."

"Again. I get to do whatever I want. God perk. So are you in? You get Violet to the Wire Pass Trailhead. Make the hike to the Wave. You see that I'm right. She will live. It'll prove I'm God."

I pace around the room. Or something pace-like. The concussion approach to pacing. I take one tiny step. Stop. Another tiny step. Another stop.

"Are you killing ants?"

"What? No, I'm pacing. So I can think."

"Oh. Looks weird."

"Listen. Hiking the Wave? That would be literally impossible." I know all about the Wave. Our career mentor, Aaron Wade, told Violet and me about it. It's an ancient granite formation with gorgeous red sandstone that swirls and twirls with waves of color. In pictures it's breathtaking. Like something you'd expect to see in a Dr. Seuss book or on another planet. To preserve the formation and to accommodate the massive amounts of people desperate to visit the "painted desert," the Bureau of Land Management issues only a few permits a day to hikers. The permits must be won through an online lottery. "First off, you can't just show up and hike to the Wave. You need a permit."

"Duh. I know."

"We don't have one! You have to apply months in advance to enter a lottery."

"Or you can arrive the day of and win a walk-in

permit. **They give away ten a day. Easy peasy lemon squeezy."**

"What are the odds we'd win one of those? I imagine hundreds line up every day. People wait years and years to get a permit to hike that trailhead."

"Is this thing on? Can you hear the words that are coming out of my celestial, cosmic mouth? I'm God. I don't normally like to brag, but I'm super psychic. Just get there. Those walk-in permits are as good as yours. God's honor."

"Okay. Second thing. And this is somewhat of a big deal." I sit on the arm of the couch. "Let's say we make it and, by some strange voodoo magic, win walk-in permits. Violet couldn't make that hike. People *die* making that hike."

"Take Michelle."

"Not happening. Michelle hates me."

"She doesn't hate you."

"Then why is she always so mean to me? She's never mean to Violet."

"That's because Violet doesn't challenge her. You do. She's not used to being challenged."

"Well, if I tell her a voice—"

"God."

"I'm not calling you that."

"No bigs. Call me Voice, then. It's growing on me."

"Great. So if I tell her a voice told me to take Violet and her failing lungs to Coyote Buttes to take a five-mile hike—"

"It's only two-point-five miles, to be exact."

"Two-point-five miles to get to the Wave. Two-point-five miles back. That's five miles total."

"Oh, look at you with your fancy addition."

"Anyway. It doesn't matter if it was one mile. Michelle won't be down for it. Plus, she has my nephews, and her husband, Drew. Not to mention she's super pregnant."

"They can come with. The whole family can come if they want."

"Like a family road trip? You're crazy!"

"Of course I'm crazy! I'm the Alpha and the Omega. The up and the down. The left and the right. The sane and the insane. The roota to tha tooda. All things exist because I am all things."

The door is pushed open. Michelle motions for me. "Dr. Dolittle signed the papers. You're okay to be released. You'll have to come back sometime tomorrow for an MRI and follow-up exam. C'mon. Drew's downstairs waiting with the van."

I look at Michelle. Like, *really* look at her. The frown lines on her forehead. The fatigue in her eyes. The aura of misery that looms around her head like a halo of Amityville-style horror.

She extends an arm. "Indigo? Are you *coming*?"

Perhaps what the family needs really *is* a good old-fashioned intervention. A message from the beyond. A direct path to the light. I grab my duffel bag from the couch, my soul strangely rejuvenated. It's official. I'm not going home to watch my sister die. Today, I'm off to find a way to let her live.

This according to the voice in my head.

CHAPTER FOUR

It's a frequent occurrence for people to ask me fun twin questions:

"What it's like?"

"It must be so cool!"

"Can you read each other's minds?"

When they ask, their eyes are alive with wonder, eager to discover some of the ins and outs of twindom:

"Do you think one another's thoughts?"

"Sense when the other is in some sort of peril?"

"Feel the other's pain?"

I've never had quick, go-to responses for what it's like to be one half of the Indigo and Violet experience. I get that twins can be seen as somewhat of a phenomenon. But imagine being inside the phenomenon. Like…okay…imagine you're the Sun. A million Earths could fit inside you. You're nine thousand degrees on your coolest day. You are a perfect sphere. You're *the* giant thing that keeps other giant things in place. Yet to think the Sun sits there reflecting on all these amazing facts about itself is absurd, right? It doesn't think. It just is. The Sun not being able to verbalize why it's so hot, or how it manages to be figuratively cool at the same time, is the best, albeit strangest, way to explain what it's like having an identical you.

But ever since Violet's been sick, and no longer attending school, there aren't so many of the fun twin questions like, "Do you guys know Tia and Tamera?" The questions have dwindled down to only a few. Or rather, the same question delivered in a multitude of ways. Some variation of: "How *are* you, Indigo?" Like that day on the bus...

"So happy to see you." Our student body president, Susie Prouty, slid into the seat beside me on the city bus, set down her overstuffed hunter-green JanSport backpack, placed her hand on top of mine and said, "How you must be feeling. I can't even imagine."

"I can help you," I answered quickly. "Imagine, I mean."

"Oh...um," she started.

"Go with me if you will. Imagine being the Sun."

"Uh...the Sun?" She looked over her shoulder, clearly searching for another seat to escape to.

"Yeah," I continued. "But pretend it's four billion years from now and you're all outta fuel. A sun with no hydrogen— *cooling.* Your sun days are almost over. Do you bow out gracefully and simply explode?"

"I..." She scratched her head.

"Or should you search for another thing to be?"

★ ★ ★

"Indigo?"

"Hmm?" Michelle snaps me back to the confines of the musty hospital elevator, saving me from a memory I wish I could dispose of somehow. Pull it from the deep recesses of my mind and dump it into a bowl of other unwanted memories like Dumbledore could. Poor Susie Prouty. She hasn't talked to me since.

"Let's keep this voice thing to yourself," Michelle whispers surreptitiously even though we're alone, as if there are elevator cameras with mics and she doesn't want anyone else to know her sister is a bit touched.

The elevator dings and the doors slide open. I follow Michelle as she moves through the vestibule, her high-heeled boots click-clacking on the shiny marble flooring of the hospital lobby. Across a carpeted seating area, through thick panes of floor-to-ceiling windows, I see Michelle's husband, Drew, pulling up alongside the curb in their silver Ford minivan.

"I just don't want anything taking away from Violet. This is her time to say goodbye. Nothing should ruin her moment. You understand."

I dare not ask the obvious question: Won't, like, her dying ruin her moment?

As we step in front of the automatic doors, the panes of glass glide along their aluminum tracks, allowing ice-cold Seattle winds to rush inside. My breath catches. Frosty air sneaks its way up my sleeves, down my collar and through every imaginable opening of my jacket as we step outside.

The memory of being up on that scaffolding returns to me, chilling me more than the Washington breeze.

Michelle turns, lays a heavy hand on my shoulder. I resist the overwhelming urge to push it off. "Indigo? We're clear, right? The voice thing?"

"I'm not hearing a voice." I'm not lying. I'm not hearing a voice. At least not right now.

"Okay?"

"I was only kidding. Ha." All right, that was a lie.

Michelle doesn't exactly look convinced or amused but nods anyway. She moves toward the front of the van, and I slide open the back door, step up and toss my bag onto the seat beside me. I'm thrilled to find the heat cranked up to a boil, not so thrilled to see my nephews, Brandon and Nam, in the back playing what appears to be their favorite game of I'm-going-to-hit-you-as-hard-as-I-can.

"Take the 90, honey?" Michelle's using her sweet wife voice. The voice she uses whenever Drew's around so he doesn't have to be continuously reminded he married a lunatic. As he speeds off toward the exit of the hospital parking lot, into the hustle and bustle of downtown Seattle traffic, she murmurs, "I'll be so relieved when this is all over. It's literally killing me."

"Post hoc, ergo propter hoc."

She spins around. "What did you say, Indigo?"

"We're studying fallacies in school. Nothing's literally killing you. Except time itself. So your statement is a fallacy. I'm not sure which one. Maybe *illogical conclusion* is a better choice than *post hoc.* Yeah. *Post hoc* is wrong."

"Indigo." She groans. "If you're gonna ramble weird facts, at least know what you're talking about, okay?"

I shrug, pull the hood from my jacket over my eyes and lay my head back against the seat, hoping the warmth of the van will ease the mounting pressure and pain permeating through every cell of my skull. Literally killing her? *Violet* is the one dying.

I feel hot breath on my neck and twist to see my nephew Brandon leaned over my seat. "I heard you jumped off a building. Aunt Indiana Jones. Get it?" He pushes his bright orange glasses up onto the bridge of his nose. "Was it fun?"

"I didn't jump. I fell. Much like you would fall, Brandon— through the windshield. If you don't put your seat belt back on."

He climbs over the seat, shoves my bag onto the floor and buckles in beside me. "Wanna hear my letter to Aunt Vee?"

"Letter?"

"Yeah." He unfolds a crumpled piece of lined notebook paper, attempts to smooth it out on his lap and adjusts his glasses. "We have to write letters." He smiles, exposing his brand-new adult front teeth that are about four sizes too big for his mouth. With his spirals of dark brown, curly hair shooting out in every imaginable direction, my nephew looks a lot like a seven-year-old Einstein. Or maybe he looks like an animation escaped from the Disney channel. "You know, before she kicks the bucket."

"Don't say *kicks the bucket*!" Nam leans over the seat and slaps Brandon across the head, causing his glasses to shoot off his face like a bottle rocket. "It's insensitive, beaver teeth."

"My glasses!" Brandon screeches. "You break my glasses, I break your face!" He quickly unfastens his seat belt, hops onto his knees and reaches toward the back, slapping Nam across the neck with a loud *thwack*. "Game over!"

"Esophaguses don't regenerate!" Nam wails. "You forfeit all hits when you break rules."

Though Nam is two years older than Brandon, he's small for his age, so they stand at about the same height and, coincidentally, have the same level of seven-year-old maturity. But while Brandon looks like his dad with his thin frame, high cheekbones and round face, Nam is a carbon copy of Michelle, right down to his dark brown skin and kinky-curly hair. Interesting how the gestational gene explosion can create so many interesting variations of human. You wouldn't even guess Nam is biracial, while Brandon has the lighter skin and softer hair to suggest he could be.

Brandon grins, slides his glasses back on and clicks his seat belt over his shoulder. "Whatever. I quit anyway."

"Mom!" Nam howls. "Brandon hit me in the esophagus."

Michelle spins around, tosses the boys a wide-eyed, maniacal glare that could rival Medusa's. "Another hit and so help me God you will both lose your iPads for the rest of the *decade*. Have some freakin' decorum. Violet's laid up in bed and you two actin' like you're inbred!" She twists back around as Drew merges onto the freeway, driving like we're racing in the Daytona 500. Sweet. The faster he drives the better.

It's quiet in the car for a good eight seconds before Brandon says, "So? You wanna hear my letter?"

"I'm sure it's great. I have a bit of a headache, though, Bran."

He ignores me and reads, "'Dear Auntie Violet. I think you're really cool and brave and I will miss you when you're dead.'" He looks up. "That's all I have so far."

"That's beautiful, honey," Michelle calls from the front seat. "Maybe say *why* you'll miss her, though." She turns to me. "You might wanna think about what you're going to say too, Indi. Everybody gets a chance to say goodbye. Jedidiah is already at the house waiting." The expression on my face must read something close to *who the hell is that and why is he at our house* because Michelle adds, "From New Faith International Church?"

Oh. *That* guy. Pastor Jedidiah Barnabas. Which simply cannot be the man's real name. No parent is that cruel. He's the pastor of the megachurch Mom and Dad force us to attend every so often. The nondenominational church of everything. A church that takes religious ambiguity to such a level, you could be worshipping Satan, for all you know. It's also held in an amphitheater so gigantic you can't even see Pastor Jedidiah when he races across the stage calling forth the archangels from all corners of the universe to infuse their energies or synergies or...whatever. Were it not for the flat-screen monitors stretched from corner to corner, I wouldn't even know what he looks like. "Why is he at our house?"

"To facilitate Violet's passing. Read her last rites. That sorta thing," Michelle explains.

"Last rites! You guys are Catholic now?"

Aaaaand The Voice returns. "We are not Catholic," I reply

nonchalantly, as if this voice booming from nowhere is now a normal thing. "We don't even go to church really."

Michelle turns to face me again. "What does that have to do with anything, Indigo?"

"I was only… Nothing. Never mind."

"You don't have to speak," The Voice explains. **"I can read your thoughts."**

"Please *don't* do that," I whisper.

"We do so go to church." Brandon scribbles onto his sheet of paper. "On Easter. That's Jesus's birthday."

"No, it's not, bacon bits for brains," Nam calls from the back of the van. "Christmas is Jesus's birthday. Easter is the Easter Bunny's birthday."

"Oh, yeah. Hey, Indi, how is this?" Brandon reads. "'I'm gonna miss you when you're dead, because you're nice, and pretty, and smart, and fun, and good, and awesome, and cool.'"

"Better," Michelle calls out. "What do you think, babe?" She reaches across the seat and brushes strands of Drew's long black hair off his shoulder. Drew's Native—from the Colville tribe, I think. He and Michelle started dating in high school and have been together pretty much ever since.

He pulls an Apple EarPod out of his ear. "I'm sorry—what?"

"Brandon's letter?" Michelle forces a smile. She's irritated Drew's not paying any attention to the subject at hand, but working hard to dial back her crazy. I wonder if Drew can see it in her eyes. Sense it.

"It's… Yeah. For sure." Drew places the EarPod back into his ear as he continues speed-racing across the freeway.

"You like it too, Auntie Indigo?" Brandon adjusts his glasses for the twelfth time since I've gotten in the van.

"Why don't you have the strap for your glasses, Bran?" I ask. "Those things are never gonna stay in place."

"It makes me look like a nerd." Brandon buttons the top button on his blue polo. "And I have an image to uphold."

"What about your giant teeth and little head?" Nam asks seriously. "That makes you look like a nerd."

I pretend my phone is ringing. "Sorry, kids, I have to take this." I hold the phone up to my ear. "Hello? Oh, yes. I can talk."

"Pretending to be on the phone? Good one."

I hunker down and whisper into the receiver, hoping the sound of the loud freeway traffic and Brandon and Nam arguing drowns out my conversation. "I just don't feel like talking to them."

"So say that."

"What's the point? They don't listen to me. Nobody listens to me. Speaking of. How exactly is this supposed to work? I show up at home and shout, 'Hey, everybody, God says we should pack up the cars and head to Arizona. I'm driving'?"

"I've seen you drive. Not a good opener."

"Are you going to help me at some point? If you're who you claim to be, you know my family. They won't entertain this. Not for one second. I need some intervention here. Shine a bright light or arch a rainbow across the sky or something."

"You've been watching way too many Hallmark movies. I don't do *any* of that."

"Then what do you actually do?" I sigh.

"I set things in motion. I'm the architect. You guys are the ones that make things happen. That's why *you* have to get her to the Wave."

"So you're seriously not going to help me?"

"What do you think I'm doing now? Think of these conversations as a cheat sheet. I'm giving you the answers to the test, but you still gotta take the test."

I scratch my head. "I'm terrible at tests."

"Okay. I'll give you another answer. A riddle, if you will."

I like riddles. Violet and I are actually pretty good at them. "All right. I'm listening."

"Solve it and you'll know where to start." The voice clears its throat. **"Roses are red. Violets are not blue. Start with Violet."**

I wait. Careful not to even breathe for fear I'll miss the rest. A long moment passes.

"Hello!" Is he gone? Will the riddle never be fully stated? The answer never revealed to me?

"Yes? I'm here."

I exhale. "Oh, thank God."

"You're welcome."

"No, I meant… Just…what's the rest?"

"What do you mean? That's the whole thing."

"What? That's not a riddle! Doesn't even make sense."

"Violets aren't blue. They're purple. Makes sense to me."

I groan. "This is madness. You're madness."

"Talk to Violet. Get her to listen. She's your ticket to winning the group over. There. The great Oz has spoken."

Talk to Violet. Something that used to be as reflexive as blinking. Indigo and Violet Phillips. Identical twin sisters and best friends since birth. We both stand exactly five feet four inches tall. Both have thick black hair that hangs past our shoulders, both weigh in at 117 pounds. At least, we used to. Violet's lost quite a bit of weight since the Fates decided to be unkind to an unsuspecting soul, snatching the very breath of life from her. We're both the exact shade of brown as the oldest Obama girl, Malia, a fact discovered when we all inadvertently got on the same elevator at the Columbia Center and her Secret Service agent was kind enough to let us take a selfie. Our Facebook pic got shared over eight *thousand* times. And Mediatakeout.com ran the photo on its website with an article titled, "Obama Has Secret Love Children Twins, Y'all! Picture Proof!" I have a mole under my left eye and Violet a mole under her right. A trait that reveals we are what's referred to as mirror twins. While some people find it fascinating that our reverse, asymmetrical features make Violet right-handed and me left, I was always more concerned with the reality that if she committed a heinous crime, I could easily go to jail for it, since we share the same DNA. We do think the same thoughts. Sometimes at least. Finish each other's sentences. Oftentimes. Definitely sense when the other is in some sort of peril. If perilous events occur. We are your stereotypical twin best friends. My shoulders slump. Or at least we used to be.

"What if she won't listen to me? She doesn't talk to me." I speak quietly into the receiver. "At least not anymore."

"Then you'll have to find a way to *make* her listen. Think outside of the box. Be bold. Be brave. I believe you can do it, Indigo. I know you can."

CHAPTER FIVE

Our tranquil street in the Columbia City section of Seattle always appears gloomy after a heavy rain in the winter. Most of the trees have completely disposed of their vibrant orange-, brown- and auburn-tinted fall leaves, leaving bare, spindly branches that hang ominously over wet gray pavement.

Drew pulls into our tiny driveway and yanks the key out of the ignition. A terrible quiet blares louder than the *pop-pop* of pyrotechnics at a rock concert. Here we all are. Ready to walk into our traditional Craftsman-style house to watch a real-life horror show. Death seems to loom in the air, thick and impenetrable. Our house certainly appears foreboding. I mean, it's always been the worst-looking house on the block anyway, with its red-painted door peeling around the edges, and faded yellow siding in desperate need of patchwork and repair. Not to mention every house in the neighborhood but ours is decorated for the holidays with glittering lights, Nativity scenes, illuminated menorahs or tacky holiday inflatables. To add to our home's appeal, or lack thereof, Mom fired the gardener because she said he wasn't doing anything but blowing leaves around, so, ironically, our front lawn is littered with wet leaves turning to mulch. I feel like people can sense there is something deeply troubling going on here. I focus on the one evergreen that stands beside the house like a beacon of hope. *Don't worry. Some things never die*, it seems to say, its pine needles blowing ever so gently in the wind.

"Indigo, Drew and I need to speak with the boys. Explain things a bit. We'll be in soon."

I clumsily snatch my bag off the floor, already over this whole one-armed Indigo situation. I pull open the van door and mumble, "See you inside," before cutting across the grass, my Uggs sloshing and sinking down into the scatters of wet leaves as I walk.

I climb up onto the porch, push open our large front door and trudge inside. Getting in and out of the house is a lot simpler now. We used to have to leave a change of clothes in a large trash bag and change in the foyer closet before we could enter the house—Michelle's orders to keep Violet's lungs free from possible infection. But ever since Vee's decided to bow out gracefully from life, the rules aren't so much enforced anymore.

I toss my bag onto the floor, kick the door shut with my foot and notice Pastor Jedidiah Barnabas sitting on the couch beside Alfred in our dimly lit den. I've only ever seen the pastor on a giant screen murmuring about energetic downloads or some other spiritual mumbo jumbo, so it's sort of surreal to see him this close. He's a short Caucasian man, with pale blue eyes and sparse strands of dark brown hair. He wears jeans, open-toed Birkenstock sandals and a tan corduroy jacket over a crisp white dress shirt.

"Indigo?" He stands respectfully. "Honored to officially meet you." When he speaks it's slow and overly articulated. He steps toward me with arms outstretched, swiftly enveloping me in a tight hug.

"Hi." I cough into his shoulder as I get a mouthful of corduroy.

He pulls away and looks me squarely in the eye since we're about the same height. "How you must be feeling."

"Yeah," I reply. "I bet you can't even imagine." I think of giving him the sun analogy but remember Susie Prouty almost falling down a flight of stairs at school to get away from me last week and decide against it.

"Since you attend New Faith International Church of Love and Light, you're aware I receive messages from the beyond." He takes a deep breath and exhales so forcibly, a blast of his breath blows into my eyeballs. I blink in surprise. "Energetic messages that are transmuted from the higher planes and downloaded into my alignment."

"That…makes sense."

"As a result, I can see into the spirit realm. I communicate with guides, ascended masters and archangels and am here to help direct Violet as she transitions. Does that sound good to you, Indigo?"

The door is pushed open. Drew, Michelle and the boys enter from outside.

"Pastor Jedidiah." Michelle slides in between us. I step aside, relieved to let her take center stage. "Can we get you something to drink? Coffee? We feel so honored and deeply blessed to have you—" she covers her mouth "—here to... to..." Tears erupt and flow like hot lava. I'd be lying if I said I didn't see it coming. Michelle bursting into a fit of tears is pretty common these days.

Pastor Jedidiah envelops Michelle in a warm embrace similar to the one I just received. Drew follows suit, wrapping one arm around Michelle while the other hand waves angrily at the boys. Understanding the signal, they too step forward and wrap their arms around their weeping mom.

I'd join in, but group hugs aren't really my thing. Besides, this is a perfect opportunity to make my escape. I surreptitiously step around them and move through the den, scooting past Alfred.

"Indigo?" Alfred holds up a sheet of typing paper. "Letter? You write it yet?"

"Not now, Alfred." I literally run down the narrow hallway across the old and fraying carpet runner that lies over our fifty-year-old hardwood floors. I make it to the end of the hall in record time, but just as I lay my hand on the antique brass knob of the guest room door, it swings open and Mom steps into the hallway, lips tightly pursed, eyes void of emotion.

"Indigo." She shuts the door before I can even see inside.

"Mother," I reply.

"How are you feeling?" She's asking the question but there

is a distance and coldness to her voice. As if she's not really present. Or doesn't care either way. Or both.

"Fine, Mom. How's Vee?"

"As well as can be expected." She glances up at my mess of hair. "I packed you a brush and hair gel, Indigo. Did you not think to use them? You could've put your hair into a high ponytail."

Did she forget that my arm is kinda broke? "I did the best I could. Sorry."

"Did the pastor see you looking like this?"

"Well…he saw me. So, I guess."

She heaves the heaviest of sighs. "I want everyone in the den so we can discuss how this is going to work."

"Now?"

"Yes, now."

"Mom, you guys aren't seriously going to let her do this, are you?"

"Indigo, I'm *not* in the mood." Her voice cracks. I sense she's approximately three seconds from one of her classic screech-and-screams. "Do what I asked you to do!"

I yank on strands of my matted hair. I don't want to push Mom to her limits or anything. And God forbid my concussion has to endure a screech-and-scream. I just want… "Okay. Let me talk to Violet super quick." I try to move around her but she blocks my path with an outstretched arm.

"You can't go in there. This is precious time for Violet and Dad."

"Oh. Okay. I won't go in." I wait. Hoping she moves because she thinks *I'm* about to move. Then I can bum-rush

Violet's room and tell her all about the voice. Mom might scream after me but who really cares. My sister's life is on the line. But Mom doesn't budge, standing like Heimdall guarding the entrance into Asgard.

"Indigo, have you lost your natural mind?" she whispers. "So help me God, child, if you don't do what I asked you to *do*."

"Yes, ma'am. I'm going." Geez luss! I shuffle back into the den, where Pastor Jedidiah now sits on the love seat beside Michelle. She's downgraded from a Category 5 cry to a tiny tropical-storm whimper. Drew hovers over the boys, who sit cross-legged on the floor in front of the fireplace, looking lost, dazed, confused and…quiet—certainly a first for them. I'm sure Michelle threatened their lives before they came in.

Alfred dangles his letter when he sees me and mouths, "Write it, Indigo!"

I look away.

"I have a message that's currently downloading from the higher realms." Jedidiah inhales dramatically and holds his breath for so long I start to wonder if he's gonna black out and hit the floor like I did earlier this morning. Michelle must be wondering something similar, because she stops whimpering and stares into Jedidiah's face, eyebrows raised.

"Pastor? Are you okay?" Michelle asks.

He exhales at last. Slowly. Painfully slow. When I begin to contemplate if he'll ever speak again, he murmurs, "Life is a stage and we are all players in the game of life. Acting out scenes, if you will, which were chosen specifically on the other side. We are lining up gems in the best possible order. In an attempt to move on to the next level."

Alfred looks up. "That sounds like *Bejeweled*."

Michelle glares at Alfred.

He shrugs. "What? It does."

Jedidiah opens a shoebox on the coffee table, with a bunch of items stuffed inside. He removes what looks to be bound sticks of wood. "These are Palo Santo Holy Sticks. Palo Santo has been used for thousands of years for healing." He ignites the sticks of wood with a lighter from the pocket of his corduroy jacket. Wisps of smoke swirl up toward the ceiling.

Alfred coughs. "You sure that stuff's safe to ingest?"

"Is it like medical marijuana?" Nam asks.

Michelle moves to open a window. Cold air blows into the den.

"Babe?" Drew asks. "Can you close that? It's freezing outside."

"But this smoke could irritate the boys." Michelle rubs her belly. "And the baby."

"No, no." Jedidiah places the bundle of sticks under his nose and inhales deeply. "See? Smoke from this species of Palo Santo is better for you than oxygen."

As the boys gaze wide-eyed at Jedidiah while he waves the sticks of Palo Santo back and forth like an aircraft marshaller, I stare at Drew as he struggles to force the window shut, recalling the year when our Christmas tree fell and smashed straight through it. Though Mom and Dad quickly got the window fixed, they never did replace the screen. I stare at the open space, thinking about the dense bushes that surround our house like a moat…a thick moat of bushes…and leaves. Hundreds and hundreds of leaves.

The voice said to do something drastic. Take control. Be bold. Be daring.

A thought occurs to me. A glorious thought to rival all the thoughts I've ever thunk. I race up the steep, creaky wooden stairs that lead to the second floor of our house and tear off down the hallway.

CHAPTER SIX

"**W**hat are you doing?"

I'm furiously pulling books from off my bedroom shelves, tossing them into a pile on the floor. "Looking for something. A book."

"**Won't any of these you've thrown on the floor do?**"

"It's a book Violet and I used to read when we were kids. It was her favorite."

"*See Spot Run?*"

"What? No." I crawl over Violet's bed. She hasn't slept here in months, so the sheets and bedding have been stripped from it. I move to our desk and start yanking drawers open, searching among the mess of papers, hair accessories and schoolbooks. "I know it's in here. I saw it not too long ago. At least I think I did."

"**Um. Hello?**"

I look up at the ceiling, exasperated. "Can't you see I'm busy here?"

"You do know I know everything, right? Since I'm God and all."

"Stop saying that! It's sacrilegious. Besides, if you were God, Jedidiah would be able to hear you too, since he collects energy from beast masters."

"Ascended masters."

"Yeah. Those guys."

"Well, suit yourself. Don't mind me. I'll be here. Knowing exactly what you're looking for aaaaand exactly where it is."

I sit on the edge of my bed. "Fine. It's called—"

"*Alice's Adventures in Wonderland*? I know."

Right. Okay, maybe this isn't a voice after all. It's only me. I'm talking to myself. Of course I would know what book I'm looking for because... I'm me.

"Would you like to know where it is? Because if you really are talking to yourself, you'd know."

"Didn't I tell you not to read my thoughts?"

"What? I can't help it."

A knock at the door startles me. I jump up. "Yeah?"

"Indigo!" It's Alfred. "Everyone is downstairs waiting for you."

"I'm finishing up my letter. Be down in five minutes."

"Mom said, 'If you don't come back with Indigo, I'm gonna go straight postal up in here, so help me God.' End quote."

"Straight postal?" I scratch my head. "What does that even mean?"

"I don't know, Indigo! Just hurry the eff up!" Alfred replies. I glance at the ceiling. "Tell me where it is. Quick."

"Oh, now you wanna know? Now you trust me?"

"Tell me. *Please.*"

"Closet. Top shelf. Cardboard box."

"Why would it be up there?"

"Your mom. Cleaning in here a few years ago. Put a bunch of books up there. Wanted to donate them and never got around to it. Typical Mom stuff." The voice snorts. **"You know how she is."**

I rush to the closet and pull the long string that turns on the light. It's a cluttered mess, clothes on the floor, shoes strewn about, school papers and old boxes crammed into corners. I carefully climb on top of a dresser rammed inside.

"If you fall, you'll break your other arm. Maybe dislocate your other shoulder."

"Don't jinx me."

"No such thing."

Another loud bang on the door. Alfred's muffled voice is more agitated than ever. "Indigo!"

"I'm coming! Geez luss!"

The dresser wobbles. Considering it's from a cheap chain store, cost $19.99 and me and Vee put it together with one of those disposable offset screwdrivers, I should be very afraid right now. I grab on to the top shelf to steady myself, stand up on my tiptoes and peek over the edge. Pushed to the far back, up against the wall, is an old, sunk-in packing box I've never seen before. I pull it forward, blow dust off the top, rip open the flaps and tip the box forward to examine the contents. Inside is a large stack of old books. I dig around until I see the weathered copy of *Alice's Adventures in Wonderland*.

"Told ya. Now do you believe I'm God?"

"Arch a rainbow across the sky or something and I might." I jump down from the dresser, fling off my shirt, tug open one of the drawers and grab a tank top. I stare at my mesh sling. "Do I really even need this thing?"

"Yes."

"I disagree." I peel up the Velcro straps, freeing my broken arm, and throw the sling onto the floor. I groan with sweet relief.

"You shouldn't have taken that off."

I move my arm slowly back and forth, trying to get used to the weight of the cast. The movement makes my shoulder throb. "I can't function with one arm stuffed inside a shirt, inside a sling." I clumsily pull the tank over my head and rush from the closet to my desk, grab a pen and begin writing furiously.

"Whatcha writin'?"

"Don't you know everything?"

"Well...yeah, but I do enjoy a good conversation."

"I'm writing my letter to Violet."

"Saying goodbye?"

"No. It's not really even a letter but you already know that. It's part of my plan. I'm thinking outside of the box like you told me to."

"You're listening to me! This is so exciting!"

I write more feverishly than I've ever written in my life. Just as Alfred kicks the door, hard, I finish.

"Indigo!"

I rush to the door and jerk it open. Alfred's baby face and gentle features are forced into a scowl. He looks down at my arm.

"What happened to your sling?"

"I don't need it."

"Indigo, your arm is broken."

"Yeah, but not in half."

"But your shoulder."

"I'll be fine."

His expression softens. "Do you think—" he pauses, flips his Seahawks cap backward "—she'll go to hell for this? And us too, for letting her do it? We could be seen as accomplices. I don't wanna go to hell, Indi."

"Tell him there's no such place."

I lurch forward and wrap my arm around him, hugging Alfred closely for the first time in like...ever. "There's no such place, little brother."

He seems a bit shocked by the burst of affection but doesn't pull away. Lays his head gently on my shoulder instead and sighs.

As Alfred and I make our way down the stairs, the smell of burning wood sticks wafts up to my nose, singeing my throat. I notice Violet. Her wheelchair is locked in place in front of the fireplace, facing the family. Her hair has been perfectly straightened, the long, freshly pressed strands pulled neatly over her shoulder. She wears a gorgeous burnt-orange sweater dress that must be new since I've never seen it. Thankfully,

Violet and I aren't the type of twins who wear matching clothes and hairstyles. We always found it to be a bit...horror movie–ish, so we made sure to stick to our own distinctive vibe. I'm more of a jeans, T-shirt and ponytail kind of a girl, while Violet is the prim and proper fashionista who spends at least an hour a day fixing her hair.

The rich color of the dress makes her light brown skin glow like the beacon of light she is. Even though her face is a bit swollen from all the steroids and she has her signature cannula wrapped around her ears with nasal prongs stuck up her nose, she doesn't look like she's dying. She looks like a princess. Both hands rest in her lap on top of her prescription. The petrifying bottle holding medicine that could painlessly end her life today. I cringe at the sight of it. Because her skin is a bit paler than mine now, the mole under her eye is more accentuated, making her look like a demure runway model. I know I have the same mole, but there's no denying it looks better on Vee. Everything looks better on Vee—my face included.

She glances up as Alfred and I descend the stairs and our eyes meet for the first time in weeks. She gives me a polite wave. It's the only communication I've had from her in at least a week. It makes my heart ache and want to burst with happiness all at the same time. She talked to me! Maybe not with actual words, but still! I wave back.

"So, what's your master plan?"

"Shh," I whisper as I settle into the cushy La-Z-Boy chair that's so old and raggedy it squeaks whenever it moves. "I need you quiet so I can do this properly."

"Oh. Gotcha. My nonexistent lips are sealed."

I look over at Mom, seated on the couch beside Dad, as Alfred settles in next to her. She gives me a perturbed stare. Did she see me talking to myself? I smile awkwardly in return.

Michelle, Drew and the boys are all squished onto the love seat. Jedidiah sits on the arm of the couch beside Alfred.

Violet passes the prescription bottle back and forth between her hands. "I—" she takes a deep breath "—love you guys."

Hearing her voice makes my eyes well. It's been *so* long since I've heard her speak. Speaking has proved difficult for Violet in the end stage of pulmonary fibrosis. The air sacs in her lungs are rapidly forming new scar tissue every day. Usually when a person breathes, oxygen moves through the air sacs to their bloodstream. But for people with Violet's condition, the scar tissue forming is so thick, oxygen cannot pass through properly. There's no known cure, and the causes vary from genetic to environmental...to no cause at all. In the end stages of the disease, you suffocate to death. A lung transplant could extend life. But Violet's not a candidate for a transplant. As a result of an experimental drug called Nathaxopril, a drug that effectively slowed the progression of Vee's pulmonary fibrosis, her kidneys are failing. So on top of her lung struggles, she now needs dialysis once a week. People with other failing organs don't really qualify for lung transplants. And besides, she's in the final stage of the disease now. Weeks away from her imminent death. I quickly dab at my eyes before tears can fall. Dad wraps an arm around Mom.

Violet adjusts her cannula, continues. "This isn't suicide. Please don't think that. This is a chance—" she takes another deep, pained breath "—to end my suffering. I'm going to be with God." Another deep breath. She pauses.

"Take your time, baby," Mom says encouragingly.

Violet sniffs. "After I hear your letters, I'll take my medicine, lie comfortably in bed and…go to sleep. The medicine takes a few hours to work but I'll sleep the whole time. No pain involved." She looks over to Jedidiah. "Right?"

"I'll be beside you the entire time, Violet." Jedidiah stands and turns to speak to the family. "I'll be communicating with her guides as she transitions into the higher realms. The more family in the room the better. Your loving energies will work as a force to direct Violet. Transitioning isn't always easy. Spirits have been known to get lost."

"Like in *The Conjuring*?" Nam asks.

"That movie was *scary*," Brandon adds.

Drew frowns. "You two watched *The Conjuring*?"

Nam points at Alfred. "Uncle Alfred let us."

Drew turns to Alfred. "Really? *The Conjuring*? No wonder they've been having nightmares."

"Go ahead, honey," Mom urges Violet, tossing Drew an evil glare. "We're listening."

Violet continues, "I will watch over you guys from the other…side." She places a hand over her chest to gently massage it. I've never seen her do that before. Maybe this speech is causing her physical pain. "I'll be your guardian angel now. I promise." She transfers the prescription bottle back and forth between her hands again. "That's all I…wanted to say."

There is a long stretch of silence. Everyone sits with dejected looks on their faces. As if maybe they thought she was gonna say, *Just kidding, y'all. I'm not killing myself today! Gotcha!*

Alfred flips his Seahawks cap backward and forward, his new nervous tic. Michelle blows her nose and wipes tears. Drew looks despondently at the floor. The boys stare at Violet with wide-eyed fascination, as if waiting for her to drop dead at any moment. All those two need is a bag of popcorn and they'd be good as gold.

"Can I go first?" Alfred jumps from the couch like it's on fire.

Violet smiles sweetly. Nods in agreement.

Crap. I wanted to go first. I *need* to go first. But Alfred's already moving to stand front and center. He takes a knee beside Violet's wheelchair.

"'Violet.'" Alfred reads from the page with visibly shaking hands. "'Please don't tell Indigo or Michelle but—'" he leans forward and whispers "'—you're my favorite sister.'"

She smiles, seemingly enjoying Alfred's letter.

He goes on, "'I know I'm your favorite brother. But you don't have any other brothers. So yeah. But even so, I wanted my letter to be your favorite letter. So I thought a lot about what to say. I was gonna do a bunch of remember whens. Like, remember when you, me and Indi snuck onto the Amtrak downtown and ended up in Portland and Mom and Dad had to drive four hours to pick us up?'"

I remember that. We were only ten and Alfred eight. Mom and Dad almost got *arrested.*

"'But then I thought...nah. Remember whens aren't all

that interesting.'" Alfred pauses, fumbles with the paper. It falls onto the floor. "Sorry everybody. Shit."

"Oooh, he said *shit*!" Brandon says to his dad.

"Now you just said *shit*, idiot," Nam replies.

"Be quiet," Drew scolds. "Both of you."

Mom, Dad and Michelle murmur things like, "That's okay, Alfred," or "Take your time. You're fine."

Alfred flips his cap forward. "'So I settled in on this. Five important dates I want you to promise me you'll be there for. In ghostly form or whatever they call it when you're dead.'" He clears his throat. "'Number one. The day I graduate from high school. Because Mom and Dad seem to think that'll never happen.'"

Mom lays her head on Dad's shoulder, wipes her eyes with a handkerchief.

Alfred continues reading. "'I want you there to whisper in their ears, "I told you he could do it." Number two. When I get married. I want you to be my best ghost. Sort of like a best man but way cooler.'"

Violet no longer looks like she's enjoying Alfred's letter. In fact, she appears downright miserable. She wipes tears as they flow freely.

"'When I get my first job because Michelle says, "That'll be the day." So I want you there to say, "Yep, what a day it is, *F-R. F-R.*"'"

Dad looks over at me and I mouth, "For real, for real."

Dad rolls his eyes.

Alfred flips his Seahawks cap backward and then forward again. "'Number four. When I have a kid, because Mom says that'll be my sweet karma and she can't wait to see how bad the kid will be. I want you there to be his or her guardian angel. In case the kid turns out like me. And lastly, I want you to be there when I die, so your face is the first face I see when I get to the other side.'" I've never seen Alfred cry, at least not before this very moment. He slides off his Seahawks cap and hands it to Violet. "It's my favorite." He cries. "I want you to have it."

Violet takes the cap and places it on her head. Alfred leans forward and the two embrace, crying onto one another's shoulders.

I look over at Mom and Dad. Mom's head is in her hands. Dad is rubbing her back. I hate to interrupt such a moment, but it's now or I'll have to sit through more sad letters. And I really don't wanna endure Michelle wailing through hers with another Category 5 cry.

I jump up. The La-Z-Boy squeaks. "I'm going next!"

Everyone seems startled at my burst of enthusiasm, but no one objects. I step in front of the group as Alfred returns to the couch. Violet fiddles with her bottle of medicine, doesn't look up at me.

I stare down at my stained boots in an effort to avoid meeting anyone's eyes, clutching *Alice's Adventures in Wonderland* tightly in my hand, my letter to Violet stuffed inside. I clear my throat and start softly. "I have lots to say but never speak. Knowledge is the thing I eat. Inside me adventures you will find. Quests and treasures of every kind. For all those that wish to visit me. Your hands are the ultimate key." I turn to Violet and ask kindly, "What am I?"

She blinks, confused. "I'm sorry?"

"It's a riddle," I reply. "What am I?"

"Indigo, what is this?" Michelle interrupts, annoyed.

"Hey." I point to her. "It is *not* your turn."

Michelle sits back with a loud, exasperated sigh.

Violet definitely seems intrigued; she flips Alfred's Seahawks cap backward. When Alfred did that, it made him look deranged; somehow Violet makes the movement seem delicate. "Can you say it again?"

"Sure." I start. "I have lots to say but never speak. Knowledge is the thing I eat. Inside me adventures you will find. Quests and treasures of every kind. For all those that wish to visit me. Your hands are the ultimate key."

"Something that has lots to say but…can't speak." Violet smiles. Like *really* smiles. She's enjoying this?

"Words on a page," Alfred pipes in.

Violet's eyes brighten. "A book!"

"Yes!" I hand her the volume I'm holding. She takes it, stares at the cover.

"How—" she takes another deep breath "—did you find this?"

"Closet. Top shelf."

She glides her fingers across the cover. "It was my favorite."

"What book is it?" Brandon asks.

Violet holds up the old and weathered copy of *Alice's Adventures in Wonderland*.

"Remember what we always talked about as kids?" I ask. "About going down the rabbit hole in search of another way to be. A magical land where the rules were undefined."

"A new life to be led." She nods. "Where the rules were, there were no rules."

"Exactly! That being said. I have another riddle." I mistakenly make eye contact with Michelle. If looks could kill. Yikes! I turn back to Violet, whose eyes are not menacing and murderous but alive with wonder. In fact, she looks more alive than she has in months. She *is* enjoying this!

"What's the riddle?" she asks breathlessly.

"Roses are red," I state. "Violets are blue. For the rest of the riddle, turn to page sixty-two."

Violet sits up tall in her wheelchair, flips open the book and turns the pages in her temperate, Violet way. On page sixty-two, a sheet of notebook paper folded in half falls out onto her lap. She looks up at me.

"Read it," I instruct her.

I stare at her as she picks up the letter, noticing she did exactly the thing I wanted her to do. She placed the bottle of death medicine on her lap. Good girl, Violet. Goooood girl.

She reads, "'Some people don't believe me. Some people want to meet me. Some people claim to be me. Who am I?'"

"Ohh. I know, I know!"

"Don't interrupt," I say reflexively.

Michelle crosses her arms and huffs loudly. "Nobody was interrupting you, *Indigo*."

"Right. Sorry." I turn to Violet. "Do you know who it is?"

She adjusts her cannula. Her own nervous tic.

"Is it a ghost?" Alfred asks.

"Nobody claims to be a ghost," Drew offers.

"A ghost would," Alfred replies.

I shake my head. "No. It's not a ghost."

"God?" Violet says to herself. Then she beams. "It's *God*."

"Yes!" I kneel at her side and place my hand on her lap, strategically over the bottle of medicine.

"Flip over the page, Vee."

She does. Grins. "*Another* riddle?"

"How many riddles are we gonna have here, Indigo?" Michelle asks.

"It's okay," Violet almost sings. "I like it."

I decide sticking my tongue out at Michelle and saying *Ha! There!* is a bad idea. Instead, I stand and take the paper from Violet's hands. "I'll read the last one." I'm using the sheet of paper to cover up the fact that I am now holding Violet's medicine. I swallow. "For the next riddle." I move dramatically toward the large window in the den while reading. "'There was a window cleaner who was cleaning a window on the twenty-fifth floor of a skyscraper. He suddenly slips and falls. He has no safety equipment and nothing to soften his fall, but he is not hurt at all. How do you account for that?'" I stop in front of the window.

Drew scratches his head.

The boys exchange confused looks and shrug.

Michelle glares.

Jedidiah nods his head knowingly as if one of his Spirit guides told him the answer already.

Mom and Dad sit there looking perplexed like...*now what is Indigo up to?* But Violet is all lit up, eyes brighter than *ever*.

"Give up?" I ask.

Violet shrugs. "How...did he not hurt himself?"

I push open the window and cold air rushes inside the house.

"Indigo, what are you doing?" Michelle exclaims. "Whatever game you're playing, we've all had enough of it."

"The reason the construction worker didn't get hurt," I declare, "is because he was *inside*. Get it?"

Violet laughs. "I do!"

My eyes bulge. Like…she *laughed*.

Mom and Dad seem in awe as well because they stare at Violet as if seeing her for the first time in a long time, then turn to one another and exchange befuddled looks.

"I have only one more riddle."

Violet smiles, and I take a mental picture of her in this moment. Almost like the Violet I've known my whole life. Full of wonder, smiling, happy, excited about life and what it has to offer. I know what I'm about to do will wipe the smile right off her face. I'm about to do it anyway.

I clear my throat. "'Roses are red. Violets are *not* blue. I'm just doing—'" I take a page out of the Jedidiah Barnabas book of life and inhale and exhale dramatically "'—what God told me to.'" I drop the letter and hold up the bottle of Violet's medicine. I twist off the cap and dump it all out the window.

CHAPTER SEVEN

The room erupts into chaos. Michelle stands, shrieking expletives. Brandon and Nam cling to Drew, crying. Alfred just keeps saying, "Oh, God, oh, God, oh, God," over and over while spinning around in circles, pulling at his short strands of hair. Mom is… I dunno what Mom is doing. A cross between a scream and a cry—a high-pitched drone and wail that makes her sound like a baby orca. Dad is shouting at the top of his lungs for everyone to *"Sit down!"* Drew is trying to calm the boys and Pastor Jedidiah is frantically lighting his sticks of wood.

"Take deep breaths!" he hollers over the roar.

I cover my ears with my hands as Michelle storms forward.

"You think you have the right?" she bellows. "You selfish little *b*—!"

"Michelle!" Mom steps forward. "You better watch your mouth in my home! You are out of line!"

Michelle spins around. "Are you freakin' kidding me? I'm not the one with the problem here."

Dad rushes forward and moves between Michelle and me. "Michelle, you let Mom and me handle this."

"You and Mom have let Indigo be a hot ass mess all these years. Why should today be any different?"

Brandon and Nam are wailing so loud, I can feel their screams resonating throughout my entire body.

Drew stands, enraged. "You are all upsetting the boys! They'll be *traumatized* after this."

"Those terrorists?" Mom shouts at Drew.

"This is a sign—" Alfred's still spinning around in circles "—that medicine is a bad omen. We gonna need an exorcist up in here. This family needs to be exorcised!"

Jedidiah exhales. "If everyone could please center and try to push out all the bad air. Follow me. Deep breath in."

"I'm sick of breathing!" Michelle points at me. "Indigo, I'm gonna kill you!" She lurches forward but Dad blocks her, grabbing her hands and pinning them carefully to her side.

"You are *pregnant*. Calm yourself, Michelle!" Dad yells. "You hear me?"

"Guys…please!" Violet's weak and warbled voice pierces through the roar of the Phillips family dysfunction.

Though it's the softest voice in the room, everyone quiets—instantly. Even Brandon and Nam promptly mute and turn their full attention to Vee. But she's not looking at any of them. Her eyes are dead set on *me*, wide with disbelief, tears streaming down her face.

"Why...?" She delicately wipes tears away. "How... could you?"

"Exactly!" Michelle exclaims. "It's not like we can retrieve it. It's a jungle out there. The yard is an absolute disaster—"

"Hey!" Mom cocks her head to the side, offended.

"Mom, I'm sayin'." Michelle shrugs. "You shoulda never fired the gardener. And it'll take days to get a new prescription. You remember all the red tape we had to go through to get that prescription filled."

I move around Dad and Michelle and rush to Violet's side, kneeling in front of her. "Please believe me, sis. I would never hurt you. I only did it to get your attention. To wake you up. So you would listen to me. Last night, I think I heard the voice of God. At least, he says he's God. In truth, I don't know whose voice I'm hearing. But it is a voice. I *am* hearing a voice."

"Indigo, stop lying." Michelle crosses her arms across her chest. "You told me you weren't hearing a voice anymore."

"Anymore?" Mom cuts in. "You mean to tell me you knew she was hearing a voice and you didn't think to tell your father and me about it?"

"Sh-she's mental!" Michelle stutters.

"I'm not!" I stand, defending myself. "I'm hearing a voice. Inside my head." I pound on the top of my head, which probably isn't helping my cause in any way whatsoever and certainly isn't helping my concussion. *Ouch.* "It's saying things to me."

"Is it telling you to kill people?" Drew asks.

"No, *Drew.* Why would I listen to a voice that's telling me to murder people?"

He breathes a sigh of relief and wraps his arms protectively around Brandon and Nam. "Oh, okay, good."

"It's telling me that Violet can live. I believe it and I can explain if you—"

"Guys." Michelle places a hand on her belly as if her being pregnant matters at this moment. "Indigo is suicidal and demented. Why are we listening to her?"

"Stop trying to tell everybody what to do, Michelle!" I say pointedly. "You're not the leader of this family."

Michelle places a hand on her hip. "And neither are *you*."

"I think we should let Indigo talk," Alfred suggests.

"I second that." Dad looks over at Mom.

"Indigo's done a *lot* of things that really don't make much sense..." Mom starts.

"Gee, thanks, Mom," I mumble.

"But she wouldn't do this for no reason," Mom adds. "She wouldn't toss medicine out a window and make up a voice in her head. At least I hope not. Something's going on. I wanna hear it."

Jedidiah steps forward in a cloud of sacred wood smoke. "I think the energy in the room is guiding us to all listen with our ears and let our hearts be receptive to Indigo." He nods at me. "Please. Proceed."

And so I do. Explaining all about the climb. Of course I leave out the part about me wanting to kill myself. Everyone listens intently. I wring my hands together. "So...believe me or not. But I was up on top of that building last night and I swear somebody spoke to me. It's been speaking to me all day. It's saying that Violet can live." I turn back to Violet. "You know me, Vee. I would never lie to you. That's not something we do. We *always* tell the truth." I look over at Mom and Dad, who both have eyebrows raised in disbelief. "I mean, at least to each other." I turn back to Violet. "The voice says that you can live. I believe it."

"How do I live," she starts, "when I'm dying?"

"The voice is very specific. It says to get you to the Wire Pass Trailhead. Get you to agree to travel to Coyote Buttes. If you can make a trek across the open desert to the rock formation called the Wave, you will live."

"Where's this at?" Mom interrupts. "What's the Wave?"

Michelle scoffs. "Mama, stop entertaining this. It's probably something she made up! There is no Wave."

"There is. I've heard of it before," Violet declares.

"Me too." Alfred whips out his phone and fiddles with it for a few seconds. When the screen loads, he holds it up for Mom to see. "There. That's the Wave."

"Well..." Mom nods. "It's certainly beautiful."

"Drew?" Michelle moves to Drew and takes his arm in her hand. "Please back me up here."

Drew runs a hand through his long strands of hair. "Michelle's right, guys." He looks at Michelle. "What else...should I say?"

"Just forget it, Drew." She sighs.

"Listen," I plead. "I know this sounds a bit out there. But what have we got to lose? What if there's some sort of magical healing waters there or something? Anything is possible."

"No." Michelle steps forward. "Anything is not possible.

79

Humans can't sprout wings. Prince can't make another album. Dogs and cats can't have a dog–cat baby."

"They can't?" Brandon asks, pushing his glasses up onto his nose.

"No, son." Drew gives Brandon a concerned look.

"Anything is not possible." Michelle shrugs. "So, guess what? *Your* statement is a fallacy. False."

"*False* is defined as something not true," I reply. "You have no firm evidence that dogs and cats can't have a dat or a cog. And Prince just released a new song. Vevo much, Michelle?"

Alfred holds up his phone. "*I-C-Y-M-I* and not to be a total buzzkill, but I just read an article that says people die making this hike."

"Let me see that!" Mom takes the phone from Alfred. Reads on the screen. "Oh, dear God."

"Not to mention, Violet can't hike," Dad adds.

"Maybe you're hearing the voice of the devil," Nam offers.

"She could use a wheelchair," I state.

"Over rough and muddy hiking terrain?" Dad shakes his head. "That's not gonna work."

"I've seen hiking wheelchairs," I explain. "Like in magazines. I've seen them."

Dad turns to Michelle. "Is that a real thing? A hiking wheelchair?"

Michelle smacks her lips. "They're called all-terrain wheelchairs and they are thousands of dollars and need to be special-ordered. You can't just go to a store and be all, 'Hi, I'll take one all-terrain wheelchair to go.'"

"We could loan you one of ours." Jedidiah places his Palo Santo Holy Sticks on the coffee table.

"The church has an all-terrain wheelchair?" Dad asks in disbelief.

"We have two. We use them for a wonderful ministry that travels into the Old Growth Forest to receive blessings and energy transfers from the trees."

"See, look!" I interrupt. "Now we have a hiking wheelchair. Everything is lining up for this. Maybe it is the voice of God I'm hearing. I mean, if God can talk to Moses, why not me?"

"Did you just compare yourself to Moses?" Michelle laughs. "Girl, you ain't no Moses."

"Who's Moses?" Brandon asks.

"One of the three wise men," Nam whispers.

Brandon nods. "Oh, that's right."

"Mom?" Violet interrupts. "Dad?"

"Yes, baby." Mom rushes to Violet's side and takes her hands in hers.

"Would it be okay if I spoke to you both...alone? In my room?"

"Of course, honey." Dad moves to Violet, unlocks her wheelchair and slowly pushes her toward the back of the house. Mom follows close behind.

When the guest room door is heard being pushed shut, everyone turns to me. No one speaks. They only gaze, wide-eyed and seemingly...*terrified.* As if God himself is standing beside me and they don't wanna piss him off.

At last Michelle breaks the awkward quiet by storming from the house, slamming the door as she goes.

It's been about an hour of uncomfortable silence as we wait for Mom, Dad and Violet to return. Thankfully Michelle hasn't come back yet either, though I keep glancing up at the front door, waiting for her to burst through it, screaming more expletives my way. My shoulder's starting to cramp, so I scoot to the edge of the chair, remembering the doctor's warning that I shouldn't take off my sling. The La–Z–Boy squeaks like a dog's plastic chew toy when I stand. All heads shift in unison. Horrified stares are tossed my way.

"I'm…going to the bathroom."

"Is God going with you?" Nam swallows and scoots closer to Brandon on the couch.

"Nope. God's not coming." I back away slowly, staring at all of them as they stare at me. No longer able to take another second of their terrified gawking, I turn and literally run. At the end of the hallway, I push through the bathroom door, gratefully moving into the isolation of the small half bath. I glance up at the ceiling. "So? What happens now?"

I feel the door being pushed open from the other side.

"Hey, I'm in here."

I turn to see a disheveled Michelle peeking her head through the crack in the door.

"What are you doing?" I hiss. "I said I was in here."

She steps inside the bathroom and twists the faucet nozzle. Loud water rushes down the drain as she shuts the door and locks it.

"Michelle, get out!"

She pushes me up against the wall.

"Hey!" I shout. She uses her thumb and forefinger to squeeze my nose shut. "What the—"

She takes her other hand and covers my mouth, pressing her body weight up against me. My eyes bulge, panicked. I can't *breathe*.

Her knee pins my uninjured forearm to the wall. I struggle to push against her but I know she's pregnant, and quite honestly (even though she's trying to kill me), I don't want to hurt her! She presses her shoulder into my recently dislocated one, sending pain searing through my entire body. My head pounds from lack of oxygen. I bang on the wall, hoping someone will hear.

God, help me!

Perhaps God's reading my thoughts and got the message to download into Michelle's homicidal brain stem because she immediately releases the hold she has on me and backs away to lean up against the sink.

I take in frenetic gulps of air. The entire ordeal must've lasted for only three seconds, but certainly the longest seconds of my life. "What the hell is wrong with you?"

"How did that feel, Indigo?" she asks coolly, one hand over her belly.

"You're a nutcase!" I scream. "A real-life demon from a Stephen King novel!"

"Stop saying weird shit and answer me! I wanna know how it *felt*."

"You were trying to *kill* me! How do you think it felt?"

"Girl, please." She snorts. "Ain't nobody tryin' to kill you. I wanted you to feel how Violet feels. That's how she *feels*! And nothing makes it better. Nobody backs off and gives her room to breathe."

I lean up against the wall, still gasping, heart racing furiously.

"She is *terminal*. Do you even understand what that means?"

"Stop…talking to me…like I'm a kid." I'm still shaking. Still gasping.

"Then stop acting like one! There is no cure for her ailment. If you get it, you die. She *will* die. Respiratory failure," Michelle goes on. "That's her future. One day she will take her last breath and choke to death while she's awake. Or maybe she'll get lucky and die in her sleep. Would you like to drown, Indigo?"

I only stare at her in response since clearly drowning is not on my bucket list.

"That is what it will be like for Vee. It will be like drowning. It'll be worse than drowning. Do you want us to watch her suffer and die the most painful death imaginable? Is that what you want?"

"Of course not. Y-you're not understanding me, Michelle. I love Violet. I only want—"

"What?" She cuts me off. "What do you only want?" She stares at me. Patiently waiting for my answer.

I have so many words to speak in response, so many things to say in my defense. But I can only manage to hang my head, ashamed. The Voice said Michelle doesn't like me because I challenge her when no one else does. But I'm no challenge to her. At least not a real one.

"Please don't take this the wrong way, Indigo." She steps forward. "But I'm about to enlighten you. You only want this so you can continue feeling whole. Without her, you're… Danny DeVito in the movie *Twins*."

I look up. *"Who?"*

"With Arnold Schwarzenegger? Never mind. Just admit that this isn't about Vee. This is about your need to feel complete. You haven't figured out how to be your own person. Because you don't know who you are."

Tears brim to the surface. I quickly wipe them away. Her words hit harder than a fastball to the gut. Didn't I just admit to Susie Prouty that I'm a dying sun searching for another thing to be? Without being one half of the Indigo and Violet phenomenon, I'll just be Indigo. And who exactly is that?

Michelle reaches into her jacket pocket and presents a new prescription bottle. My heart skips a beat. "I made a call. Was able to pull some strings at the pharmacy around the corner. She *can* continue with her plans today."

"Michelle, you can't give that to her!"

"Watch me." She turns, yanks open the door.

"Well, I guess you win, huh? 'Cuz it's always gotta be your way. Right, Michelle? Whatever makes *you* happy."

Michelle turns back. "Not my way this time, Indigo. It's Violet's way."

Hot tears blur my vision. "I'm hearing a voice. The voice says it's God. I know you don't believe me. But it's true."

"Oh, yeah? And what's God saying now? Give me one word from God. That's all I'm asking. Give me one word and I'll believe you."

I listen. Hoping the voice doesn't say something silly like *hickory dickory dock* or *roses are red and eyeballs are blue.* I wait. And wait. And wait.

"What's the voice saying, Indigo?"

Tears spill down my cheeks. I don't even bother to wipe them away. "Nothing."

"Not surprising at all." She moves through the door; it clicks shut after her.

I lean over the sink and look up at the ceiling. "You've always got so much to say!" I wail. "Couldn't think to offer a word to Michelle?" I pound my fist onto the sink. "You just left me hanging! Why did you *do* that?"

The voice sighs. **"Indigo."**

"Oh, welcome back! Now you want to speak?"

"You'll learn this eventually. I know you will. The most important words...they have to come from you."

"Whatever, okay? I'm not in the mood for your cryptic prose. Get out, please. I need to be alone."

"Uh, where should I go? I exist in all places?"

"Fine. Don't go anywhere. Just leave me alone, I guess." I slump down onto the floor of the bathroom, curl into a ball around the toilet and cry my eyes out like I'm a toddler who just scraped her knee and is experiencing real pain for the first time.

That's certainly what it feels like.

★ ★ ★

I must've fallen asleep wrapped around the toilet because a knock at the door startles me awake. I jump up when I hear Dad's deep voice resonating through the thick wood door.

"Indigo?"

"Yes?" I stand and smooth out my wrinkled tank top.

"Everyone is in the den. Join us when you're ready, hon."

"Coming, Dad." The weight of my cast feels like an anchor trying to pull me back down to the floor. I sneak a quick peek at myself in the bathroom mirror that's mounted over the sink. I look worse than I did at the hospital, if that's even possible, especially now that my eyes are swollen from crying. Note to self: avoid all mirrors for the time being. I swing open the door and move down the hallway, slowly shuffling my feet along the carpet runner. As I step into the den, I keep my eyes glued to the floor. My peripheral vision's enough to let me know everyone is staring at me. I slide back into the La-Z-Boy chair. It squeaks.

"So…" Mom starts, standing beside Violet's wheelchair, a hand resting on Violet's shoulder. "Violet's decided she wants to take the trip to the Wave after all."

I look up. Jaw drops. Mind…*blown.*

A series of gasps erupts from the family.

It *worked*? Nothing that I do works. But Violet… I mean, she must believe me. She *believes* me?

"I do…have conditions," Violet adds, almost as if she's reading my mind.

I sit up on the edge of the La-Z-Boy. Of course it squeaks

and everyone turns to stare at me some more. I ignore them and tap my feet on the floor in excitement.

"One. We leave tomorrow," Violet articulates. "First thing in the morning."

"Tomorrow?" I whisper excitedly to myself. My feet tap faster.

"Number two," she goes on. "The whole family comes with. No exceptions. Everyone."

"Everyone but us." Michelle raises her hand. "Sorry. I'm not going. And the boys have school and Drew has work."

"No, I don't," Drew admits. "Livewire just submitted the graphic proposal to PlayStation and none of the staff can do anything until we get our budget. I'm actually off. I could go."

"Fine, Drew. Go if you want." Michelle shrugs. "But the boys are staying here with me. They can't miss school."

"Why not?" Mom asks. "It'll only be a couple of days. What are they gonna miss? Coloring and ABCs?"

"Grandma, I'm in the fourth grade." Nam snorts. "We're doing long division and fractions."

Mom smacks her lips in response to Nam. "It's all work-sheets and recess. Y'all can miss a few days of school."

"Yeah," Brandon agrees. "All we do is go to recess."

"No, you don't," Drew stresses. "You're in school for seven hours a day. That's absurd."

"Please, Mom?" Nam tugs on Michelle's shirt. "I wanna go."

"Chelle?" Violet begs. "This trip can't happen without you. You have to come."

All eyes are on Michelle as she sucks her teeth, staring straight ahead.

"You'd deny her this opportunity?" Dad asks, incredulous.

"What opportunity?" Michelle turns to Dad. "I'm not trying to be contrary. But a family trip to Arizona in December to take a dangerous hike because Indigo is claiming that God is speaking to her. Am I the only one who thinks this is absurd? What if something terrible happens?" She looks at Violet. "Vee, what if you need emergency dialysis? Or have another episode where you can't breathe? We'll be stuffed in a bunch of cars and—"

"The church has a paratransit bus," Jedidiah cuts in. "Sorry to interrupt. I don't see why you all couldn't use it for your trip."

"That's awfully generous of you, Jedidiah." Dad's deep voice resonates in the cramped den. "But who could drive it? Mom let her commercial driver's licenses expire and I got a torn rotator cuff. I can lift just fine, but turning the wheel of a bus would be tough for me."

"I could drive it," Jedidiah replies. "I have a commercial driver's license. I'd be happy to drive you all to Arizona."

"You'd come with us?" Violet smiles.

"It's a sixteen-passenger paratransit bus. Not to be confused with a charter bus. Those have bathrooms and are a lot bigger. But this could still fit the whole family, medical supplies and up to two wheelchairs easily."

Violet looks over at Michelle. "Chelle, please? This…means something to me."

Michelle sits silently, contemplating what we know she'll

eventually agree to. If Michelle hates me to negative ten, she loves Violet to positive one hundred. It's anything for Vee. It's always been that way.

"This is what you really want?" Michelle asks.

"It's what… I really want," Violet declares breathlessly.

"I won't let you down, Violet," Michelle whispers.

Nam and Brandon high-five each other. "No school!" they squeal in unison.

I dare not move a muscle. Knowing the moment has come at last for Violet to actually speak to *me*! Like, really talk to me. She'll have to ask me questions. We'll pack together. Work out the details for the trip. Maybe we'll even stay up all night chatting like the old days. I can't help but smile so big. I'm all lit up inside like a happy troll doll.

Violet turns to Mom. "Could you help me pack?"

I deflate. She wants *Mom* to help her pack?

Mom squeezes Violet's shoulder. "Of course, honey."

"I'm a bit tired, you guys." Violet sighs. "Didn't sleep much last night. So… I'll see you all tomorrow. I'm excited for… this new adventure."

I can't believe it! Is she seriously still not going to talk to me?

I get my answer right away because with that, Mom pushes Violet's wheelchair toward the back of the house.

Drew taps the boys on the shoulder. "C'mon."

"Where are we going?" Nam asks.

"Home," Michelle explains. "If we're leaving tomorrow, you guys need to pack and get things in order."

"I'll call the school." Drew kisses Michelle on the cheek. "You want me to grab you anything?"

"Everything I need is here." Michelle adjusts Brandon's glasses, bops him on the nose. "Make sure they pack boots, gloves. It'll be cold."

"In Arizona?" Nam scratches his head.

"Yes, in Arizona," Michelle replies. "It's winter all over the country and we'll be one of the only fools on a dangerous hiking trail in the cold and rain."

She looks over at me when she says *fools* and her eyes widen as if to make sure I know that I'm the biggest fool of all.

As Dad walks Jedidiah to the door, Alfred moves toward me, leans over the chair and whispers in my ear.

"Thanks, Indigo. That was... Indi, that was *everything*. F-R. F-R."

He rushes up the stairs before I have a chance to respond. I watch him go. He looks happy. It's a look I haven't seen on Alfred in days.

When I turn back, Michelle and I are alone in the den. She steps over to me. Stands directly in front of the La-Z-Boy.

"What?" I ask finally.

"Well, I guess you win, huh?" she says sarcastically, mimicking my words from earlier. "'Cuz it's always gotta be *your* way. Right, Indigo? Whatever makes *you* happy."

"It's not my way. It's Violet's way." I mimic her right back and smile even though I feel like crying. "And I am happy. Happy we're not all singing 'Kum Ba Yah' at Violet's bedside while she drifts off to the fifth dimension."

"The family is putting their lives in your hands."

I swallow.

"And at the end of this road, when there is no voice of God and no cure for Vee, what will you do then?"

"Everything will work out," I say with about as much confidence as Ron Weasley circa year one. "You'll see."

"I will see. That's for damn sure."

She moves off down the hallway, and I sit alone in the den feeling more disconnected from Violet and the family than ever before. I lean back and sigh.

The chair squeaks in response.

CHAPTER EIGHT

When Violet and I were fourteen years old and starting our second semester at Silver Line Big Picture High School, I convinced her to join a support group for pet obesity prevention. Silver Line accepts twenty students into each grade, for a total student body of only eighty. Needless to say, getting in is competitive. Big Picture high schools focus on learning through internships. On Tuesdays and Thursdays, students go to internships in their field of interest. On Mondays, Wednesdays and Fridays we attend one class a day called an advisory. It sounds simple, but inside *and* outside of the classroom, the curriculum is a lot of work. Especially since the internships can end up feeling more like full-time jobs on top of the laundry list of school obligations. And being a member of at least one off-campus group was one requirement I was desperately trying to find a way out of.

"Violet? You down for this?" I shut my laptop computer

and stuffed it inside my desk drawer. "Preventing pet obesity is an important issue in this country."

"We don't have pets." Violet lay across my bed, her feet dangling over the side, staring up at the ceiling, kicking the metal frame to the rhythm of Beyoncé's "Single Ladies."

"I know. But if we ever do get one, we don't want it to get fat."

She laughed and rolled over onto her stomach. "You just wanna annoy Mr. Guyere."

"What makes you think that?"

"You Googled 'dumb groups you can join.'"

I grinned. "I really do care about pet obesity, though."

"You do *not*." She howled with laughter.

Mr. Guyere was our guidance counselor and the man responsible for making sure all students satisfactorily met Silver Line requirements. He micromanaged and dictated so much of my school experience that I truly was looking forward to seeing the look on his face when I told him about my new after-school commitment. And what a look it was:

"Pet *obesity* prevention?" Mr. Guyere lowered his head and glared at me over the rims of his glasses. "Miss Phillips, need I remind you that organized off-campus groups must fit into the category of academic, charity or hobby." He scanned his file folder, flipping through loose-leaf sheets of paper. "To review, Violet is a member of UNICEF, National Honor Society, National Beta Club, Future Business Leaders of America, Phi Beta Lambda…" He slid off his glasses and set them on his desk. "The list goes on, quite honestly. But you—"

he held up one sheet of paper "—are a member of the Seattle division of Pet Obesity Prevention?"

"Yes, sir." I folded my hands in my lap. "That's correct."

Violet covered her mouth to stifle a giggle.

"Precisely how does preventing pet obesity fit into one of our recommended categories?"

"It's a hobby, Mr. Gruyère."

He frowned. "It's Gu-yere."

"Oh. Right. *Gruyère* is cheese. Sorry about that." I slid the signed forms across his desk. "Anyway, a hobby is defined as an activity done regularly in one's leisure time for pleasure. Watching people discover ways to correct their pet's over-sizeness? I find that pleasing. That's the very definition of a hobby, sir. Dictionary.com it, and you'll see."

He glowered and angrily stamped a sheet that said I'd met my club requirements for the semester.

Only my original plan of signing in to meetings and then sneaking across the street to stuff myself silly at Ezell's Famous Fried Chicken got dramatically foiled. Because the veterinarian who headed the Seattle division of Pet Obesity Prevention had a seventeen-year-old son named Troy Richmond, and Troy didn't have an obese pet, but boy oh boy did he fall hard for Violet. So I was stuck sitting through each and every meeting. What dumb luck.

"Is *that* what you're eating for breakfast?"

It's still dark outside as I stand, slumped over the Formica kitchen counter, tearing open a new box of strawberry frosted toaster pastries. I clumsily peel off the foil wrapping, slide both of the pastries into the toaster and rest my aching head in my hand.

"Why? Is it bad for me or something?" I grumble.

"It does have TBHQ in it. Which is made from butane. Which isn't so bad. If you're a *diesel* engine." The voice laughs.

I place a hand over my chest and rub it the way Violet did yesterday. Maybe this will be my new nervous tic. Alfred has a few dozen. I've earned the right to have a nervous tic.

"Indigo?"

I turn, surprised to see Violet standing at the entrance to the kitchen sans wheelchair. She's dressed in leggings, with an olive-green shirt hanging off one shoulder and calf-high leather Frye boots, and her oxygen tank is strapped to her back like a backpack in a pretty purple canvas cover. Only Violet could make an oxygen tank look like the newest, most coveted accessory. Her hair hangs in soft waves, like she woke up an hour ago to style it, which... I'm pretty sure she did. I woke up an hour ago too, and certainly didn't bother fancying up my hair. Though Mom will be thrilled to know I managed the high ponytail she was pushing on me yesterday. The pastries pop up from the toaster with a loud snap. I grab one and present it to Violet.

"Would you like a smoking hot pastry?" I blurt awkwardly.

"I'm not hungry." She steps forward to flip on the kitchen light. A warm, luminescent glow floods the room. "Who were you talking to?"

"Oh." I transfer the food to a paper plate. "Just myself."

"It's okay if you were talking to...God."

"You don't think it's weird?"

"You kidding? I wish…God would talk to me."

"The Voice."

"Huh?"

"He says it's okay if I call him Voice. You can call him that, too." She slides into the bench at our kitchen table and it suddenly occurs to me… "You're walking?"

"I feel so good today. Michelle…gave me three shots of Nathaxopril."

"Nathaxopril?" I move to the table and plop into the seat across from her. "Isn't that the stuff that made you even sicker?"

"It helps me breathe. Yesterday was…bad." She clears her throat. "Worst day, honestly. Today, I feel normal. Almost, I mean."

"But it's the reason your kidneys are failing."

"It…has some side effects. To say the least." She tenses. "I don't want to talk about it, if you don't mind. I want to enjoy feeling good." She pulls at the yellow plastic tablecloth Mom bought to hide the scorch marks from when Brandon and Nam were trying some sort of DIY YouTube science experiment. An experiment that ended up with the Seattle Fire Department sending arson investigators to the house to interview Mom and Dad.

"I'm sorry. I didn't mean to pry." I stare down at my non-matching socks, one blue, the other black with green stripes. A tense moment passes between us. Now there are secrets, something that never used to be. I never had to think about saying the right thing when it came to my twin sister. I knew the ins and outs of how she felt, understood her moods and behaviors. These past few months she seems to hold back from me. She keeps her distance. Has strange walls up. Did I do something wrong? Have I offended her in some way? I take a bite of my butane-infused breakfast treat. It somehow manages to be hot, chewy, crumbly, delicious and disgusting all at the same time. Violet places a folder on the table and pulls it open.

"I mapped out a course for us." She spreads out sheets of paper.

"You did what?"

"Seattle to Coyote Buttes? It's a nineteen-hour drive. I broke it up into two days. I included best-reviewed rest stops and restaurants..." She pauses. Rubs her chest. I rub mine as well. "I thought we could stay at an Airbnb in Hodell. A lodge near the trail for the second. I booked everything already. The flights out the next morning are—"

"Flights?" I interrupt.

She rubs her chest again. I rub mine, too. "Sorry. I meant when we drive out, it should be early to avoid traffic. Does this all sound good, Indigo?"

A twinge of guilt rises up my throat like the heartburn I get after eating cheesy crust pizza. Violet mapped out a course for us. Booked hotels? Yelped *rest* stops? And what did I do last night? Watched *Key & Peele* comedy skits on my iPhone until I fell asleep.

"It wasn't a ton of work or anything," Violet says as if reading my mind. "I used Kayak. And the Airbnb is a little remote. But everything is cheap. Mom and Dad will appreciate that."

"They do appreciate cheap things."

Mom and Dad are retired. Both worked as Seattle City bus drivers for over thirty years. Retirement has made them… frugal. Putting it mildly. Mom prints online coupons like those extreme couponers on TLC. We currently have a garage stocked to the brim with paper towels, toothpaste, bars of soap, and tiny bottles of Herbal Essences shampoo and conditioner. If a zombie apocalypse struck, we'd be the cleanest family in the new Seattle dystopia. And Dad seems to be on a mission to stick it to Skyway Water and Sewer. He spent six months building a water-recycling shower in the upstairs bathroom. A shower that cuts off after three minutes and shuts *down* for ten minutes after each shower. More than once, I've had to finish washing up in the sink so I wouldn't be late for my internship. Still, it lowered our water bill. So the Phillips family might be dirty, but at least we can be proud of our water footprint.

Violet fiddles with her cell phone, heaves a sigh. We're not as connected as we once were, but I know something's off with her.

"What's wrong, Vee?" As soon as the question escapes my lips, I shake my head. "I mean…that was a dumb question." Of course something seems off with her. She's dying. "I shouldn't have asked that."

"It's okay." She sets her phone on the table. "Why do you think he doesn't call?"

"You mean Troy?" Of course she means Troy.

She drums her nails on the table and I notice they're painted green to match her olive-colored shirt. It's the *color of the day* but I don't bring it up. *Color of the day* is a phrase Violet and I came up with when we have one of those twin accidents where we dress alike. I'm wearing a green T-shirt and leggings, too. Painting my nails would've been a nice touch. Certainly looks good on Violet.

"Not one call?" she murmurs in disbelief. "Not even a message? No one could be that cruel. Could they?"

"He's a good guy, Violet." I bite the dead skin around my thumbnail. I do this when I'm lying. Violet knows this. But since she's not paying me much attention these days, she doesn't seem to notice. "Everyone deals with grief in their own way. Disconnecting is his way of dealing with it." I close my eyes and imagine Troy strapped to a train track with a local Amtrak approaching at a high speed. The thought makes me smile. But when I open my eyes, I see Violet's are red and her bottom lip is quivering. "Violet?"

A tear slides down her cheek. She wipes it away in her delicate manner.

"Please don't cry, sis."

"It's pathetic, right? Thinking about a boy at a time like this? I really miss him."

Here Violet is near *death*, and the main thing on her mind is stupid ass Troy Richmond. I'd shove him off a cliff if it wasn't morally irresponsible.

I remember knocking on the door of his posh Lincoln Tower condo in downtown Bellevue. A condo gifted from his dad when Troy graduated from Seattle U. He pulled open the door and stared at me with a horrified look on his face. Troy was classically handsome: dark brown skin, tall and lean, deep dimples, hazel eyes. The dream boy for sure. But dreams can take a drastic turn. Dreams can go bad. Fast.

"It's *Indigo*."

He shrugged, like *duh, I know that*, but I could tell for a second he thought I was Violet. Sure, I have the mole under my left eye, and she her right. And yeah, her nails are always done, her hair typically straightened to perfection—but it's *still* hard for people to tell us apart. Plus, I was wearing my North Face bomber jacket that covered up a T-shirt that had EVERYONE POOPS in bold letters across the front. Would've been a dead giveaway to my identity.

"What do you want?" Troy asked. He was wearing True Religion jeans and a light brown button-up shirt that matched his light eyes.

"Oh, you're here." I looked over his shoulder. You could see the Seattle skyline from his floor-to-ceiling windows, Mount Rainier, the waterfront. It was a stunning view. He didn't deserve it. "I thought you died."

He frowned. "Why would you think that?"

"Did you lose all your dad's money and your cell phone got cut off?"

"What?"

"Are all your fingers broken?"

"Indigo—"

"You in the early stages of dementia?"

"*Indigo*. Why are you here?"

"If you're not dead, your fingers aren't broken, you still have your dad's money to pay your phone bill and buy five-hundred-dollar True Religion jeans and you're *not* displaying warning signs of early dementia, why haven't you called my sister?"

He moved to shut the door. I stuck out my foot so he couldn't.

"How'd you even get up here? We have security. You have to be on the list."

"The security guard thought I was Violet. We're identical twins, dumbass."

"Look. We broke up. I don't have an obligation to her."

"Funny. I don't have an obligation to do the Hokey Pokey. But I do it anyway. Because my seven-year-old nephew thinks it's fun."

"This isn't the Hokey Pokey, sweetheart. I'm not cut out for bedpans and bedside vomiting, okay. I pray she's well. I really do. I want only the best for Violet. She's a good person."

"I know."

"And I'm—"

"An imbecilic addlepated mongrel?"

"A what?"

"Half-wit. Lame brain. Loser. Dope. Dolt. All synonyms for *moron*. Thesaurus much, Troy?"

He was standing so straight and poised. Damn him and his perfect posture.

"I'm consciously choosing to move on with my life. Trying to absorb all the happiness I can. I want to be *happy*. One day, I'll be on my own deathbed. And I can look back on my life and say I had a good one." His cell chimed in his pocket. He grabbed it and looked at the screen. "Look, you gotta go."

"So you're seriously not even gonna call her? Just to say you

care? Doing that will mean everything to her. Please, Troy."
I was pathetically begging to one of Seattle's biggest piles. I
didn't care. I only wanted to see the look of pure joy on Violet's
face when Troy Richmond's name scrolled across the screen
on her cell. "Please call her. She needs to hear your voice. I
have no idea why, but she loves you."

"Troy?"

I turned. There was a female standing behind me in the
hallway. "Who the hell are you?"

"I was about to ask you the same question." She was drop-
dead gorgeous. Long black hair that hung to her waist. Curves
that stood out even though she was dressed in a fancy Bur-
berry coat and matching rain boots. I mean, Violet and I…
we're cute, for sure, but standing next to her, I looked like a
homeless waif.

"I'm Indigo. Your turn."

"I'm Corina," she said with a dramatically rolled *r* as she
moved around me, entered the apartment and kissed Troy
right on the mouth.

My jaw dropped. "You're Troy's girlfriend?" I asked breathlessly.

She raised a concerned eyebrow. "Obviously."

"How long?" My heart was racing.

She laughed. "I'm sorry?"

"I wanna know how long you and Troy have been together."

She turned to Troy. "*What* is going on?"

Troy said nothing. Only stared at me. His eyes begged me

to leave. *Say nothing. Go. Adios. Sayonara. Arrivederci, sister. You don't have to go home but get the hell out of my hallway.*

"I'm...with the Department of Health and Homeland Security," I started slowly. "Letting you know the inspectors will be here later today to check the pipes. Troy's are full of shit. The smell is permeating through all the units and making the residents puke."

Corina grimaced. "That's disgusting."

"You said it, girl." And with that, I turned and walked away.

"Violet," I start. "I got to know Troy during the time you two were together. He's probably so heartbroken." I chew more of the dead skin around my thumbnail. "He doesn't know what to say." I down my entire glass of milk. "What to do." I stuff half a pastry in my mouth and mumble, "Or how to even feel." I swallow. "I *know* he loves you, though. I know this is killing him."

"I'm sure you're right, Indigo."

Violet and I are more distant than I thought if she believed that load of crap. I choke on a pastry crumble.

"You okay?" she asks.

I nod and clear my throat. "Crumb went down the wrong pipe. My bad."

She rubs her chest again. I resist the urge to ask her if *she's* okay. But then she starts to cough. And it's not your average cough. It's more like a series of coughs that won't stop. She covers her mouth with both hands. I can resist no more.

"Violet, are you okay?"

"It's fine." When she moves her hands, they're covered in splatters of crimson red blood.

"God," I breathe.

"Don't worry." She rubs her hands on her pants, smearing blood and dirtying her leggings. "Side effect."

I move to the sink, wet a paper towel and pump soap onto it. I rush back to the table.

"It's not a big deal, Indigo."

I wash off the blood with the soapy paper towel. Her hands are shaking, so I squeeze them in mine. "You're so cold, Violet. Maybe you're not getting enough oxygen. You need your wheelchair."

"Maybe you're right."

"Of course I'm right."

"Indigo." She pulls her hands away, adjusts her cannula and stands. "I'm fine, okay." She hands me a sheet of paper. It's a spreadsheet with my name on the top, a breakdown of our trip with scheduled stops, hotel name and Airbnb info... She even included the Yelp star rating next to every restaurant we're planning to eat at. It looks like something a CEO would hand out to his staff.

"I'm going to see if I can relax a bit before Pastor Jedidiah gets here with the bus. I'm so tired."

"I can sit with you. We could talk. Don't you have questions? About the voice and stuff? It's like we never...get to talk anymore."

"On the trip, we'll have lots of time."

"But are you mad at me or something?"

"Why...would you ask me that?"

"I dunno, Vee. We haven't really talked for weeks. Sometimes I think you're mad at me."

"Not mad…" She pauses, seemingly gathering her thoughts. "I mean, I *already* feel different. I do. And not just because of the shots of Nathaxopril. I can't wait to see how things turn out. I do think I can live, Indigo. I'm excited to live. I really am." She squeezes my shoulder and slowly exits the kitchen.

True to his word, Jedidiah pulls in front of our house with a paratransit bus. Alfred and I peek out the living room window, watching him park in the driveway.

"Sweet baby Jesus Christ in the manger, on Christmas morning layin' in a pile of cold hay," Alfred whispers.

Every square inch of the bus, aside from the front and rear windows, is painted. Rainbow colors are swirled around… eyes. Like…there are hundreds of tiny *eyeballs* painted onto the bus.

"It's satanic!" Alfred hisses. "Ain't no way I'm getting in that thing, Indi. Somebody from school could see me. They'd think I was in a cult or something."

"Nobody can see inside," I point out. "The windows are all covered with eyeballs."

"Why, though?" Alfred flips a different Seahawks cap backward since he gave his favorite to Violet. This one is lime green too, but I swear it's almost glowing. I seriously can't understand why the Seahawks colors are fluorescent lime green and blue. That doesn't even go together.

"Maybe it means something." I try to comfort Alfred. "He's

always talking about interdimensional travel and ascended masters. Maybe the eyeballs represent, like…heaven."

"Or hell." Alfred scratches his elbows. "Thing's giving me the creeps. Looks like eyeball pox. I gotta talk to Dad. This ain't gonna work, man. Maybe we can follow behind you guys in the car."

"Alfred." I call after him but he's already rushing up the stairs two at a time.

When I look back out the window, Drew has pulled up and parked on the side of the street. The back door slides open and the boys jump out onto the pavement, their matching backpacks strapped to their backs. They stare at the van in a mixture of awe and terror. Drew steps out of the van next. His jaw pretty much drops. Watching the three of them gawk at Jedidiah's psychedelic paratransit experiment makes me laugh a little. My Canon Rebel T6 is hanging around my neck with a strap. I grab it and take a few snapshots of their horrified expressions.

Click-click.

"Good morning, Indigo."

I twist to see Michelle looking bright and refreshed, dragging a giant suitcase behind her, holding a large bottle of water.

"Hi," I mumble and turn back to the window, letting my camera dangle around my neck once again. She looks over my shoulder.

"That's the bus?" She laughs. "Has Alfred seen that yet?"

"He called it eyeball pox, started scratching his elbows and ran off to find Dad."

She laughs. Hard. "Oh, this is gonna be real interesting. Did you sleep well, Indigo? How's your head?"

I give Michelle a perturbed eyebrow raise. "Um… I didn't sleep well. My head hurts. Not as bad as yesterday, but it still hurts."

"That's a good sign. If it hurt worse, I'd be worried." She reaches into the pocket of her dark blue jeans and hands me a baggie with two white pills inside. "If anybody asks, I didn't give you these."

"What are they?"

"Pain medicine."

I stare at the bag of pills.

She laughs. "Girl, I'm not poisoning you, if that's what you think. Dr. Dolittle prescribed you something similar but we haven't had a chance to fill your prescriptions. This isn't something you want to get in the habit of taking, but it's fine for a day or two."

I'm still not convinced these pills won't kill me. It must be written all over my face because she says, "Look, Indigo. You want your headache gone. Take 'em. Or don't, and have a headache all day. But that bus looks kinda old, so I doubt the shocks are new and improved. Might be a bumpy ride."

I take the pills from her.

"And here's some water." She hands me the bottle of water.

I throw caution to the Seattle winds and hope to God they're not laced with arsenic. I down the pair with a gulp of the water.

"I'd drink it all. It'll help 'em go down easier."

I down the whole bottle.

She takes the plastic bag from me and stuffs it back into her pocket. "How's everything else? You feel light-headed, dizzy? Any brain fog?"

I set the empty water bottle in the windowsill. "No. I feel okay, other than the headache, I mean." *And the voice in my head.*

"How was taking a bath with the cast?"

"Easier than I thought. I just rested it on the side."

"Big improvement on your hair."

I motion to the fact that I'm not wearing my sling. "Two hands are better than one."

"Careful with your shoulder." She nods. "Let me go find Alfred so he can help us load Violet's medical supplies up on the bus." She laughs again. "Eyeball pox."

I watch her disappear up the stairs.

"See?"

I look up at the ceiling. "See what?"

"She was being nice. Told you she doesn't hate you."

I shake my head. "She wasn't being nice. She was doing her job."

"What job?"

"She's a nurse. Duh."

"Yeah. But is she *your* nurse?"

"Trust me. Nurses take a Hippocratic oath to uphold the sick even if they'd rather see them dead."

"That is not in the Hippocratic oath."

"Well, it's something like that." I pull on my North Face coat, move to the door and head outside.

It's cold, cloudy, dismal: Seattle at its finest. My shoulder throbs. My head *pounds*. What a day for a road trip. Jedidiah and Drew are loading luggage up onto the bus. Jedidiah is wearing a heavy coat, gloves, a wool hat…and open-toed *sandals*? Unbelievable. He pushes his palms together and bows when he sees me. I move to stand beside Nam and Brandon.

"Namaste, Indigo."

"Namaste to you too, Pastor," I reply even though I don't know what the hell *namaste* means.

"She's a beauty, isn't she?" He pounds on the side of the bus. "I got her nice and warm for you."

"Morning, Indigo." Drew smiles as he advances down the stairs of the bus to stand beside the boys. "How are you?"

"Better," I say.

"What do all the eyes mean?" Nam yanks at the hanging tassels on his hat.

"The all-seeing eye." Jedidiah rolls back on his heels. "Also known as the third eye or the sixth chakra. You see with your eyes but you *see* with your *eye*." He points to his forehead and closes his eyes. "The eyes on the bus represent my spiritual vision and the vision you can all attain if you work hard enough."

Nam looks up at Drew. "I wanna see with my third eye."

"Yeah, Dad." Brandon yanks on Drew's coat. "I want three eyes."

"Focus on the two eyes you've got and get on the bus." Drew pushes Nam and Brandon up the stairs and climbs up after them, dragging the last suitcase behind him.

As I approach the doors of the bus, Pastor Jedidiah places both hands on my shoulders.

"How are you today, Indigo? How are you feeling?"

"I'm good, Pastor."

"Please. Call me Jed."

"Uh…okay." There is no way I'm calling this man Jed.

"I am honored to guide the Phillips family on this pilgrimage." He reaches into his coat pocket and extracts a bottle of Trader Joe's extra-virgin olive oil. "This oil has been blessed by the spiritual masters in our Himalayan division at New Faith International Church of Love and Light, Nepal." He turns the bottle, allowing a few drops of oil to drip onto his finger. "I bless thee and thou." He pushes his grease-soaked finger onto my forehead.

"Um."

"Thou and thee."

"Thank—" the oil drips down my forehead "—you." I move past him and up the stairs into the bus. Once I'm sure he can't see me, I wipe the oil off with the back of my hand. With my luck, I'll have sprouted a giant pimple right on top of my third eye. Trader Joe's olive oil is *not* meant for your face. I don't care how many Himalayans blessed it.

I scope out the inside of the bus. It's actually quite nice. Small. About sixteen seats total just like Pastor explained yesterday. The aisle is wide to accommodate a wheelchair moving up and down. In the back is a large empty space. The motorized all-terrain wheelchair is strapped to one side, sporting some seriously high-tech 4x4 wheels. And there's room on the other side for another wheelchair.

I sink into one of the polyester upholstered seats and lean my head back. I blink. On the ceiling, one giant painted eyeball surrounded by glittery gold lettering that says, "See it, Grab it, Love it."

"Cool slogan, right? You like it?"

"It sounds pornographic," I whisper.

Nam stands over me. "How come your forehead looks all greasy, Aunt Indigo? Did you forget to wash your face?"

"I've been blessed by thou and thee," I reply. "Not to be confused with those idiots thee and thou."

"Who are thee and thou?" He sits beside me.

"Hey!" Brandon whines. "I was gonna sit by Auntie."

I stand. "You guys should both sit here. Together. Away from me."

"Why?" Brandon pushes his glasses up onto his nose. "So you can talk to all the voices in your head?"

"No. Because Rosa Parks and a bunch of other people fought hard so you could sit in the front of the bus." I move to the back before they can object, scoot into a pair of seats and stretch out my legs, a clear symbol for nobody to sit by me. I stare out the window. At least I try to stare through the spaces between all the third eyeballs. Violet is being wheeled out of the house by Dad. Mom and Michelle follow close behind. Alfred trails even farther behind, lugging a bunch of Violet's medical supplies, staring at the ground, shaking his head back and forth and muttering to himself, one hand over his eyes like it's a bright sunny day and he's trying hard to block out the sun. I feel like I should climb down to help or, I dunno…stare at them so it looks like I'm involved and assisting Violet, but I'm sure I'd just be in the way.

"How you hanging in there, champ?"

"I'm…" I look over the edge of the seat at Brandon and Nam; they're completely engrossed in their iPads and Drew is talking on his cell. I look up at the ceiling. Thankfully, it's a portion not filled with eye. "I'm nervous," I whisper. "A lot is riding on this. I'm guiding everyone to Arizona. In some weird and crazy way, I'm in charge. I'm *leading*."

"No. *I'm* guiding everyone to Arizona. I'm in charge. I'm leading."

"Yeah, but it's on me if this is a disaster. Not you."

"Road trips are never disasters."

"Be for real. Road trips are notoriously terrible."

"Only in the movies. Not in real life."

"If you say so."

"Plus, you got the Jedi Master on the wheel. He's a good driver. Best in the whole state."

"Yeah?"

"Yeah, man. Plus, Violet planned every detail. What could possibly go wrong?"

"We could get a flat tire and drive off a cliff, we could break into a closed theme park and hold the security guard at gunpoint, or someone could die and we could stuff them in the trunk while I do a stripper dance to win the Little Miss Sunshine pageant."

Brandon and Nam are now peeking over their seats, staring at me.

"I told you Aunt Indigo was crazy," Brandon whispers.

"Stop lookin' at me!" I snap. They quickly dip below their chairs and turn around, mumbling about what a wacko I am, I'm sure.

Mom and Michelle are the next up the stairs with enough luggage to *move* to Arizona. Both have Trader Joe's brand blessed olive oil dripping down their foreheads. Both look none too happy about it either. Mom's hair is pulled up into her signature, impeccably neat, silver bun on top of her head. When she sees me in the back she nods. I nod back. I feel like instead of mother and daughter, she's Alexander Hamilton and I'm Aaron Burr and we're about to have a death duel. Or an epic rap battle.

When Alfred climbs up the stairs behind them, he stuffs a bunch of Violet's supplies under a pair of empty seats, moves all the way to the back, tosses his bag onto the floor and slumps into the seat across the aisle from me.

"I thought you and Dad were gonna ride *behind* the bus," I call over to him.

"Dad said no." He covers his head with his hoodie and puts his head in his lap. "Wake me up when we get to Arizona."

I turn my attention back to the front. Violet is being carried up the stairs by Dad. He gently sets her on one of the seats near the front. Then wipes the oil dripping down his face.

We all wait while Jedidiah has Violet's wheelchair lifted with the fancy wheelchair lift. He secures it in place and moves to stand beside Dad. Next to Dad, Pastor looks about two feet tall.

"Can I pray now and we declare Divine order over our travels?" Jedidiah asks.

"I want to say a few things first." Dad unbuttons his tan wool coat. "I'd like everybody's attention, please."

Everyone turns their attention to Dad. Brandon and Nam slide their oversize headphones off their heads.

"This is a sensitive situation here," Dad starts. "I got my entire family on this bus. All the people I love the most. So we're respectful of each other's space. We give Pastor Jedidiah the peace he needs to drive us all safely. Everybody stays seated when the bus is moving. We're courteous always. And I don't need to remind you all that we got Violet with us, who isn't exactly feeling well. Let's try to remember that when we make our planned stops. She gets off first. We are conscious of her and her needs. Am I clear?"

Everyone nods.

Jedidiah points to me. "Indigo. Would *you* like to say something before we declare Divine order over our travels?"

"Me?"

"Good idea. You should definitely say something. Yeah. This'll be good."

"What should I say?" I whisper out of the side of my mouth.

"Um…you asking us?" Mom asks in disbelief.

Nam and Brandon exchange knowing looks and shake their heads.

"Just repeat after me. And make sure your voice is booming. People always trust a booming voice."

I stand.

"Good morning, family."

"Good morning, family!" I shout.

"Why are you *screaming*?" Brandon covers his ears.

"Sorry." I clear my throat. "I was trying to be booming."

"Say what?" Michelle asks.

"Just keep going. Repeat after me: I am glad you're trusting me as we embark on a holy mission ordained by Almighty God herself."

"I'm not saying that," I whisper.

"Just say it!"

"Uh…" Everyone gawks at me. "I'm glad you're trusting me!" Now Nam covers his ears, too. I lower my voice a bit. "As we embark on a holy mission ordained by Almighty God…"

"Herself."

"Herself."

"God's not a *girl!*" Brandon shrieks.

"Tell him I am neither boy nor girl."

I clear my throat. "No! It doesn't matter. Just…let's continue. What else should I say?"

"Indigo?" Dad rubs the bald portion of his head. "You sure you all right now?"

"No. I mean…yes." *Voice, I'm tanking here.*

"And justice for all. Amen."

I groan. "That's it. Thanks for trusting me. That's all I want to say."

I slump back down into my seat.

It's quiet for a few seconds.

"Wow." Jedidiah finally speaks. "Thanks for sharing those beautiful thoughts and insights, Indigo. And now we declare Divine order over our trip by all repeating after me." He pushes his palms together over his heart. "I declare Divine order over our trip."

Everyone repeats it.

"Excellent." Jedidiah sits in the driver's seat and the loud *beep-beep* of the bus sounds more like the pop of a starter pistol at the beginning of a race. He pulls off down the street and we are officially on our way.

CHAPTER NINE

We've been driving for less than a half hour when it strikes me. I forgot to go to the restroom. I pull Violet's typed schedule out of my pocket and scan the page to see what time our first scheduled stop is. Uggh. That's a long time from now. There is no way I can hold it for much longer than a few minutes. Damn Michelle for making me drink that entire bottle of water. Although... I rub my temples. Whatever she gave me...well...it worked.

I stand and scoot down the aisle to kneel beside Dad and Violet. Dad reads news on his phone. I tap him on the shoulder. "Dad?"

He turns to me. "Hon, you need to be seated."

"I know, but I have to, uh, go to the bathroom."

Violet looks over at me.

"Sorry, Vee. I know it's not a scheduled stop. But I really have to go bad."

"It's no big deal," she replies. "We don't have to follow it, like…perfectly. It's to help keep us on track is all."

"But we're not even out of Seattle yet," Mom calls from across the aisle. "How are we making a stop already? Indigo, you didn't go to the bathroom before we left? You're eighteen years old and need to be reminded to go to the *bathroom*?"

"I did go. But then Michelle gave me a bottle of water."

"Oh, this is my fault?" Michelle laughs. "Girl, bye."

"No. I'm just… Look, I gotta pee. Bad."

"Jedidiah?" Dad leans forward. "You mind swinging by a gas station so Indigo can run to the bathroom?"

"The gas station urinals are connected to terrible fields of disturbed energy." Jedidiah expertly switches lanes. "Let's stop at a café—5-Point Café is right off this exit."

"Okay, Indigo. We're stopping. Now go sit down," Dad orders.

I return to my seat.

Jedidiah exits the freeway and we glide along in heavy morning traffic. Just as a large truck is leaving, we pull into an empty spot on the street, right in front of 5-Point Café and Bar.

"I have good parking space karma," Jedidiah explains. "Never fails. Always get the best spots."

"I wouldn't turn off the bus, Jedidiah." Dad turns to me. "Indigo, in and out. Hurry up."

"Does anybody else have to go?" Mom turns to look at Brandon and Nam. "Go now. We don't stop again until—" Mom reads from Violet's schedule "—Oregon."

Nobody says a word. I walk the gauntlet alone. "I'll be super quick. I swear."

The bus doors open and I rush down the stairs into Seattle winter.

I wash my hands at the sink and grab a paper towel. The restroom at 5-Point Café isn't anything fancy but at least the toilets are clean. I push back out into the restaurant. On Saturdays and Sundays this place is usually packed with a line down the street to get in. But since it's a random Tuesday morning, most people are at work or school. I move toward the door and hear a familiar laugh. I pause. I *know* that laugh.

I turn to see Troy in a booth. "Dear God, no." He's not alone. He's with the girl I saw at his apartment. *Corina.* I back slowly away. "Don't let them see me. Please, don't let them see me."

"Hey, excuse you," someone barks.

I twist around, almost slamming into a waiter carrying a tray of smoking hot breakfast food. "Shoot. My bad." I sneak a quick peek at Troy. He and the girl are holding hands. My blood must be boiling because I have to wipe sweat from my forehead and the restaurant's not even all that warm.

The waiter clears his throat. "*Excuse* me? I need to get around you."

"Oh, right." I turn back to the waiter and say softly, "Could I get a knife?"

He gives me an odd look.

"I ordered the steak and eggs and I didn't get a knife. Like, I need a really sharp steak knife. One that could puncture through tires. Though I'm not going to puncture tires. I'm going to cut my steak…and eggs."

The waiter reaches into his apron, hands me a bundle of silverware wrapped tightly with a thin paper towel and quickly moves around me.

I stuff the silverware into the pocket of my coat and rush to the door. A few people moving into the café stop to stare at the eye-mobile. I hear a girl say:

"Dude, that is some weird shit."

I push past them and scurry around to the side alley before anybody on the bus notices me. I scan the street and easily spot Troy's pearl-white Jeep Wrangler. Thankfully, it's parked on a secluded section of Fourth Avenue, in front of a giant inflatable Santa. I rush to the car, ducking low so that Mom or Dad won't catch a glimpse of me through the hundreds of eyeballs on the bus windows.

Once I make it to Troy's Jeep, I slide and squat *Mission: Impossible*–style behind the Santa. The silverware clanks loudly onto the pavement as I rip off the paper towel. I grab the steak knife and examine it.

"Uh? Hello? Girl, what is you *doin'*?"

"Assisting karma."

"The universe is perfectly balanced. Karma doesn't need assistance."

I ignore the voice and examine the knife. It has a round tip? Stupid safety knives. How come people don't make steak knives meant for jabbing things anymore?

"You're gonna get arrested."

"Cool. Never been to jail."

I try sawing at the tires but it's like taking a toothpick to concrete. These are not your average tires. I scan the silver-ware on the pavement.

"A butter knife won't work either."

"I wasn't going to try that."

"A spoon? Nah."

"Could you be quiet, please? I need to think."

The fork suddenly stands out to me. I take it and stab at the tires.

"Literally never seen anybody do that before. And I'm God. I've seen everything."

Fork's not working. I look around to make sure no one's paying any attention to me. It's a busy morning and traffic is heavy, but thankfully, I'm almost completely obscured by Santa. I sigh. Where can I find something that can puncture through a tire?

"If you bend all the other prongs, so only one fork prong stands, you might be able to push it through."

I study the fork. That's actually a pretty good idea. "Wait—you're helping me?"

"Eh, when in Rome."

I bend the fork prongs down by pushing them onto the concrete. It takes a massive amount of effort, but after a min-ute or two, I'm finally left with three bent fork prongs and one that stands erect. With all my strength, I stab into the grooves of the tire. Again and again and again, until finally, I hear the *tsssss* of air seeping through rubber. "Yes! I did it!"

"Congratulations, Indigo. You've just committed your first felony."

"Thank you!" I move around and do the same thing to the other tire that's hidden by Santa. Two flat tires should serve him well. Happy Tuesday, Troy.

I stuff all the silverware back into my coat pocket and run back to the bus; the doors open as I approach. Michelle's rushing down the stairs.

"Michelle." I'm all outta breath. "What, uh, are you doing?"

"Girl, you took so long, we ordered a dozen of those breakfast muffins they make."

Crap. If Michelle sees Troy she'll make a scene. Violet will know about Troy and his new girlfriend. The trip could be ruined before it even begins!

I hold out my hand. "Oh, you stay on the bus. I'll get the muffins."

"I have to pay." She holds up her credit card.

I snatch it out of her hand. "I got it. You relax." I take off before she can respond, rushing across the pavement and pushing through the doors back into the café.

A hostess with short jet-black hair shaved on one side is returning from seating a family. "Hi. Can I help you?"

"Yes. To-go order for Michelle Delacroix?"

She studies a computer screen at the host stand. "Yeah, I see it. You ordered a dozen of the blueberry oatmeal muffins?"

"Yep." I thrust the card at her.

She takes it.

I stare over her shoulder, tapping my feet anxiously as she rings up the order. Thankfully Troy's back is to me and it looks like he's not even halfway through his meal. As long as he doesn't turn around, I'm good.

"Would you like napkins and utensils?"

"Uh…maybe napkins." I think of Brandon and Nam. "Make it lots of napkins."

"Got it. System is so slow today." She hands me back the card. "Receipt should print out in a second. You can have a seat. I'll let you know when they're ready."

Ugggh. They're muffins. Aren't they already made? Shouldn't they have a muffin vending machine in this place? "Can you check? We're in a bit of a rush, if you don't mind."

The receipt prints out. She pulls it out of the machine and slides it across the counter. "Can you sign? Customer receipt hasn't printed yet. Like I said, system is slow."

I scribble something illegible at the bottom. "And can you check? Please?"

She sighs. "I guess. Yeah. Be right back." She takes off at a snail's pace.

I glance back over at Troy's girlfriend. Our eyes meet. *Shit.* She saw me! Her brow furrows. She leans forward and says something to Troy.

He starts to turn toward me but I duck behind the counter before he can see, pretending to tie my shoes even though I'm wearing Uggs.

"He didn't see me. He totally didn't see me."

"But she saw you."

"But maybe she didn't recognize me."

"Nah, she totally recognized you."

"Stop being so negative!"

"Indigo?"

I look up. Holy shitballs, Troy is standing in front of me.

Wearing another pair of expensive True Religion jeans, with a snow-white T-shirt. Looking like he comes from money.

"What are you doing?" he asks.

I pop up. "Troy Richmond. What an unpleasant surprise."

"Are you...following me?"

"Troy, do I look like I have private detective equipment in my pockets? I don't know where you go on a day-to-day. I don't know what you do. I'm here for the muffins, man. The fact that I've run into you is simply an unfortunate co-incidence."

He eyes me suspiciously. "But it's a school day and you don't even live in this part of town."

Thankfully the hostess approaches with a giant to-go bag.

"Here you go, Mrs....Delacroix?" She hands me the bag. "A dozen blueberry oatmeal muffins to go, extra napkins."

"Mrs. Delacroix?" Troy says to the hostess.

"Oh, did I pronounce it wrong?" the hostess replies as the customer receipt finally prints out. She grabs it and reads. "Michelle Delacroix?"

"Yep. That's correct." I snatch the receipt out of her hand. "Thank you, miss. Have a great day." I turn to Troy. "Can you move out of my way?"

"You're with the family? Is Violet with you?"

"Dang, boy, stop being so nosy. Move around."

I scoot past him and rush from the restaurant back into the Seattle cold. I climb onto the bus.

"Everything all right?" Mom asks.

"Sure. Yeah." I hand the bag of muffins and credit card to Michelle.

"Oh, thanks. Did you get utensils?"

"For what?"

"The boys need forks."

Who eats muffins with a fork? "Oh, yeah. I asked but they ran out. Sorry."

I tap Pastor on the shoulder. "We can go now. Let's drive away from this place. Fast."

"Wait a second, Pastor." Michelle hands him a steaming hot muffin. "Try one. These things are so good."

"Don't mind if I do." Pastor Jedidiah peels off the paper. He takes a giant bite, closes his eyes and murmurs, "These *are* delicious."

"Told you." Michelle passes muffins out to the rest of the family.

I take a seat in the back and slump down. Why aren't we *moving*? Why is Pastor eating so slow? Why? Why? *Why?*

After what feels like a trillion years, Pastor crumples up the muffin paper, tosses it in the trash behind his seat and exhales dramatically. "That was the best muffin I've ever had in all my life. Thank you, Michelle."

Just as Pastor flips on the blinkers and checks his mirrors, banging on the side of the bus startles everyone.

"What on Earth was that?" Mom stands, peeking through the glass on the doors.

"Indigo!" a muffled voice shouts from outside.

I slump farther down in my seat. It's Troy. I'm caught. I'm dead. Jail-bound for sure. Federal prison, here I come.

Mom gasps. "Is that Troy Richmond?"

"What?" Violet looks dumbstruck. "*My* Troy?" She peeks through the window. "Who's the girl with him?"

Now everybody moves to a window.

Jedidiah pulls the lever that makes the doors swing open and Troy takes a step back. "Goooooood morning. We're not taking passengers. I know it looks tempting."

"Indigo!" Troy shouts. "I know it was you who fucked up my tires! I want you to know I called the police."

Mom and Dad turn to me.

"What is he talking about?" Mom asks.

"I—" I scratch my head "—may have forked his tires."

"Forked? What is that? Is that slang for something?" Dad asks.

"No, I literally stuck a fork into two of the tires on his Jeep."

"Indigo!" Dad bellows. "When?"

"Just...um...now."

"Those were thousand-dollar tires, sir," Troy calls up to Dad. "I really have no other choice but to press charges when the police get here."

"Let me talk to him." Violet struggles to stand. "Dad, can you help me? I don't...wanna get too winded. If I do it on my...own. And I don't...wanna use the wheelchair."

"You sure, Violet?" Mom asks nervously, clearly not wanting Violet to be exposed to any more pain and heartache.

"Either I talk to him...or Indigo gets in big trouble." She looks up at Dad. "Please?"

Dad nods, carefully lifts Violet into his arms and walks her down the stairs.

Everybody clumps together at the doorway. Troy looks like he's about to shit his pants when he sees Violet. He freezes. Spooked.

"Hi, Troy," she says softly.

Troy stuffs his hands into his pockets and mumbles, "Hello."

"Good to see you." Violet extends her hand to Corina. "Hi, I'm...Violet. Nice to meet you."

A confused Corina shakes Violet's hand.

"We're on our way to Arizona," Violet explains. "It's a really important trip. Is there any way you could...maybe call *off* the police? I can pay you for the tires."

Troy stares down at the pavement, too ashamed to even make eye contact with Violet. "Uh, yeah. That would be okay."

"What do I owe you?"

Troy shakes his head. "Nothing. Look, Violet. I couldn't take money from you. It wouldn't feel right."

"But I have a few thousand dollars in savings. I don't mind. I only want to keep peace. Indigo...sometimes she does things without thinking... She's sorry."

I roll my eyes. Maybe I do things without thinking but I am definitely *not* sorry.

"Violet." Troy clears his throat. "I won't take money from you, all right? Let's forget it. Call it even."

"Call what even?" Corina interrupts. "That random girl damages your property and you're going to let it slide? Is there something I'm missing here?"

"She's not random. Don't get involved in business that's not yours," Troy snaps at Corina. "Go wait by the car."

Corina's jaw clenches in anger.

Dad steps forward. "So then we're good here, Troy?"

"Calling it even." Troy scratches the back of his head. "Yeah."

"Maybe not even," Violet adds with a sigh. "But at least… the police don't have to get involved."

"I agree." Troy runs a hand across his cheek. "I'm sorry, Violet."

This would be the point where *I* would lurch forward and kick Troy in the balls, but though Violet and I share identical DNA, we don't share an identical approach to love and life. She's probably standing there, imagining all the ways Troy is good, while I'm imagining him with a wounded nutsack. She's forgiving him for all the pain he caused her over these last couple of months. I'm concealing the prong of a fork in the pocket of my coat.

She steps forward and hugs him tightly. He rests his head on her shoulder.

"I really am sorry, Violet," he whispers. "I'd take it back if I could."

"I know you would." She pulls away, turns to Dad. "I'm ready."

Dad picks her up and we all part to make room as they climb the stairs. The doors to the bus slam shut. Leaving Troy and Corina alone in the cold. I watch them through a window next to Violet's seat. They're in a deep conversation that seems to be escalating pretty quickly. Corina removes the lid from the cup in her hand and hurls it in Troy's face, storming away. He hangs his head, dripping with orange juice, and walks in the opposite direction. I guess…back to his inoperable vehicle? Maybe he'll call a Lyft or a tow truck. Not sure how he'll get around on two flats. Not sure I care either. Maybe the police can give him a ride home.

Violet's staring out the window, too. She adjusts her cannula with trembling hands.

We're all silent. Watching and waiting to see what Violet will do. What she will say. Is she going to burst into tears? Yell and scream at me? I knew Troy had a girlfriend and didn't tell her the truth. Then I put our entire trip in jeopardy by damaging Troy's property. I was careless, reckless and melodramatic to the tenth power. She has every right to be angry.

As if reading my mind, Violet looks up at me. "You…"

"Violet, I know what I did was wrong. I wasn't—"

She holds out a hand to silence me. "You *forked* his tires?"

I pull at my ponytail. "With a fork. Yeah."

She's quiet for a moment. Then she starts to laugh. In fact, she laughs until she's nearly bent over. It's the first time I've seen her laugh in *months*. My jaw drops.

"*S-M-H,*" Alfred says while literally shaking his head. "Man, Indigo, you crazy." He laughs, too.

Mom and Dad exchange looks, then burst into laughter as well.

Even Michelle cracks up. "Did God tell you to do that, Indigo?"

"No. He told me not to," I declare with an embarrassed shrug.

Soon, the entire family is howling with laughter.

A familiar smell wafts up to my nose. We all spin around

to see Jedidiah holding one of his prayer sticks. Its swirls of smoke drifting into all corners of the bus. "Should we have Indigo confess assault with a deadly fork? Or full speed ahead to the Wave?"

"Full speed ahead, Pastor." Violet laughs, wiping tears from her eyes. "Right, Indigo?"

I grin. "Definitely full speed."

CHAPTER TEN

"Whatcha reading?"

"You're God. Shouldn't you already know?"

"Humor me? I do enjoy a good conversation."

"The thesaurus." I turn the page.

"Is it good?"

"It's not good like a regular book or anything." I shift in my seat, trying to find some sort of comfortable position. Michelle was right. It has been a bumpy ride so far. I stretch out my back and yawn. "I know it's weird, but I like finding new ways to say things. Like, you could call someone smart, or you could call them keen, nimble, crafty and resourceful."

"Or you could call them sprambly."

"Wait." I flip to the *S* section. "What's *sprambly*?"

"You won't find it. I made it up just now. It means keen, nimble, crafty and resourceful."

I set the book down on the empty seat beside me. "You can't be makin' up words like that."

"Of course I can. You do know all language is made up, right? Trust me. I made up a lot of it. Making up words is fun. Try it."

"Indigo?"

I glance up. Alfred is standing in the aisle. "Could I talk to you for a second? I mean…if you're done talking to yourself."

"Uh, sure."

Alfred sits beside me as the bus speeds along the highway, forests of evergreens in the distance whizzing by in a blur. He cracks each individual knuckle. Flips his cap forward.

"Alfred? What's up?"

"I have to tell Mom and Dad something, and I don't know how they're gonna take it. I'm scared. I need to practice my confession, *I-R-L*."

"In real life? On *me*?"

"I need someone who is sort of disconnected from reality."

"Gee, thanks."

"No, I mean…you won't judge me."

I stuff my thesaurus into my camera bag on the floor at my feet. "You really think this trip is a good time for an in-real-life confession?"

"Not really, but…" He cracks his knuckles again.

Hmm. He looks *super* tense. What could warrant a practice confession? I drum my fingers on my cast.

He's gay.

He identifies as a girl, wants to change his name from Alfred to Allie.

He's certainly not pregnant. That's a plus.

Oh! He might have gotten a *girl* pregnant. Yikes.

Alfred clears his throat and cracks his neck.

"Alfred Phillips, if you don't speak!" I whisper. "This is making me solicitous about your well-being."

"What's that mean?"

"It means I'm nervous, I think. Just hurry up."

"Dang. Fine. Chill." Alfred licks his lips. "So at school. There's this boy…"

All right, great. He's gay. I can handle this. I love gay people. I'll be excited to have a gay brother. Someday, I'll have a gay brother-in-law. They can adopt gay children. I'll go to gay pride parades. I'm already named after a color of the rainbow. It all fits.

"His name is Mikey."

"Nice. Did you guys have sex?"

"What?" Alfred flips his cap forward. "What the holy hell?"

"Sorry. I thought you were gay."

"Why did you think I was *gay*?"

"I dunno. You licked your lips and then said, 'There's this boy named Mikey,' so I assumed."

"So to clarify—" Alfred neurotically applies ChapStick to his lips "—I said, 'There's this boy named Mikey.'"

"*And* you licked your lips. Don't leave that part out. I thought you were…you know. Thinking about him."

"No offense, Indigo." Alfred shakes his head. "But I worry about you. A lot."

"Fine. Whatever. You're not gay." I lean back in my seat. "But if you ever become gay, I'm cool with it."

"How progressive." He rolls his eyes. "Can I finish my practice confession?"

I mime zipping my lips.

"Okay, Mikey—a friend I never have nor ever will have sex with—he had the answers to the algebra test. And he was selling them for forty-seven dollars."

"Why forty-seven dollars? That's such an odd number. Why not fifty?"

"Indigo? Can you *please* listen?"

"Sorry. Keep going."

"I paid him forty-seven bucks on Venmo. And he texted me the answers. Anyway, long story short. The teacher found out. His phone got confiscated, and all the people who he texted the answers to got…expelled. It was six of us total, including him."

I sit up. "You're an *idiot!*"

"Shhhh!" Alfred whispers.

Mom and Michelle turn around.

"Sorry." I wave. "I thought I saw a possum running across the highway. Idiot possum!"

I yank on Alfred's jersey and pull him down so we're below the seat and no one can see or hear us. "You got expelled from school? Mom and Dad are going to go apocalyptic on you. How could you be so *stupid*?"

"I thought you said you weren't going to judge me?"

"*You* said that. I'm judging the hell out of you!"

"That makes me feel really bad."

My face twists into a scowl. "Good!"

"Whatever, man." Alfred stands.

I grab his arm and pull him back down again. "Do not—I repeat—do not tell Mom and Dad this mess until we get home. Do you understand?"

He snatches his arm away. "I wish I would've told Violet instead of *you*. She would be calm and rational. *She'd* help me."

I wince. He's right. She would. She might even know how to fix this. But I can't exactly ask for her opinion. Not without everybody else finding out, too. And if everybody else knew Alfred was currently expelled from school, this trip would be over. I bite the inside of my bottom lip. "I thought you got a D on your Algebra test anyway?"

"Yeah. So?"

"So how did you get a D if you cheated?"

"I think the answers were wrong."

"Forty-seven dollars for *wrong* answers?" I want to call him an imbecile. Idiot imbecile. Imbecilic dimwit. But WWVD. What would Violet do? I don't want Alfred to feel the pain of having to settle for the least favorite sister. At least not yet. "Maybe something can be done. Maybe you don't have to be expelled."

A small bit of hope springs back to his eyes. "You think?"

"Maybe. I dunno. Just gimme some time to figure it out. Okay?"

"I hate to interrupt this warm and touching conversation, but I think something's wrong with the Jedi Master."

"Something's wrong with Jedidiah?"

"What's wrong with Pastor Jedidiah?" Alfred asks.

"I dunno." I stretch my neck to check him out at the wheel. Sure enough, his face is pained. He's shifting uncomfortably. Grimacing. Gripping his stomach.

"You might wanna tell Michelle. The man needs to be *examined*."

Jedidiah grabs a microphone from off the dash and presses a button. "Goooood morning, ladies and gentle ladies. Fun fact about Oregon—it's known for having more ghost towns than any other state." He pauses. The sound of his stomach rumbling can be heard through the mic. "Uh-oh." He clears his throat as a noise from somewhere deep within Pastor Jedidiah's rectum erupts like a foghorn. His neck turns red.

"Ewwww," Brandon cries. "He *farted*!"

"Pastor, you feeling all right?" Michelle stands.

"I'm..." He hunches over and cries out in pain.

"Jedidiah, you should pull over!" Dad stands.

"Copy that..." Jedidiah still has both hands on the wheel. "You're still safe in my hands. We declared Divine order, so everything's in alignment with the universe." He switches on the blinkers and pulls onto the shoulder of the road. Once he turns off the engine, he doubles over, whimpering in pain.

Michelle rushes to his side. "Dad, help me."

Dad and Michelle each take a shoulder and push Jedidiah so he's sitting back up.

"Did you go to the bathroom today?" Michelle asks, kneeling in front of him.

"I tried. I could only go a little."

"Did it smell funny?" Michelle asks.

"Now that you mention it."

Brandon giggles. "Super gross."

"Smelly pee." Nam laughs. "Nasty."

Michelle turns and points to Brandon and Nam. "Another word from you and I'll throw you off this bus. You understand? Right out the window!" She turns her attention back to Jedidiah. "Okay, where's the pain?"

Jedidiah points to his side.

"What about here?" Michelle pushes on his stomach. He whimpers. "And here?" She pushes on another side of his stomach. He groans.

"It's kidney stones for sure."

"Pretty sure it's kidney stones." Michelle sighs.

Jedidiah lets another one rip.

Nam and Brandon cover their mouths to contain their laughter.

"Should we take him to urgent care?" Mom asks.

Michelle shakes her head. "Nothing urgent care can really do. With kidney stones they have to pass. Plus, he's… passing…gas. And that's a good sign. Means things are moving. The stones will pass eventually. We should turn around and take him home, though."

"No!" Jedidiah speaks through clenched teeth. "I refuse to abandon this mission." He points to the small trash can near his seat. Michelle quickly grabs it and hands it to him. He extracts the muffin bag from the café and pukes into it. "So sorry," he mutters between retching.

"My Lord." Mom grimaces.

Michelle fiddles with her phone. "There's a pharmacy close

by. I can call in a prescription that might help them pass quicker. And get you something to help you sleep and settle your stomach." She places a hand on Jedidiah's knee. "You really wanna be on this bus trying to pass kidney stones? You sure you don't wanna go home, where you can have privacy? It's gonna be painful. And by painful... I'm putting it nicely."

"I can take pain." Jedidiah winces, still hovered over his bag of puke.

"That's easy to say now." Michelle stares at her phone. "But people say passing kidney stones is as painful as giving birth. And from personal experience, I can tell you I wouldn't have wanted to give birth on this bus."

"When I commit to something, I see it through," Jedidiah articulates through clenched teeth. "I'm not leaving you. Not abandoning Violet."

"We'll stop at this pharmacy in Urlington, then." Michelle studies her phone. "Google Maps says it's five miles away. I'm sure there's a restaurant nearby. We can eat there, too. That'll be our first rest stop."

"I didn't research Urlington." Violet perks up. "The rest stop in Pendleton is better. It's star-rated with good reviews. How far away is that?"

Michelle studies her phone. "About twenty miles. I'm sorry, Violet." She rubs her tired eyes. "We need a pharmacy ASAP. Urlington is closer."

"Who's gonna drive the bus now?" Drew asks.

"I could certainly try," Dad says without much confidence.

"Isaiah, now, you know better." Mom shakes her head.

"Last thing you wanna do is reinjure your rotator cuff. Doc says one more tear and you'll have to have surgery."

"It's fine." Violet's head slumps. "We can forget it…if you guys want. I feel like I'm causing everyone trouble and now… Pastor is sick and—"

"No, Violet. It's no trouble at all, hon." Dad wraps an arm around her, kisses her on top of her head.

"I can drive." Mom stands confidently.

"Babe, you can't. You don't have a driver's license."

"So what, Isaiah?" Mom shrugs. "I still know how to drive a bus."

"But, Mom, what if you get pulled over?" Michelle interrupts.

"Oh, pish tosh." Mom waves her hand dismissively as she sits in the driver's seat and adjusts the mirrors.

Nam grunts. "Now we'll never get to Arizona."

"Excuse me, Nam?" Mom's annoyed. "What is that supposed to mean?"

"He might be referring to how—" Drew swallows "—slow… you used to drive."

"Drew, I drove the speed limit. Just because you drive like a bat out of hell."

"*Mom.*" Michelle shakes her head. "Drew is a very good driver."

"Son-in-law? How many moving violations have you gotten so far?"

"In my life?"

Mom unbuttons the sleeves on her red dress shirt and rolls them one at a time to her elbow. "Just this year, for starters."

"Maybe two." Drew shrugs.

"And like three last year." Alfred cuts in. I elbow him in the side. "What? It's true."

Drew hangs his head in shame. "And they were speeding tickets. You're right, Mom. I'm sorry for letting the family down with my irresponsible driving."

Michelle rolls her eyes. "Really, Drew? You're apologizing for driving irresponsibly? At a moment when you're *not* driving? That's absurd. Get a spine! Stop apologizing all the damn time."

"Right. Sorry," Drew says.

Michelle groans.

"Transporting people was my profession for thirty years," Mom explains as if we don't know that. "And I was good at it. Never had one write-up. Never had one ticket. Never missed a day of work. I know what I'm doing. Driver's license be damned."

"Driver's license be *needed*," Alfred whispers to me.

Michelle helps Jedidiah stand. "C'mon, Pastor. Let's get you to the back of the bus. I'll sit with you if you need."

Jedidiah snivels in pain as Michelle leads him to the back and helps him into the two seats Alfred was sitting in.

"I was actually sitting there," Alfred explains.

"Not anymore." Michelle snaps her fingers at me. "Indi, grab me a few blankets so the pastor can lay down. And grab me my phone so I can call the pharmacy."

I run to the front, dig around Michelle's large bag and retrieve the two small blankets stuffed inside. When I go to grab her cell, an email loads on the screen. I don't mean to pry, but I mean, it's on the screen. From someone named Nathan Marshak:

A few papers left to sign for you and Drew. We might be able to have your divorce finalized before the New Year. Mazel Tov.

They're getting a *divorce*?!

"Everybody sitting down?" Mom looks at me through the rearview mirror. "Indigo? Do you think that you need to find a seat?"

Another nonrhetorical rhetorical. "Yes, Mom. I do." Violet's staring at me quizzically. Does she know? That Michelle and Drew are in the middle of a *divorce*? That Alfred's been *expelled* from school?

Pastor Jedidiah starts hurling into his paper bag again.

"It smells in here!" Nam mumbles. "Can we open a window?"

Brandon uses two fingers to plug his nose.

I press the side button on Michelle's phone so the email disappears and shuffle to the back with the blankets as Mom revs up the engine. Her silver bun the only thing you can see at the top of the driver's seat as she inches into traffic. And I do mean inches. I could get out and run faster than this.

I hand Michelle the phone and the blankets. She covers up the pastor as he winces in pain, laid out across the two seats, sandals hanging out into the aisle, face hidden inside a bag of puke.

Michelle calls out to Mom. "Take Exit 21C."

"Copy that." Mom continues her crawl down the highway.

I slide around Alfred and plop down in my seat, peeking through the eyeballs on the window. Cars whiz by us in a blur. An elderly couple in a pickup truck zooms past. The wife on the passenger side sticks her head out the window and screams:

"Get off the damn road, you damn buffoons!"

I shake my head.

"Arizona?" Alfred huffs. "We might not even make it to the next exit."

"Helen." Dad leans forward. "You can speed up a bit."

"I'm driving fifty-five, Isaiah!"

"The speed limit is seventy." Dad's speaking softly but we all can hear. "You'll get pulled over driving this slow. And then we'll really be in trouble."

"Isaiah, please let me do what I do. Safe driving is the key to a long life." Mom continues at a snail's pace.

I look back out the window as a school bus packed with young children zips around us.

I raise an eye to the ceiling. "I thought you said nothing could go wrong?"

"I meant wrong wrong. Trust me. Everything's gonna be fine."

CHAPTER ELEVEN

It feels like years since Mom took the wheel. Brandon and Nam are literally banging their heads against the window, Alfred is frenetically coating his lips with strawberry Chap-Stick and Michelle, Drew and Dad all look like they're about to scream: *Get me off this damn bus before I jump out the window!* When, at last, the bus inches off the highway.

"Man, I feel like I aged a thousand years since Mom took the wheel," Alfred declares.

"I know, right? Welcome to Burlington."

"Urlington." He stands, stuffs his tube of ChapStick into his back pocket. "I gotta talk to Drew."

I grab the bottom of his Seahawks jersey. "Not a word about the expulsion."

"Not even to Violet? She'll know what to do. Violet always knows how to fix things."

I shrug and mumble, "I don't want to upset her. So I guess you're stuck with just me this time."

Alfred only nods in reply, moves down the aisle and slides into the seat beside Drew. Since Drew makes video games for a living and Alfred's a big gamer, they're more like best friends than brothers-in-law. I observe them for a few seconds as they chat it up like two teens. Alfred will be inconsolable when he learns about the divorce. But he won't be the only one in a rotten mood. When Mom discovers that pregnant Michelle is set to be a divorcée *and* single mom, there will be no containing the screech-and-screams. And how the hell am I supposed to manage getting Alfred unexpelled?

I twist my neck to stare out the window as we turn into a gravel covered parking lot. Urlington looks…barren. Like one of those industrial towns time and most people forgot. Or should forget, anyway.

"Be nice. Good people in this town."

"Hey. Didn't I tell you to stop reading my mind?"

"Look here, Indigo. As God, I can't help but know everything. My bad, okay? I'm sorry that I'm so smart and all-knowing."

Dad stretches his legs out into the aisle and rubs his shoulders. "Everybody off."

Jedidiah whimpers like a wounded animal.

"Except Pastor," Dad adds sympathetically.

"The restaurant at the corner looks like it could be good." Mom pulls parallel into a couple of parking spaces. "We can eat there."

Across the street, what can only be described as a dilapi-
dated barn has a sign that reads Big's Bison Burgers.

"We'll use the restrooms, and while we wait for the prescription for Pastor to be filled, we can eat lunch. We stick
together," Dad instructs us. "We are a part of the Phillips family. That means we have a responsibility to the family name.
Be kind. Be courteous. Be aware of the needs of others."

Everyone waits patiently as Dad assists Violet down the
aisle. Once she's situated in her chair, Dad rushes outside and
Mom lowers the lift.

"I'll bring you back some food, Pastor." Michelle gath-
ers her purse and slides on her boots. "Try to get some rest."

"No rest for the weary." Jedidiah tosses off the blankets.
"I need to go with you. Must—" he pulls himself up "—pay
attention when the universe guides me."

He stands. Sort of. If you can call it standing.

"Pastor, you can't even straighten up." Michelle slides on
her gloves.

"Don't worry. Feeling fine!" He speaks as cheerfully as one
can when they're bent over at a ninety-degree angle.

Michelle watches Pastor shuffle awkwardly down the aisle,
then motions to me. "Ready, Indigo?"

I take my camera out of the bag at my feet, sling it over my
shoulder and move toward the exit. As I descend the stairs, I
take in such deep gulps of ice-cold air, my chest burns. The
outdoors is intoxicating, a welcome change from the dry heat
blasting on the bus for hours. Plus, Pastor's bag of vomit was
a bit of a damper on the indoor air quality. Putting it mildly.

I stare up at the layers of silver clouds through the lens of my camera.

Click-click.

I love taking pictures of clouds. These are so thick it seems as if they're all working together: conspirator clouds, determined to keep us shrouded in darkness. Like they're getting a big kick out of our lack of vitamin D. I lower my camera, close my eyes and visualize warm rays of sunlight enveloping every inch of my skin. The thought heats me up inside. Up this way, the sun disappears during this time of year. Darkness gets into your bloodstream and ferments. Depression lingers in the air at every turn. You even stop dreaming in color. I can't help but wonder if the lack of sunlight played a part in Violet's conclusion that suicide was the best option for her. I wonder if it played a part in mine.

"This isn't suicide," Violet explained to the family the day she announced that she was opting to end her life. "Please don't call it that. Besides, I'm only assisting the plan that's been laid out for me. It's dying with dignity. It's the law. And it's my right."

The gravel crunches beneath my Uggs as I turn a full circle, taking in all of Urlington. Though, there isn't much to take in. A few old houses down the road.

Click-click.

A terrifying-looking rusted bridge stretched across a dried-out riverbed off in the distance.

Click.

Big's Bison Burgers has a few pickup trucks in their driveway. And Carlson's Drugstore seems as though a strong wind could blow it over at any given moment. It's an old wood-sided building with paint that was probably blue at some point. One of the windows is cracked. Metal-framed doors look slightly off their hinges. Sitting underneath the dismal sky, the drugstore kind of reminds me of the house Dorothy landed in Oz.

Click-click.

Nam doesn't seem to mind that the store is lacking in the feng shui department. He's chasing Brandon around the nearly empty parking lot, laughing and hurling insults at him, Dad's speech completely on deaf ears with those two.

"Booger boy! Booger boy! You eat boogers for diiiinnnner," Nam sings.

Brandon has a hand over his butt as he runs. "Stop it. You're gonna make me poop my pants."

Michelle rushes ahead of everyone. "I'm gonna run inside and speak to the pharmacist." She disappears inside the store.

I hurry to Violet's wheelchair and cut in front of Dad. "I'm with Violet, Dad. You should check on Pastor. He doesn't look so good."

Jedidiah takes baby steps, hunched over, in full salute to the gravel. He attempts taking one of his signature deep breaths, but one inhalation and he's grabbing his stomach in pain. He stumbles forward. Dad speeds toward him.

"Jedidiah, you sure you should be walking?"

"Without pain we don't grow and expand, Isaiah. If you place silica, soda ash and limestone into a furnace at three thousand degrees, do you know what you get?"

"I can't say that I do," Dad replies.

"Glass."

"Ahh." Dad rubs the bald portion of his head. "Oh, I see. I get it."

He clearly doesn't get it.

"I'm in the furnace," Pastor explains. "Heating up to something marvelous. I can't wait to see what I turn into."

A perturbed look stretches across Dad's face as he follows behind Jedidiah. Probably imagining the pastor as a glass sculpture, bent over for the next few decades.

I struggle to guide Violet across the thick layer of parking lot gravel, my camera banging against my chest as it sways back and forth, shoulder throbbing.

"I have a weird feeling about this place," Violet murmurs.

I grind my teeth. "Yeah, me too," I agree just to appease Violet. She likes to stick to her schedules and plans. Any sort of deviation is unsettling to her. But the truth is, it seems bleak here for sure, but not exactly dangerous. I pause to rub my aching shoulder.

"Do you think you could use some help, Indigo?" There's a slight hint of amusement in Mom's voice.

"Nope." I wipe my forehead, simultaneously ice-cold and sweaty. "I'm fine. I got this."

Violet holds up her phone. "See? It only has a one-star Yelp rating. You don't wanna go anywhere with a one-star rating."

Alfred holds open the door. "Violet, people who live in towns like this don't Yelp. They drink beer and smash the empty cans over the tops of their heads."

"Alfred Phillips!" Mom calls out from behind us. "I'm sure

Urlington has wonderful people who live here. That's insensitive and rude."

An old lady with pink sponge rollers in her graying blond hair and a dusty mink coat that looks like she found it in a box in her basement pushes past Mom.

"Excuse you." Mom stumbles back.

The old lady turns around and hisses at us, exposing her only two teeth. We all recoil. "Did I *ask* to be excused?" She scurries past Alfred, an evil glint in her eye.

"See." Alfred gestures toward the woman as she disappears into the store. "Told you."

Drew rounds up the boys and we all head inside.

Carlson's Drugstore is about what I expected it to be. Scuffed tile flooring that's yellowing in spots. Old, dusty shelving. There is only one checkout counter with a cashier who appears to be about a hundred, watching one of those box TV sets from the olden days.

"Where's the enemas?" Sponge Roller Lady hollers as she scoots down an aisle.

The cashier doesn't move an eyeball from the TV screen, or even move a muscle, to be honest. "Aisle three. Bottom shelf." He speaks so slowly I wonder if he's a robot. Like the Urlington version of Amazon's Alexa.

Toward the back, you can see a small pharmacy with a lone female pharmacist who seems as if she's about had it with Urlington, Carlson's Drugstore and especially Michelle. The two are having a heated discussion. I stretch my neck, eavesdropping on their conversation.

"So I guess your measly bachelor's degree trumps my two master's degrees? Girl, bye," Michelle declares.

Yep. Classic Michelle. "Hey, Violet, you want anything?"

"Maybe some VapoRub." We both rub our chests in perfect synchronicity. "It always helps and we forgot to pack it."

"One VapoRub comin' up, sis." I push her up an aisle, thrilled to, at last, be of some assistance to Violet. (In a way that doesn't involve committing a felony, I mean.) To my left, old, grimy-looking shelves are stacked with packages of ramen noodles and different varieties of soups, to my right… motor oil. "Interesting pairing." I push Violet to the next aisle, where we almost run into Nam. He's holding a plastic container of Red Vines.

"Auntie Indigo, can we get these?"

"Why you asking me?" I shrug. "I don't care if you get sick and all your teeth fall out. Ask your dad."

"He's on the phone."

At the far end of the store, Drew is having another hushed conversation. He's been on the phone almost this entire trip so far. Probably talking to his lawyer. *Divorce.* I whistle. Is it because after all these years, Drew discovered Michelle is mean and hateful? Did he cheat on her? Is Michelle pregnant by another guy?

"Ask Grandma, Nam," Violet offers sweetly.

"She'll say no," Nam whines. "She says no about everything."

Violet takes Nam's hands into hers. "Try this. Say… 'Grandma, Aunt *Violet* wants these, but I don't think she should have them.' Then ask her what she thinks." Violet grins. "She'll buy them. Watch."

Nam lurches forward and hugs Violet. "Thank you, Auntie Vee! You're the best."

He skips off, blissfully clutching his giant bin of Red Vines. Nam's right. She *is* the best. All I did was basically tell Nam to get lost. She was patient and even found a way to help him get what he wanted. Maybe I *should* ask her what we should do about Alfred's situation. She'll know what to do. She's so much better than me.

"Geez luss, Indigo! Self-deprecate much?"

"What? It's true!" I reply.

"What's true, Indigo?"

"Oh, uh… I was just sayin' I gotta stop being so mean to Nam and Bran."

The front doors to the store are pushed open and a young man steps into the flickering neon lighting. He's got greasy brown hair and dull gray eyes that match the color of the thick layers of clouds outside. He's in his early twenties, maybe. He stops abruptly after moving through the door, eyes darting back and forth like someone high on something. I lift my camera and quietly twist off the lens cap as he steps to the cashier.

Click-click.

"Can I get a pack of Lucky Strikes?" His voice is deep and raspy.

Without taking an eye off his tiny TV set, the cashier reaches behind him to unlock a glass case. "Be just the pack?"

Click-click.

"Yeah." The man stuffs his hands into his pocket.

I lower my camera and hold my breath, nervous about what could be in his pocket. There's something about him. Almost like he could go full-on serial killer right before our eyes. He extracts a crumpled ten-dollar bill from his coat pocket.

"Is he okay?" I look up at the ceiling. "Am I being paranoid?"

"Definitely. He wouldn't hurt a fly. Okay, maybe a fly. But nothing bigger than a cricket."

"Look at that man, Violet."

She looks up. "What about him?"

"Something seems off with him. Don't you think?"

"Now that you…mention it." Violet pauses to take a deep breath. "He looks so *sad*. Poor guy. The winter months… get everybody down. Indi, I'm pretty sure this isn't the right aisle."

I scope out the shelves. One side is stacked with baby diapers, wipes and lotions. The other side, wine and hard liquors like tequila and whiskey. "Oh, yeah. Let's try another."

When I turn my attention back to the mysterious man, he's exiting with his pack of cigarettes in hand. Yep. Definitely being paranoid. I return to the task at hand and we make our way down another aisle.

"Yay, we found it." Violet leans forward to study the items placed neatly on the shelves.

There are a variety of medicines like cough syrups, Tylenol and other, off-brand painkillers. I kneel. "What about this one? It's called—" I snatch up the box "—Chestix Rub."

"I guess it's like the generic of Vapo?" Violet runs a hand

through the ends of her hair. "Let me Google it to see if Chestix is a good brand."

"Violet." I smile. "Chestix is probably *not* the best brand, but it's all they have."

"I'm being a total ESTJ, aren't I?"

I have to take a second to remember that ESTJ is a personality type—extroverted, sensing, thinking, judging.

Violet groans. "I wish I could be more like you."

"Me?" My eyes bulge. "I'm sorry? *Why?*"

"Because...you're not an ESTJ, anal-retentive like me."

"You're right. I'm not ESTJ. I don't even know what I am, because I pretended I had to go to the bathroom and hid there until class was over when we took that stupid personality test at school."

"See? I'm always trying to do what's best. What's *right*. But...what difference does it even make? What good has it done me?" She leans back in her chair. "Sometimes I hate caring so much."

"And I hate not caring."

"We should switch brains. Okay, that settles it. I'm not gonna Google Chestix. Let's just get it!"

"Look at you, Vee." I squeeze her shoulder. "Living on the edge."

She laughs. Her second laugh of the day! It warms me up better than thoughts of the sun.

Pastor Jedidiah shuffles past us. Dad trails behind him.

"Pastor," Dad mumbles. "Why don't you go on and sit down somewhere? I'm pretty sure they don't sell kava kava tea. Try the one I showed you. It was English breakfast."

"That wasn't tea. It was a well-marketed packet of dust is what it was. Kava kava is rich and delicious and a *wonderful* natural remedy for pain. You should try it for your rotator cuff." Jedidiah is basically speaking to the floor as he shuffles around the corner with Dad looking none too happy to trail behind him.

The front doors are pushed open again, causing my muscles to tense and harden like petrified wood. It's the man. He's back. He steps over the threshold and into the light. His eyes do a quick scan, like he's looking for something. Maybe that's it. He forgot something. I look to the ceiling. "Why is he back?"

"Didn't I tell you he was as harmless as a declawed cat? Girl, when are you gonna start listening to me?"

"Why is who back?" Violet asks.

"That creepy-looking guy."

"Oh, yeah." Violet sounds genuinely sympathetic. "The sad one."

Mom chucks a bunch of items onto the counter, including the large container of Red Vines. While she looks at the magazines, Brandon and Nam sneak bags of Sour Patch Kids and candy bars into her basket.

"Violet," I whisper. "I think this guy is a bad egg."

"Really? Why?"

Before I can explain the sensation I'm getting deep within the pit of my stomach when I look at him, the man unzips his heavy winter coat and extracts a gun. I've watched Alfred play enough *Battlefield* on his PS4 to be able to properly identify a fully automatic. Rapid-fire guns where a single pull of a trigger can kill a room full of people. "Everybody on the floor!" He holds the gun in the air.

It's instant pandemonium as a variety of high-pitched screams reverberate throughout the cramped store.

Dad rushes to Mom and the boys.

Nam and Brandon drop their bags of candy and slump to the floor, screaming at the tops of their lungs.

Pink Roller Lady hollers "Sweet Jesus, he's gonna kill us all!" before she slams onto the tile, covering her head with her hands like it's an elementary school fire drill instead of an armed robbery.

The man grabs Drew by the collar, pushes him down and places a steel-toed boot onto his back. He points the gun directly at the back of Drew's head. "Everybody to the front of the store. On the floor! Now! Do as I say, and nobody dies."

"Daddy!" Nam screams.

"Don't be scared!" Drew's voice quivers. "Do what he says."

Mom and Dad put their arms around the boys and hunch together, splayed out on the dirty tile.

"Hurry up!" The man points the weapon at Michelle and the female pharmacist as they walk slowly to the front, their hands raised. "On your stomachs!"

Clearly Michelle can't lie on her stomach but she quickly gets down on her side. The pharmacist sprawls out beside her. Both are visibly shaking and teary-eyed.

He motions to Violet and me with his free hand. "You two! Get on the goddamned floor like I told you to do."

Violet is holding her chest. Barely breathing. Face turning dark red.

"It's okay, Violet. *Breathe.*"

At last, she inhales, and I kneel beside her wheelchair, watching as the color slowly returns to her face.

"Remember what Michelle said. Take in slow breaths. Slow. Like this." I imitate for her.

"Stop talkin'!" He points the gun at us. "Hurry up!"

Violet's entire body is trembling as I help her slide out of the wheelchair. Once we're situated on the cold, scratchy laminate, I wrap my arm around her so we can huddle as close together as possible, hoping my cast doesn't feel too heavy on her thin and frail frame, resisting the urge to cry out in pain as my shoulder throbs from the movement. My eyes focus on the gun and a lump forms in my throat. The last time I thought of dying it was at my own hand. Now, with my life in the hands of someone else, I can't help but think how foolish I was. I wanted the right to take my own life. Now I want the right to live.

The man turns the gun on the cashier. "Old man. Get *up.* I want all the money!"

The cashier stands as slowly as he speaks. "We don't really got no money."

"What?" The rifle jiggles in the man's trembling hands. "What do you mean?"

"Well," the cashier starts with his hands raised. "Everybody usin' that chip thing. State made us switch over last month. We don't got much cash, but you're welcome to what we do got."

"Give it to me, then!"

The cashier lowers his hands to open the register. Removes a small stack of bills and some change. "Here's the lot of it."

The man keeps the gun pointed outward as he shuffles to the counter and takes the money with his free hand. He counts it. "This is *forty-one* dollars!"

"And some cents, too." The cashier nods. "Don't forget the cents."

"There's a safe! I know you got a safe where you keep all the money." He stuffs the small amount of cash into his coat pocket.

"No, sir. No safe. Like I said…everybody usin' those chip cards. No cash to keep."

"I want wallets and purses! Take them out!"

I watch Dad extract his wallet out of his back pocket and toss it forward. Drew does the same. Alfred tosses his wallet forward as well, though I don't know why, since I'm sure there's no money in it. Michelle pushes her purse forward.

He turns the gun back on Violet and me. "Gimme the camera. Now!"

I pull the strap from around my neck. My Canon is a three-thousand-dollar piece of equipment, though Mom and Dad got it for half-off on Black Friday. Still, it's not to be slid across dirty laminate tile. If it's going to be on the Urlington black market Craigslist, it shouldn't have scratches on it. I gently place the camera in front of me, lens facing up.

"What's that on her back!" the man asks.

"Oxygen," Dad calls out. "She's my daughter. She needs it to breathe."

The man eyes the pack on Violet's back. "I don't like it."

"It's nothing but *oxygen*," I repeat.

"I said I don't like it. Take it off!" he orders.

Dad shoots daggers at me, his eyes saying the words his mouth can't speak. *Be quiet, Indigo. Do what he says, so nobody gets hurt!*

Surprisingly, Violet is calm as she sits up and begins to remove the canvas backpack that holds her oxygen. Though I can't say the same for Michelle. She's a mess, tears streaming down her face, sobbing uncontrollably. It's so loud and obnoxious that even the gunman is exasperated.

"I can't even think, you're so damn loud," he says to her. "Shut *up*!"

"I'm sorry. I apologize." Michelle cries frenetically. And it's that pathetic, sniveling, snot-faced cry. I feel like screaming at her to get a spine the way she screamed at Drew. She always acts so dang tough. Now it's *time* to be tough. Or at least pretend. And what's she doing? Whimpering like she's the one with the damn kidney stones. Which reminds me. Where is Pastor Jed?

"Voice?" I whisper.

"Yup. Here."

"We're being *robbed*!"

"I know. Ca-razy."

"Help us!"

"I told you, I don't do stuff like interfere. It's not really my style, yo."

"You could've at least told us not to come here!"

The man points his gun toward me. "Who the hell are you talking to?"

"She's talking to God." Jedidiah has appeared, scooting down the aisle toward the gunman, still bent over. "You know, the One Infinite Creator of the Universe?"

Now the gun is turned toward Jedidiah. "Stop right there!"

Only Jedidiah doesn't stop. He takes another step forward. "I'm unarmed and unable to even stand due to hard deposits of minerals and acid salts sticking together in my concentrated urine."

"What?" the man yells.

"I am no harm to you. I only ask that you put the gun down and stop scaring these good people."

"I'll shoot you first, if you don't get down."

"See, that's where we have a problem," Jedidiah explains. "I *can't* get down on the floor. In too much pain. Kidney stones. Can you believe it? Of all the distorted fields of energy to walk into."

"I don't care if you got rabies. Get *down*!"

"Suppose I had one hundred sheep and lost one of them?" Jedidiah asks.

"Wh-what?" the man stutters, seemingly thrown off by Jedidiah's lack of compliance.

"Doesn't seem like it would make a whole lot of sense to leave the ninety-nine and go after one sheep. Who cares, right? One sheep is...no big deal."

"I don't know what you're talking about, but if you don't shut your mouth I'll shut it for you."

"Wanna know what I would do?" Jedidiah appears completely unfazed by this entire ordeal, continuing to move toward the gunman peacefully. "I'd go after that one sheep.

That one sheep means as much to me as the whole ninety-nine. Perhaps even more."

Everyone watches with trepidation as Jedidiah takes a final step. The rifle is now resting on top of his head. I close my eyes and imagine Jedidiah's head exploding like the soldiers in Drew's newest WWII game.

"I don't want to kill you," the man articulates. "But I will."

"I don't believe in death," Jedidiah explains. "I'll simply travel into a new dimension. Take a new form. But know this. I will spend the rest of *your* life guiding you to make better choices. Whether in this dimension or another. Whether by your side in physical or spiritual form. I pledge to be with you. I'm on your side either way, my friend."

"I will kill you, man. I swear to God, I will."

"Even then you can't get rid of me." Jedidiah's speaking so softly, but it's deathly quiet in the store, so we all can hear. "You're my one sheep. You matter more to me than the whole lot. I promise you do."

And then something stranger than a voice piercing through the dead of night, to speak to me on top of an under-construction building, occurs. The man lowers his gun and begins to cry.

Everyone is startled for a moment, but Dad quickly seizes the opportunity, rushes forward and carefully extracts the weapon from the man's hands just as the crying turns to Michelle-style uncontrollable sobs.

"Get rid of it, Isaiah!" Mom cries out.

Dad studies the weapon. "It's…"

"A paintball gun!" the man wails. "It's not even real."

"I'll be," Dad declares. "It *is* a paintball gun."

Mom breathes a sigh of relief. "Oh, thank God."

I grab my Canon from off the floor and hold it tight. Violet secures her pack tightly on her back.

"He oughta still be locked up!" Pink Roller Lady screeches, still lying facedown.

Drew rushes to Brandon and Nam, who are sniffing and wiping tears, but they still held up better than Michelle, who has *yet* to recover. Still frozen in her spot on the floor, wailing like somebody died from a rapid-fire paintball to the forehead.

"I'm so sorry." The man hands the forty-one dollars and cents back to the cashier.

"No need for apologies." The cashier takes it and sets it on the counter, slowly counts it.

Pastor Jedidiah calls out to me. "Indigo?"

"Uh, yes, Pastor?"

"Be a dear and reach into my pocket. Grab me my wallet."

I sling the camera strap around my shoulder so it dangles safely at my side, rush to Jedidiah and extract a brown leather wallet from his back pocket.

"Open it."

I do.

"Give our friend here all the cash that's inside."

"Seriously?" I say.

"Seriously?" Pink Roller Lady calls out.

"Seriously," Jedidiah replies.

I take the cash, which could easily be a few hundred bucks, and hand it to the man. Up close he doesn't look like a man.

He looks...like a *kid*. Maybe because I was looking at him through the lens of my camera, I didn't really notice at first.

He wipes his nose, still blubbering like a fool. "No way. I can't take this."

"How old are you?" Dad asks.

"Fourteen years old, sir." The boy sniffs.

"Fourteen." Mom repeats it in shock. "Where on Earth are your parents?"

"He can still be tried as an adult at that age!" Pink Roller Lady hollers.

Drew swoops up Brandon, who wraps his legs around his dad's waist and lays his head on his shoulder.

"What's your name?" I ask.

"Willy." He sniffs. "The kids at school call me Willy Wonka. They make fun of me 'cuz of the way I dress and 'cuz I...smell."

"I don't smell you." Alfred stands, brushes off his jersey.

"I sweat a lot." Willy wipes his snotty nose. "Even when it's cold outside. Nothing I do works. I wanted money so I could move away from here. Just wanna go somewhere far away where nobody can smell me. Maybe I'll be better then."

"Where are your parents?" Dad asks.

"Don't got a mom. Jefferson May's my dad."

"Jefferson May? That good-for-nothing!" Pink Roller Lady yelps. "No wonder you turned out so bad."

"Lady, you're not helping the situation," Michelle says, finally dialing down her blubbering and picking herself up off the floor.

"Are you planted in a church, William?" Jedidiah asks.

The boy shakes his head. "No, sir."

"How would you feel…?" Jedidiah pauses to moan in agony.

"You okay, Pastor?" Dad steps forward.

"Right as rain." Jedidiah grunts. "William, how…would you feel about a long bus ride on Sundays? We could send the bus down to Urlington. Maybe your dad could join us, too?"

"You'll find him at the local tavern on Twelfth and Main." Pink Roller Lady slides a Christmas reindeer tote bag over her shoulder. "Where he practically lives. The bum."

The boy wipes his nose with the back of his hand. "He never been to church before neither."

Jedidiah claps his hands together. "Aren't you both in for a treat! I want to make sure you're making better choices in life. Getting planted in a church is a good start. Why not the New Faith International Church of Love and Light, Seattle?"

"Is he gonna get arrested, Mom?" Brandon asks.

"Oh, police ain't comin'," the cashier says calmly. "Urlington police is clear on the other side a town. Teamsters is on strike at the Omni plant. It's a mess over there. No point in even callin' 'em."

"Well, there you go," Jedidiah says. "The Universe always provides."

Willy turns to Dad. "Can I have my paintball gun back? It's my pop's. He'll be mad at me if something happens to it."

"No." Dad grips the paintball gun tightly with both hands. "Doesn't sound like you *or* your dad need any kind of gun."

"Yeah." The boy nods. "You're probably right, sir."

"My good friend Michelle." Pastor points to Michelle.

"She's a nurse practitioner. She can examine you when you're in Seattle next and we get to the bottom of this smelly and sweaty situation. Right, Michelle?"

"Absolutely, Pastor." Michelle gives Willy a sympathetic head tilt. "Sounds like maybe you have hyperhidrosis, Willy. We see patients with that condition all the time."

"It has a name?" Willy replies in awe.

"Everything has a name," Michelle replies.

As Willy and Pastor exchange numbers, I turn to Violet.

"You okay, sis?"

She nods. "I knew he was sad, Indigo. I *knew* it."

Of course she knew. *I* judged him. Thought because of his greasy hair and shifty eyes he was here to wreak havoc. But Violet saw straight through to the heart. It's what she always does. God, I should be the one in that chair with the failing lungs. Maybe I shouldn't have been climbing that building. But I'd give anything to trade places with her.

"Indigo, *stop*. I swear to me, you are driving me nuts with the self-loathing."

"You're driving me nuts, too!" I whisper. "So there!"

I help Violet stand. It's not self-loathing. It's practical thinking. If Violet lives, the world will be a better place because of it. But what am I destined to be? Like the world needs another heartless photojournalist. Taking pictures, a safe distance away from the dregs of society. Writing stories as if I care about anything more than the accolades that come with it. The Twitter followers, the Facebook likes. Violet would be the type of photojournalist who takes photos of what she sees, and reaches out to touch it as well. To her, every little thing in the world is beautiful. Even Willy May—the paint-ball gun bandit.

As Willy waves goodbye, I notice he has a golden glob of Trader Joe's olive oil sliding down his forehead. "Sorry again about the scare, folks." He looks over at Violet. "I'm real… sorry."

And with that, Willy leaves the store.

Pink Roller Lady takes her basket to the counter. The cashier rings her items up as if nothing happened.

"You have a nice day, ma'am." The cashier places her items in a bag and hands her a receipt.

"Well, now that the juvenile delinquent is gone, I probably will!" She pushes through the doors.

Michelle turns to Dad. "This is nuts. We just got held up at gunpoint!"

"At paintball gunpoint." Alfred flips his cap backward.

"It doesn't matter if it was a water gun," Michelle goes on. "This is insane. Pastor is sick. This trip is a bust. Let's call it what it is and go home. I don't wanna play this game anymore. Nobody should have to play this game anymore."

"It's not a game," I reply defensively.

"Indigo, please," Michelle says. "Nobody actually believes this is real."

"Speak for yourself," Dad interrupts.

"I don't want to go home," Violet pleads. I help her back into her wheelchair.

"But, Violet, be sensible?" Michelle begs. "So far we've run into Troy and his new *girlfriend*. Indigo damaged his property with a damn fork, which Mom and Dad could potentially

166

have to pay thousands of dollars for. Pastor has *kidney* stones and we got robbed!"

"Almost robbed. With a fake gun." Alfred's putting Chap-Stick on again. "My dude Willy, though. Feel sorry for him."

"I know, right?" Violet echoes.

"Are you guys kidding me with this right now?" Michelle shakes her head in disbelief. "I feel sorry for *us*."

"Look, I'm glad he almost robbed us with balls of paint." I step forward. "If he hadn't, then who knows what would've happened to him. Suicide maybe?"

"You an expert on suicide now, Indigo?" Michelle asks with a knowing smirk.

"No," I state defensively. "I only mean the kid is dealing with some heavy stuff. How would you like to be sweaty and smelly all the time, Michelle?"

"The boy didn't mean us no harm," Dad adds with a shrug. "No harm, no foul."

"He did mean to *rob* us, though," Michelle says. "That's foul."

"Only to get the hell out of Urlington. Can't say I blame him." The pharmacist brushes off her dingy white lab coat.

Michelle turns to her. "Shouldn't you be filling our pre-scription?"

"Oh, right." The pharmacist turns and heads toward the back of the store.

"Everything doesn't always have to make sense, Michelle," I offer. "Sometimes you have to throw caution to the wind and take the damn blue pill."

"If you talkin' about *The Matrix*, it was the red pill," Alfred declares.

"Listen, I don't say this often," Dad starts. "But Indigo's right."

"Is that supposed to be a compliment, Dad?" I ask.

"Of course it is. I say we stay on course," he replies.

"I wanna keep going, too." Drew sets Brandon down. "Let's take a family vote."

Michelle turns to Drew. "You can't be serious."

"Aren't you the one who told me to get a freakin' spine?" Drew raises his hand. "Team red pill."

"I vote we continue." Alfred raises his hand. "Taking the red pill. Gulp. Glug."

Although I have a feeling Alfred would do anything to avoid going home to being expelled from the tenth grade, I'm still happy to have him on my team.

"I wanna keep going, too." Brandon raises his hand.

"I'll take whatever pill keeps me out of school the longest." Nam raises his hand and shrugs.

"Mom?" I ask. "What do you think we should do?"

Mom nervously wrings her hands together, gives Michelle a sympathetic pat on the shoulder. "Sorry, Michelle. I'm not siding with Indigo over you. I'm...going with God."

"Oh, that's right." Michelle smirks. "Because Indigo is hearing the voice of God."

"Yes, she is." Jedidiah winks in my direction. Or more like a wink at the floor, but the top of his head is pointed toward me, so I think it was meant for me.

"Let's get back on the bus," Drew suggests.

"What about lunch?" Mom asks. "I thought we were gonna eat at Big's Bison Burgers. I'm starving."

"After almost getting robbed—" Alfred yawns "—I'm not really in the mood for bison."

"It's unethical to eat bison." Nam grimaces. "That's like… eating a horse."

Dad picks his wallet up off the floor and hands the paint gun to the cashier. "No offense to Willy Wonka, but let's get the hell outta Urlington."

"Dad." Violet gives Dad a chastising look. "It's Willy *May*. The mean kids call him Willy Wonka."

"I happen to like Willy Wonka." Dad stuffs his wallet in his back pocket. "Willy Wonka was a CEO of a Fortune 500 company. He was millionaire genius. How's that even an insult?"

"My mouth was waterin' for some bison, but fine." Mom sighs. "Let's go through the McDonald's drive-through. I got coupons."

"Coupons for McDonald's?" Alfred frowns. "Why? Everything's a dollar."

"Are *you* paying for McDonald's, Alfred?" Mom asks.

"Uh…no." Alfred flips his cap forward.

"Then I'll use my coupons, thank you very much!"

Brandon squeals with delight. "I want chicken nuggets!"

"Big Mac for me," Nam sings.

"I like Burger King better but whatever." Alfred moves toward the exit with Brandon and Nam.

As Dad takes over control of Violet's wheelchair and Mom pays at the front for the items she was purchasing, Michelle and I stand face-to-face, right where Willy stood when he tried to rob us with a pretend gun.

I wait for the onslaught—for the "Indigo, you're a mess and your life's a mess and you invented the word *mess* and blah blah, yada yada." But there is no onslaught. She only moves slowly toward the pharmacy in the back of the store. I watch her go, spooked by Michelle passing up on a perfect opportunity to make me feel small and insignificant. I look up at the ceiling.

"Voice?"

"'Sup?"

"Making sure you're still with us." I grip my camera. "Kinda...getting used to you."

"Still with you. Always and forever. Also, not to be all, 'I told you so,' but...did I tell you Willy was harmless, or did I tell you Willy was harmless?"

"You told me Willy was harmless."

"Told you I'm God."

CHAPTER TWELVE

After we crossed from Oregon into Idaho, and forests of evergreens were exchanged for landscapes of multi-colored rock formations, the next couple of rest stops go according to Violet's schedule, easing all remaining anxieties from the mock robbery.

Michelle has duct-taped blankets to the ceiling of the bus around Pastor Jedidiah's seats so he has a private blanket cubicle, and the trip has continued without any more incidents.

I lean my aching shoulder up against the window. The sensation of the moving bus is comforting for the pain, like a massage almost, but makes my head feel like it's in a blender. I need Michelle's pills. She has to know they've worn off by now. I look between the space in the two seats in front of me. Behind the driver's seat, she's hunched over her phone, typing away. Is she emailing her lawyer back? Finalizing divorce plans? Maybe she doesn't have any more pills. What if she gave me the two only to tease me with comfort and relief, so that when the pain came *back*, I'd feel it tenfold? This was her diabolical plan all along—my head in a bus blender. I close my eyes instead of humbling myself and begging Michelle for more meds like some sort of fiend. Before I know it, I'm drifting to sleep:

In my dream, it's the first day of college. Violet and I step onto a lush, green university campus.

"It's the color of the day," Violet squeals as we approach the front doors of the admissions office.

I look down at our matching orange T-shirts and slap my hand against my forehead. "Dude. Now people are going to think we're those weird freak-a-zoid twins who dress alike."

She laughs.

I feel a tap on my shoulder and turn to see a male professor in dark sunglasses carrying a briefcase.

"Young lady." He straightens his striped tie. "Why are you two dressed alike?"

"We're twins."

"Fraternal?"

"What? No. We're identical. Obviously."

"That can't be." The professor backs away, strangely spooked. "She doesn't look anything like you." He rushes off.

"What the hell was that about?" I turn to Violet and gasp. Her face has morphed into something barely human. Maggots crawl in and around her decaying skin. I back away, stumbling over my own feet and falling onto the grass.

"What's wrong, Indigo?" She stands over me, empty eye

sockets boring into my soul, filling my heart with horror. "What's wrong?"

I wake with a jolt to see Violet sitting beside me on the bus. "Indigo?"

I sit up.

"What's wrong? You were trembling."

"I was?" I wipe my forehead, slick with sweat.

"You had a bad dream, didn't you?" She coughs, covering her mouth like a demure geisha girl.

"Yeah." I bite the dead skin around my thumbnail. "Can't even remember what it was about, though. Weird colors and shapes." I blink, struggling to erase the image of my decomposing twin sister.

She hands me a plastic baggie with two of Michelle's pills inside and a tiny bottle of water. "Michelle said to take these."

"Oh, thank God." I gratefully take the bag and water from her hand.

"You're very welcome."

I ignore the voice in my head, swallowing the pills with a giant gulp of water.

"Sorry you had a bad dream." Only she doesn't look sorry. She looks downright giddy. Her face is all lit up, and she's tapping her feet like she's about to jump out of her seat and hit the roof.

I stuff the bottle of water and empty plastic baggie into my camera bag. "Did we win the lottery?" I push a finger into one of her cheeks and grin. "You look happier than a troll doll."

"I am." She grabs my hand. "Indigo. Look out the window!"

I peek through a pair of eyeballs. "What am I looking for?"

"Look harder." She squeezes my hand. "Don't you see it!?"
Suddenly I *do*. "Violet!"

"I know, right?!"

"It's the *sun!*" Blindingly bright beams of sunlight glimmer and sparkle over the layers of rugged hilltops. The golden rays appear supernatural, like Zeus and the other Olympian gods are tossing around bolts of light for sport, their recreations creating a dramatic display of all-encompassing sunshine. My chest swells; my heart races like I drank an entire pot of coffee. I lean my forehead against the cool pane of glass and imagine for a moment that I am a bird, ready to catch a passing breeze…spread her wings…and fly.

Violet wraps her arms around me, hugging me for the first time in months. "Indi, I haven't seen the sun in so long."

If only I could whip out my Canon and capture *this*. My sister hugging me this close is like taking a magic pill that fixes everything: highly addictive, sold out in most stores—the twin pill. The throbbing in my head miraculously dissipates. The stiffness in my shoulder softens.

When Violet pulls away, she's wiping tears. "Indi. How pathetic are we, huh? Who gets this excited about the sun?"

"People from Seattle, that's who." Tears slide down my own cheeks. I wipe them away.

"Maybe we can get Mom to pull over and we can all lay out on the side of the road."

"We'd get arrested. A family of black people sunbathing on the shoulder in the middle of nowhere?"

Violet laughs. "We got one Native."

"Wouldn't matter. We'd all go to jail."

"Even Bran and Nam?"

"*Especially* Bran and Nam."

She laughs. "What about Pastor? They wouldn't arrest him."

We turn to look over at Pastor Jedidiah. Since he's surrounded by his wall of hanging blankets, all we see are his feet dangling out into the aisle, and all we hear is his snoring.

"Guilt by association."

She laughs again and we turn our attention back to the proud display of sun.

"Violet."

"Hmm?" She's still soaking it all in. If pure serenity and peace could be defined by a facial expression, it would be hers.

"I could give you a kidney, you know."

She adjusts her cannula, securing it behind her ears. "Indi, I've already told you how I feel about that. It's too much of a long shot."

"Why? It would get you back on the lung donor list."

"*If* the kidney transplant was successful."

"Why wouldn't it be successful? We have the same DNA. Same blood type. As far as a genetic melding of bones, skin, blood and brain tissue...we're the same."

"Interesting...way to put it." She coughs—it's a guttural, hacking cough that sounds like she has pneumonia. I'm no doctor, but I'd say her cough sounds like it's getting worse.

"So? What do you think?"

"I'd still have to live through the surgery. That's not guaranteed." She rubs her chest. I rub mine, too.

"But let's say you do. If you live through the surgery and if my kidney adjusts fine to being in your body—"

"So many *ifs*, Indigo." She shakes her head. "Besides, I hate the idea…of waiting around for someone else to die…so I can have their lungs and live. Not to mention if it all fails, you're left with *one* kidney."

"So what? One kidney is all we need. Two kidneys is over-kill. It's like buyin' a Lamborghini. Who needs a freakin' Lamborghini?"

"There's more to it than that, Indigo. I'd rather…go with God. Let's try this first. The hike to the Wave. God says I can live… I believe it."

"And if it doesn't work?"

She wrings her hands together. "It's *already* working. I feel different. I feel amazing." She inhales. "I can *breathe*."

"I mean, I'm just saying. What if we leave the Wave and get back home and X-rays say your lungs still have all the scar tissue and—"

"You believe the voice, Indigo?"

"I do. But—"

"Stop doubting. I…believe it, too." She places a hand on my shoulder to steady herself as another round of guttural hacking explodes from her frail frame. It makes my own chest ache to hear her cough this way.

"Vee, can't you take some cough medicine? You don't sound so good."

"Indigo, cough medicine doesn't help." Her voice is strained, annoyed even. "If it did…don't you think I would've taken it already?"

"Sorry." I've offended her. Damn me and my *idiocy*! "I'm stupid for even suggesting it."

"Indigo, you're not stupid. Look, I don't want to be negative. Can we...not be negative? Is that too much to ask?"

And just like that, all the tension that seemed erased by the dramatic display of sunlight returns. Bricks are stacked high and slathered with sealant to re-form the wall Violet is determined to keep between us.

She stands. "I'm gonna go share the awesomeness of sunlight...with Mom and Dad. You wanna come with me?"

I shake my head. "They don't like me."

"That's silly. They're your parents."

"So? Haven't you ever seen that documentary on Netflix about parents who hate their own kids?"

"Indigo, that's not a real thing."

"Well, it should be. Mom could narrate it."

"Mom likes you. She loves you."

"Mom loves me because she has to. Like me? That's debatable. All she does is criticize me. My hair. My clothes. My grades. Everything I say. She's... I dunno. She's weird to me."

"I'm sorry you feel that way. I think if you made more of an effort, you'd see the love. You'd feel it for sure." She moves slowly down the aisle, leaning on the seats for support until she's able to slide back into her spot beside Dad.

I watch them for a moment as they converse. Mom's driving, but she's still a part of the conversation, cracking up and interjecting her words of wisdom. It's a natural, effortless banter. Mom never talks to me that way. Mom talks *at* me. I can't help but think back to two years ago, when one of the happiest days of my life took a dismal turn.

I burst through the door one Sunday afternoon after learning that *I* was one of the three chosen to have dinner with a famed photojournalist. Mom was sitting in the living room, watching *Game of Thrones*.

"Mom, guess what?" I rushed to where she lounged on the couch, dressed in cozy navy-blue sweats, covered up with a blanket, a rare moment when her hair wasn't in its signature bun, so loose curls of silver rested on her shoulders, making her look years younger.

"Shh, Indigo. I'm watching my show."

I grabbed the remote and pushed Pause. "This'll be worth it! I have amazing news."

Mom checked the screen on her phone. "Make it quick. I like watching it in real time so it doesn't get spoiled on Facebook."

"So stay off Facebook."

"Just...*what*, Indigo?"

My stomach tightened, the well of joy feeling a bit run dry. "Um..." Mom folded her arms across her chest and sat up on the couch. "I won a contest."

"Oh. Great, honey."

"Yeah." My excitement started to grow again. "I took photos downtown of a police officer telling a homeless couple they had to leave this public area where they were sleeping, and I wrote a piece about the homeless crisis in Seattle. It's all going to be featured in the *Seattle Times* and I get to have dinner at *Canlis*."

"Oh, now, that's fancy. It's like two hundred dollars a plate to eat there."

"I know, right? And guess who we're having dinner with? Lynsey Addario!"

"Who is that?"

"A photojournalist." I sat on the couch beside Mom. "But, Mom, she's amazing. The photographs she takes inspire me. For her, taking pictures is about forming relationships, you know? She's all about human rights and she's this badass… oops, sorry, language…but she's a total feminist. You know that gorgeous photo of the two Muslim women dressed in electric-blue burkas and they're alone in the desert? Or at least, it looks like they're alone. *She* took that photo! And I get to have dinner with her!"

"And Violet, too?"

I swallowed. "Um…well, Violet submitted…but her photo wasn't chosen this time around."

"She didn't get chosen?" Mom smacked her lips in annoyance. "Those people at that school don't know nothin' about nothin' if Violet didn't win, too."

"It's a city contest. Not the school." I shifted. "Do you want to read my story? I can show you the photo that's going to be in the paper. It's probably one of the best pictures I've ever taken."

Mom took the remote from my hands. "Sure, Indigo. I'll look at it as soon as *Game of Thrones* goes off."

I thrust my phone at her. "At least look at the photo. It'll take like five seconds."

"Later, Indigo. I've worked all day and I'd like to relax and watch *Game of Thrones*. Is that too much to ask? I'll look at everything when it's over."

"It's on Pause, though. I don't get it."

"Of course you don't get it. You're sixteen years old. I've cleaned this house from top to bottom. Done eight loads of laundry. Cooked breakfast, lunch, and soon I'll have to throw something together for dinner. I work harder in retirement than when I was driving a damn bus all day. All I want is an hour of peace to enjoy my show. And you're in here talking about some woman I don't know nothin' about. Lynsey Adaggio."

"Addario."

"Indigo, I don't care right now. I just don't care."

I stood up. I wanted to scream, *Sorry to have interrupted pretend people in a pretend world, played by actors who are probably listening to their families while you watch their dumb show!* But instead I said, "Okay, Mom."

She unpaused the TV and a whooping, hollering Westeros sword battle serenaded my ascent up the stairs to my room. When I pushed through the door, Violet was lying down, reading a book. She literally leaped up and stood on the bed when she saw me.

"Dude! You're home!" She jumped up and down like a seven-year-old who just found out they were going to Disneyland. "I heard the news at school! Congratulations!!"

I shrugged. "Whatever. It's no big deal." I threw my bag into the corner and slumped onto the edge of the bed.

"No big deal!" Violet plopped down beside me. "It's Lynsey Addario. She's a...total badass."

"Funny, I literally said the same thing to Mom."

"Wait. You already told Mom? When?"

"Just now."

"Oh?" Her expression clouded. "What did she say?"

"She said, 'Indigo, you're the best daughter in the whole world and I wish I could splice you into four parts and cryogenically freeze three of you to save for my next lives on Earth.'"

Violet leaned back on her hands. "What did she really say?"

"She told me to go away because she was watching people rape and pillage."

"Indi...you shouldn't have told her while she was watching TV. Especially *Game of Thrones*. That's her show."

"Oh, really?" I turned to look Violet square in the eye. "I didn't know there were rules I have to follow to get my mom to *talk* to me."

"A better time would've been tonight at dinner, or while she was cooking. You could've said 'Mom, can I help?' And *then* told her."

"Good to know. Next time I achieve something great, I'll check her TV schedule, then consult with you on what's the best way to approach conversation."

"Yeah. That's a good idea."

"Vee, I was being sarcastic." I lay back onto the bed. Violet lay beside me and rested her head on my shoulder.

"Some people are set in their ways, Indigo. Finding a way to reach people is important. You gotta get on Mom's level. Learn her love language."

"I try to talk to her. I really do."

"About photojournalism, shutter speed and... I dunno... apertures. She can't connect to that. Talk to her about what *she* likes."

"And what about me, Violet? Why doesn't she find a way to reach me? To connect with *me*? She's the adult in this scenario."

"Like I said...she's set in her ways. But if you take the first step, I know she'll come around."

I remove my camera from the bag at my feet, snatch off the lens cap and load up a new battery, taking snapshots of Dad and Violet as fast as my shutter speed will allow.

Click-click.

Violet smiles when Dad seems to get excited.

Click-click-click.

Nods when he pauses.

Click.

I stretch my neck to see if I can hear what Dad is talking about.

"And boy oh boy, when Al Jarreau got on stage, you ain't seen nothing like it." Dad leans forward. "Helen, am I right or am I right?"

Mom nods as she crawls through traffic like we're in a funeral procession. "Oh, Violet, Al Jarreau was our Justin Bieber."

"Helen, you can't mention Justin Bieber in the same sentence with Al Jarreau! Justin Bieber's toe can't compete with Al Jarreau."

I frown. Al Jarreau and Justin Bieber really *shouldn't* be mentioned in the same sentence. I lower my camera and study Violet's expression. She seems completely engaged. Appears to be hanging on to every word as our parents ramble incessantly about the legendary jazz musician. Could I endure a convo with Mom and Dad about Al Jarreau? Is Violet right about me? Have I not taken the time to really get to know them? Am I not invested in them? Am *I* the one with the problem?

"Iceberg, right ahead."

My eyes shoot up. "Sorry?"

"There's an accident up ahead. Y'all are gonna be in traffic for *hours*." The voice snorts. **"Sucks to be you."**

"Not if I can help it." I stuff my Canon back into its bag and scoot down the aisle. Michelle is playing sudoku across from Violet and Dad. I sit beside her and lean forward.

"Mom?"

"Yes, Indigo?"

"There's an accident up ahead. I think we should exit the highway and take the streets to get around it."

"An accident?" Mom looks over her shoulder at Dad. "Isaiah, is that true? Check Google Maps."

Dad checks his phone. "I'll be. It's about ten miles down. Looks like traffic is bad already. It's all red on the map. Long delay, it's sayin'."

Mom switches on her blinkers. "Thank you for checking that, Indigo. You saved us."

"A couple of hours at least." Dad smiles at me. I smile back.

We all sit in a peaceful silence as Mom inches off the highway and down a ramp. I clear my throat as we round a corner, crawling deeper and deeper through a quaint Idaho town with well-kept lawns, historical houses and old, rustic, red-brick office buildings.

"You know what I really like?" I declare boldly. "Buses."

Dad tosses me a side eye. "What do you mean you like buses? What kind of buses?"

"All kinds. Especially the Seattle City Bus Company. It is so on *point*. It's particularly…adept at getting people around the city."

Dad stretches his eyes wide. "O-*kay*."

"With all the hills and stuff. Seattle is a mess. And those buses be workin'!" I slap my knee and laugh. Violet stretches her eyes as wide as Dad's. She's looking at me like I've lost my mind. But why is she looking at me like that? I'm taking her advice! "If I wasn't going to be a photojournalist, and travel the world, I'd definitely drive a bus like you guys did."

Dad twists his body so that his legs are in the aisle. "Let me get this straight. You wanna drive a *bus*?"

"I mean, I think it would be cool because buses are the way of the world. Name a country. I bet there's a bus in it."

"Indigo, you have got to be kidding me." Mom looks at me through the rearview mirror. "All that money we paid for cameras and photography classes. All the research we did to get you and Violet into Silver Line, and now you want to drive a bus!"

"Indigo, your mother and I worked hard. We sacrificed a

lot to give you kids a better life. Driving a bus isn't as glamorous as you might think."

"I don't think it's glamorous! I...don't even want to drive a bus!"

"Then why did you say you did?" Dad asks.

"I dunno. Just forget it." I take a deep breath. Yeah, that was a fail. Let's try another, nonbus route. "I was listening to Al Jarreau this morning."

Michelle laughs as she flips a page in her sudoku book. "Indigo, girl, you need to stop. You were not listening to Al Jarreau."

"I was. And his music—" I place a hand over my chest "—it spoke to my heart. I was like...dang, this man can sing!"

"What song was it?" Michelle smirks. "That touched you so."

Dad looks at me, waiting. Violet, too. Even Mom perks up.

"It was... You know, now that I think about it, I can't remember the name."

"How did it go?" Dad asks. "I know everything Jarreau."

"It...um...it went like... Ba-da-ba-ba-ba—"

"I'm lovin' it," Michelle sings. "That's the McDonald's theme song, Indigo."

"I wasn't *done*. It was like da-da-bi-di-bum-bum. And then it was melodic after that. With a crooner...harmony riff."

Violet stares at me, concerned. Dad smirks. Mom's lookin' perturbed through the rearview mirror. Michelle just shakes her head.

"Anyway, I'm...gonna go back to my seat now."

I stand and rush back to my seat, slumping down so no one can see me.

"Wow. That was crazy awkward, yo."

"Which part?" I put my head in my hands.

"The whole thing really. Da-da-bi-di-bum-bum was probably the highlight."

"See? Admit it. I'm a mess. I *suck*. I can't even have a normal conversation with my parents."

"Of course you can have a normal conversation. I mean, *that* one wasn't normal."

"*So* embarrassing."

"Why didn't you say, 'Hey, Dad, tell me what it was like being a bus driver'? Or, 'I heard you talking about Al Jarreau. What's your favorite song? Play it for me.'"

"Oh. That would've made more sense. See? Loser alert. I have the social skills of a four-year-old."

"There you go, self-deprecating again. Your name shouldn't be Indigo. It should be Selfina Depricana."

"It's not self-deprecating if it's true."

"Look through the contacts on your phone."

"Why?"

"Humor me."

"Fine." I take out my phone and scroll through the contacts. "What am I looking for?"

"Fourth name in the A section."

In that exact spot: Lynsey Addario. I smile at the memory of her and me chatting it up like old friends. We talked for so long, the restaurant started closing around us. The waiter finally had to politely ask us to leave. "What about her?"

"She didn't give the other two winners her number. She didn't tell them to look her up if they were ever in New Delhi. She didn't tell *them* to keep in touch. She liked *you*."

"Maybe she likes weird people."

"Or maybe she likes people who are awe-inspiring, formidable, impressive, wondrous and wonderful. All synonyms for *awesome*. Thesaurus much, Indigo?"

"I thesaurus more than anybody. You know that."

"Then pick a word for *loved, respected and adored by her family*."

"*Adored* is a stretch. *Respected* is laughable. If anything, I feel like I'm letting everybody down."

"And how exactly are you doing that?"

"I'm living." I sigh. "And she's *dying*."

"Look at Violet. Look at her right now."

I do. She's laughing so hard she's bent over. Mom and Dad crack up, too.

"Looks like she's the one livin', if you ask me."

CHAPTER THIRTEEN

I'm not sure what part of Idaho we're in now, but the rugged hills that have been our landscape for the past few hours have morphed into full-on mountain ranges. They're dazzling against the horizon. I opt to take a mental picture instead of reaching for my camera, soaking it all in *I-R-L*, as Alfred would say. To think, all this magnificent land exists for the world to enjoy. Here it is on full display and...well...not a soul in sight to bask in its glory. Aside from the cars zipping by on the highway, it's a barren wasteland of unimaginable beauty.

"Doesn't bother me."

"Hmm."

"People ignoring all the amazing stuff I created. Girl, I don't even trip."

"I don't think God would necessarily be bothered. But at least annoyed. It's like taking all seven Harry Potter books and using them as fire logs. J. K. Rowling would be majorly offended."

"Nah. I know Jo Jo. She ain't like that. Jo Jo wouldn't care if you sprinkled Harry Potter books with salt and ate them for dinner. People don't create something great so that other people can stand over it and gawk. True greatness isn't concerned with being admired. *True greatness is great, because it's got nothing else to be.*"

Pastor Jedidiah's moaning and groaning interrupts my conversation with The Voice. Even though the sounds are muffled by the blanket cubicle, it's still like nails on a chalkboard. Doesn't seem fair that a man as nice as he is is suffering inside a den of hanging blanket torture on a stuffy paratransit bus.

I scope out the rest of the family.

Brandon, Nam and Drew are all playing Uno. Only instead of yelling "Uno" when they get down to one card, they shout, "Butt-meister-meister-butt." Which… I don't get it.

Alfred is on his iPad. Hopefully he's Googling schools in the Seattle area that take kids with as many learning disabilities as he's accumulated over the years.

Dad's sitting in a new seat, legs stretched out, earbuds in, swaying, listening to music. I wonder who he's listening to. Al Jarreau, I bet.

"Maybe Al Green."

"Or Al Sharpton?"

"Oh, you got jokes?"

I laugh. "Says a voice who's *always* got jokes."

Violet is sleeping, head pressed up against the window.

Michelle sits beside her, engaged in a deep discussion about politics with Mom. Or maybe it's an argument.

"Mom, I don't wanna be labeled. Why is that a bad thing? I don't wanna fit into any political categories. I'm not completely conservative. I'm not completely liberal. I'm somewhere in between."

"Oh, pish tosh, Michelle. You sound like those people who get together and bang drums at the park."

"How do I sound like someone at a drum circle?"

"Because a bunch of people banging drums together at a park is senseless and so is what you're talking about. You've got views. Everybody's got views. Pick a party. It's easy."

"But, Mom, my views are all over the place. Not to mention, I have Native children."

"What's that got to do with anything?"

"America was founded on bloodshed. I don't *want* to be a part of *any* party."

"Then move to Canada, Michelle. I'm done talking about this. You're a Democrat and we need gas. Eye of the Tiger's running a little low."

Eye of the Tiger is what everyone's been calling the Eye Mobile. I whip out Violet's schedule from my back pocket. We're not set to stop again for another hour. Vee won't exactly be thrilled with another deviation. Especially since the last time we deviated from the schedule, we got held up at paintball gunpoint. The one before that, I committed a felony with a fork. But I guess Mom isn't asking for permission to stop, since Eye of the Tiger is already moving down an off-ramp. The bus turns a corner and crawls past a Shell station.

"Mom, why didn't you stop there?" Michelle asks. "That was a perfectly nice gas station. It was right off the highway."

"I don't do brand-name gas—you know that. The oil industry is one of the most corrupt in the world. Corporate thugs. Most of those CEOs and higher-ups should be in prison, you hear me? I stick to off-brand."

As we move through the small town, hundreds of locals crowd a city street that's blocked off and lined with those metal crowd control gates.

"What do you think's going on here?" Alfred asks with a yawn as he sits up and gazes out the window.

"A parade?" I say more to myself than anyone.

"Nope. A marathon."

"It's a marathon!" Nam points. "Look, Dad, I see runners!"

Sure enough, a large group of runners are rounding a corner, approaching a finish line decorated with a high standing aluminum truss. The truss has a green-and-red sign stretched from one side of the street to the other that reads, 26-MILE WINTER FUN RUN. Family and friends, photographers, coaches, even newscasters with their camera crews in tow huddle around runners as they cross under the colorful canvas banner.

"What's fun about running twenty-six miles?" Brandon asks.

"A *marathon*?" Violet's waking and rubbing her eyes. "Where?"

Mom pulls into a local gas station right across the street from the action, and everyone rushes to the windows to peek out, observing as the next group of runners approaches.

"I've always wanted to run in a marathon." Violet yawns

as she stares dreamily out the window. "Crossing a marathon finish line is one of my dreams."

It's true. As if Violet couldn't find more ways to be different from me, she had to go and take up running and biking as extracurricular activities. She was actually planning to register for the Seattle Marathon before she got sick. I watch as more runners cross under the banner. Their exhausted excitement is infectious. I wouldn't run a marathon if somebody paid me, but crossing a finish line *would* be amazing…

"You know, y'all are pretty dang close. If Violet wants to cross a finish line…let her cross it."

We *are* close to the actual finish line. If we jumped over the barrier, it would be only about a hundred yards before we "finished" the race.

"But wouldn't that be against the rules?"

"Geez luss, Indi-Pindy. Rules are made up. You don't actually have to follow them. Everybody knows that."

I stand. "Cross this one, Violet! You can't run a marathon, but you can certainly cross a finish line."

Everyone turns to me. I expect bewildered and confused looks, like the way my family typically looks at me, but this time, their expressions are receiving the words that are coming out of my mouth. Even Pastor Jedidiah's blanket tent parts, and he peeks his head out to nod in agreement.

"Yeah!" Nam squeals. "Cross this one, Auntie!"

"But…" Violet covers her mouth as she coughs. "I'm not… registered. Couldn't we get in trouble?"

"How so?" Alfred asks. "Ever heard of somebody gettin' arrested 'cuz they snuck into a marathon?"

"No duh, no one's ever heard of that, Uncle Alfred," Brandon chides him. "Because no one sneaks into marathons."

Violet peers out the window. "I can't do it. It's…too many people. Plus, I don't see any wheelchairs. Mine…would be in the way."

"Alfred and I can carry you," Drew offers.

Alfred cracks his knuckles. "Yeah, man. I can do that, for sure, for sure."

Violet claps her hands together. "Really? Mom, Dad… can I do it?"

"I don't see why not," Mom says.

"Yeah," Dad agrees. "Do it. Have some fun, honey. You've earned it."

Violet coughs into her sleeve for a long moment before clapping her hands together excitedly.

I know her coughing is "normal." I mean, I guess it is. I know that if I asked her if she's okay, she'd probably get annoyed. But the coughing does *not* sound good. It must be worrying for Michelle too, because she says, "I dunno, Vee. Let me check a few things. You coughin' a lot. I think you need to rest." Michelle reaches under the seat to retrieve one of her medical bags.

"Michelle, I'm going to be carried across a finish line. You don't need to check my vitals for that."

"I'm not checking your vitals. I'm making sure your blood is getting enough oxygen. In other words, doing my job. If you're fine, you're fine, and all is well."

Violet taps her feet while Michelle places a sensor on her

finger, watching a screen on a tiny medical device that looks like a cross between a tablet and a walkie-talkie.

When I peek back out the window, a female runner with a long blond ponytail catches my eye. She's wearing a T-shirt with a giant pink ribbon attached to the back. I grab my camera and zoom in as she runs into the arms of a man. They embrace and kiss. Lettering underneath the ribbon on her shirt reads, "I run because I lived."

Click-click.

That will be Violet and me someday. She'll be finishing a race she ran the whole way through. I'll be waiting, cheering her on. Because she will live. She will.

"What's wrong?" Mom asks.

I turn my attention back to the family.

"Oxygen saturation levels are low," Michelle replies. "Not good."

"It's because I'm excited!" Violet takes off the sensor and hands it to Michelle.

Michelle shakes her head. "Low O2 is not caused by excitement, Violet. O2 sat was above ninety this morning. Now it's dipped *drastically.* Let me increase the amount of oxygen."

"Good God, Michelle," Violet snaps. "If you want to be a doctor so bad maybe you should've went to medical school."

Whoa. Alfred and I exchange befuddled looks. Violet acting...*mean*?

Michelle winces. You can tell she's a bit stung by Violet's strange temper since Violet never snaps at anyone, especially Michelle. But despite being visibly wounded, Michelle stands her ground. "I need to increase your oxygen. It's not a question."

Violet groans while Michelle fiddles with the gauge on her oxygen tank.

"I'm about to fulfill a lifelong dream. I'm gonna finish a marathon and you're being crazy paranoid."

"It's not finishing if you're cheating," Brandon cuts in.

"She's not cheating, Brandon." Jedidiah's head is still peeking through the hanging blankets, face red, forehead slick with sweat, looking like all the Spirit guides he chats with have left the building for sure. "She's been running this race for a long time. It's about time she crossed the finish line."

"See? Thank you, Pastor." Michelle finishes with the tank and Violet slides into her leather Frye boots. "Very well said."

Jedidiah whimpers in pain and disappears behind the blankets once again.

I step into the aisle and sling my camera over my shoulder.

"I'm not trying to rain on Violet's parade or anything," Michelle explains. "I'm really not. But my advice is that she rest and let's see how the increase in oxygen affects the O2 sat." She places a hand on Violet's knee. "You need to relax. I think the trip's taken its toll on you."

"Drew, you sure you and Alfred can carry me across the finish line?" Violet's using a new tactic to completely ignore Michelle.

Drew flexes his nonexistent muscles. "Sis, you weigh about a hundred pounds. I bench-press that in my sleep."

I look at Drew's belly, slightly protruding over his black jeans, his pale, skinny arms poking through his *Star Wars*

T-shirt. The only things Drew bench-presses are Seattle's Top Pot doughnuts. Or maybe he does biceps curls with them, lifting apple fritters into his mouth while he stares at his computer screen.

"Oh, yeah, Vee. We got you. You good." Now Alfred's flexing *his* nonexistent muscles. At six-one, Alfred might be tall, but he's only about a hundred thirty pounds. Between the two of them, Violet might be in better hands if Brandon and Nam carried her across the finish line.

"Hop on." Drew steps in front of Michelle so Violet can climb onto his back.

As Mom pulls the lever to open the doors, Michelle throws her hands up, giving in to Violet the way she always does. "Y'all be careful. Get my sister back in one piece, *please*."

"As opposed to bringing her back in pieces?" Alfred grins.

Drew moves down the stairs and we all follow.

I hop onto the pavement and let warm rays of sun soak deep into my skin, stretching out my legs, observing the festivities through the lens of my camera. The crowd control gates are set up on both sides of the street, providing the runners with a safe and clear path to the finish line.

Click-click.

"I'll fill 'er up, hon." Dad moves to the pump.

"And I'll take the boys to the bathroom." Mom turns to Brandon and Nam. "You boys need to tinkle?"

"Grandma, I'm not three." Nam rolls his eyes.

Mom places a hand on her hip. "Next time, I'll ask if you need to urinate. Or how about this? Do you and Brandon need to have a bowel movement or defecate?"

Alfred laughs. "Do you and Brandon need to excrete fecal matter through your air-locked buttholes?"

Dad elbows Alfred. "Alfred, manners, son."

"You want me to come with you guys?" Michelle seems to be making one last-ditch effort to reach Violet. "I can supervise."

I cringe, imagining Michelle at the finish line checking Violet's blood pressure and running diagnostic tests.

"*No.*" Violet wraps her arms tightly around Drew's shoulders. "It's a silly wish of mine." She waves as Drew takes off toward the race. "Take a break, Chelle!"

"Yeah. We got her. We'll take good care of her." Alfred's walking backward, slathering on ChapStick. His lips look like he just ate a bucket of greasy fried chicken from Fat's Chicken and Waffles.

"Alfred," I start. "Walking backward like that, you're gonna—"

He trips over the curb and tumbles onto the street.

"Yep." I nod. "You're gonna do that."

"Alfred, boy, you can barely walk forward!" Dad bellows. "Make better choices, son."

He shoots up off the ground. "I'm okay, everybody!"

I follow after them, the roar of the crowd energizing our simple sojourn. Up ahead, rows and rows of spectators are lined around the gates that block off the street. I'm not confident we'll be able to push through to the front.

"Don't worry," Alfred says as if reading my mind. He cracks his knuckles. "I got this." He steps in front of us and taps a lady on her shoulder.

She turns. "Yeah?"

"Are black widow spiders the ones that are poisonous?"

She shrugs. "I dunno. Why?"

"Because," Alfred explains, "I saw one crawling in your hair."

"What?" she screams, shaking her long chestnut-brown tresses wildly. "Spider!"

"Where?" The friend beside her screams, too.

"Help me!" The lady drops to her knees and the crowd parts to make room for her tantrum.

Alfred looks back at me and pops an imaginary collar.

"Clever," I whisper as I step around the screeching woman, throwing her hair back and forth like a headbanger at a rock concert.

Thanks to Alfred's blatant lie, there is now a clear path and we easily make it to the front. Drew's face is a little red and, yeah, he does look a bit winded with Violet on his back, but he doesn't complain. Taking one for the team. He's such a good brother-in-law. I'm gonna miss him. Or maybe we can keep him and send Michelle away after their divorce.

Click-click.

I snap shots of Violet and Drew.

"What do we do now?" You can barely hear Violet's tiny, winded voice over the roar of the crowd.

Alfred hops over the barricade.

"Hey, you can't do that!" someone yells.

"Funny, 'cuz I just did." Alfred taps his shoulders. "Hop on, Violet."

Violet stretches out her arms and Drew carefully guides her over the barrier and onto Alfred's back. A few people stare, but now that Violet is involved, no one else says a word. There's something that happens when people observe a young person wearing a cannula with an oxygen tank strapped to their back. They dare not ask questions. You could be doing the Milly Rock at a baby christening. They wouldn't even look twice. Perhaps they figure if you need a travel pack of oxygen to get through the day, the least they can do is get the hell out of your way and let you do whatever you want.

Click-click.

Drew jumps over the crowd control gate.

I peek down the runners' path. The end is only about a hundred yards away. It's the perfect distance for a hijacked marathon dash for the finish line. Violet wraps one arm around Drew, another around Alfred, and they each hold one of her legs.

"Indigo...look at us." Violet laughs. "We're six-legged racers."

Click-click.

"Ready, set, go!" I cry. "Go, go, go!"

Drew and Alfred take off as fast as they can walk, what with each being responsible for one half of Violet. She throws her head back. Her expression is a mixture of exhilaration, poise and confidence: basically Violet in a nutshell.

Click-click.

"Giddy up, boys!" She squeezes their shoulders.

I shuffle along the barrier gate, sneaking through openings in the crowd, following as they move Violet toward her goal.

"Excuse you!" a lady says as I ram into her. She protectively pulls a small child out of my way.

"I'm so sorry." And I am. But what am I supposed to do? I

can't miss this moment 'cuz I'm trying to be polite to strangers. I push past her and her kid, keeping my focus on Violet. She's radiant.

Click-click.

Drew holds up one of his hands in victory.

Click-click.

"You can do it, you guys!" I call out.

Click-click.

They're inches from the finish line. I'm snapping pictures so quickly, I worry I might run out of memory on this card. But I can't stop to check. Capturing this for Violet is everything. In Lynsey Addario's book, she said that when she's taking pictures, she's doing her work. And when she's doing her work she is *alive*. "'I'm sure there *are* other versions of happiness,'" I whisper, staring at them through the lens of my camera while quoting my favorite excerpt from Lynsey's book. "'But this one is mine.'"

They're now inches from the finish line.

Click-click-click-click.

"Go, Violet!" I scream, scooting in front of another group of annoyed people. "Sorry. Excuse me."

Click-click.

I'm certain I'm imagining it, but the roar of the crowd seems to intensify when they move under the canvas banner and step onto bold painted letters that say FINISH. Or maybe I'm *not* imagining it. Perhaps the roar of the crowd *is* louder. The sky certainly seems bluer. The sun...shinier. Maybe on some level, the entire *universe* understands how important this is to Violet, and every atom, molecule and ion has awakened to cheer her on, too.

Click-click-click.

Drew and Alfred raise Violet's hands in the air. She turns to me. "We did it!"

"I know!" My eyes well with tears. "You did it, Violet!"

"Woot-woot!" She pumps her fist.

They move away from the path of oncoming runners to a patch of grass beside the sidewalk. I rush to meet them as they gently set Violet down on her feet.

"That was crazy!" Alfred exclaims excitedly.

"Such a high," Drew agrees, running a hand through his hair. "Much easier on my back than running the whole marathon."

"We set a world record!" Alfred offers. "First six-legged racers to cross a finish line in a marathon they didn't actually run."

Violet coughs. "We were the best...six-legged racers ever! You two are my new heroes."

I scroll through the photos on my camera, each one more vivid than the one before. Such light and life on Violet's face. Something I haven't seen in so long. Something I haven't captured...ever...to be honest. I'm always trying so hard to be as good as Violet when it comes to taking photographs that tell a story. It's not often I've looked at *her* through the lens of my camera. It's like seeing...

"You?"

I look up at the sky.

"It's like seeing you, isn't it?"

"Yeah." I smile. "I guess you're right. Like an extension of me, for sure."

When I lift the camera to take a few more shots, Violet's coughing pretty violently again.

"Vee? You good?" I can't help myself. I just need her to say, *I'm fine.* She can even yell at me like she did Michelle. Anything to calm my nerves. Something doesn't feel right. Only she doesn't yell in reply. She only looks at me, her eyes narrowed in confusion. I take a step forward. "Violet?"

"Where am I?" she asks as she methodically rubs her chest.

"You're joking, right?" Alfred and I exchange worried looks.

Violet looks around, eyes still narrowed in confusion. "Seriously! Where am I?"

Her speech seems slurred.

"Indigo, go get Michelle. Hurry."

I've never heard The Voice sound anything but relaxed… almost taunting. Like he's on a perpetual quest to fuck with me, rather than actually guide and assist. But this time, The Voice sounds *serious.*

"Why? What's wrong?"

"Nothing's wrong with me!" Violet screams as she turns to Drew. "Don't touch me, man!"

"Indigo, go get Michelle! Now!"

It happens so suddenly, I jerk back in response. Violet clutches at her chest and falls to her knees, pulling at her shirt like she's trying to rip it off.

"Violet?" Alfred kneels beside her.

She pounds her fists into the grass, chest heaving, thrashing her head around like she's got rabies.

"Indigo, get Michelle!" Drew scoops her up. "Go!"

In my entire life, I've never run so fast. My camera bounces against my chest as I race across the pavement. "Michelle!!!" I scream. *"Michelle!"*

Michelle is coming out of the convenience store with Brandon and Nam. When she sees me, she literally drops the plastic bag she's holding in her hands. The sound of glass bottles breaking on the hard concrete rings louder than the noise of the marathon.

"Where is she?" Michelle cries.

I turn and point. Drew is approaching, expression pained, racing with Violet in his arms, trying his hardest to keep a good hold on her as she continues to flail about.

"Jesus! Get her on the bus!" Michelle exclaims. "Hurry!"

Drew rushes up the stairs with Michelle and me at his heels. He lays Violet across a pair of seats and swiftly steps out of the way. Mom, Dad and the boys climb onto the bus.

"What's happening?" Mom screams.

Pastor Jedidiah scoots down the aisle. "Is she okay?"

"She will be." Michelle grabs a medical bag. "I want everyone off this bus except Mom and Indigo!"

Michelle means business and the family knows it. Dad assists Pastor as everyone disembarks, leaving us three girls alone.

"Indigo, grab her feet. Mom, you grab her hands."

Violet's body is convulsing. She's using her fist to pound on the seat. Kicking her legs and tossing her head about like a scene out of *The Exorcist*.

I clutch on to her legs, but I barely have enough strength to contain her—she's freakishly strong in this moment.

"What's happening, Michelle?" Mom wails.

"She's hypoxic." Michelle takes scissors and cuts Violet's T-shirt down the middle, exposing her chest. "It means her body isn't getting enough oxygen."

"Are you sure?" Mom replies.

"I'm mostly sure." Now Michelle holds a needle in one hand; with the other hand she uses her fingers to push around on Violet's chest. "But I like to cover all bases."

"What's that?" Mom cries.

"If she's not hypoxic, her throat's closed and she can't breathe." Michelle thrusts the needle into the spot where her fingers rest on Violet's chest. Violet's body jerks in response.

"Indigo," Michelle says sternly. "In my suitcase, under the seat, grab my other medical bag. Hurry up!"

I rush to the suitcase and easily spot the red medical bag. I grab it and push it forward, observing as all that Michelle is not gets pushed to the side to present all that she is—and that's one hell of a nurse. When Michelle works, she's like a machine. She's precise, her attention to detail like nothing I've ever seen. Her focus overpowers her emotions. She's in tune, rapt and determined to carry out her mission. And her mission in this moment is clear: keep Violet *alive*. She places a face mask over Violet's mouth and nose and pushes a button on a portable machine that revs up as loud as a motorcycle engine. As a vapor emits from the mask, Violet begins to calm. Her body seems to relax. Fists unclench. The color slowly returns to her face.

"Mom." Michelle wipes her forehead, dripping with sweat at this point. "I need you to set the timer on your phone."

"Timer? I don't know where—"

"Forget it! Indigo, start the damn stopwatch. Hurry."

I whip out my phone and press the buttons to start the stopwatch app. The seconds fly past on the screen. "It's going."

Michelle preps another needle, carefully inserting it into Violet's arm. I recognize this one, as I had something like it protruding from *my* arm not too long ago in the hospital. Michelle connects tubing to an IV bag. She stands, handing the bag to Mom. "Hold this."

Mom holds it as high as she can while Michelle studies numbers on a device now connected to Violet's finger. After a few moments, she exhales with relief. "Stop the time, Indigo."

I press the red button on the screen to stop my phone timer.

"What's it say?" Michelle asks fearfully.

My hands are trembling. "Fifty-three seconds."

"We need to get her to a hospital. Mom, call for an ambulance."

Violet's eyes are open but she seems far away, staring up at the ceiling of the bus like she's not exactly in her body. "No," she whispers through her plastic mask. "I won't go."

The machine that's emitting the vapor seems to churn and percolate like a defunct coffeepot. Michelle turns to Mom.

"Her sat measurement was reading under eighty-five for at least fifty-three seconds. God only knows when it started. Too much time has passed. Hypoxemia longer than a minute is dangerous. Deadly. Other organs can start shutting down. She needs more than what I can offer on this bus."

"An *ambulance*?" Mom is full-on hysterically sobbing. "But maybe she's okay now."

"Mom, she is not okay! Violet could be dealing with a number of things as we speak. Liver damage. God only knows what else. Dial 911! Do it now!"

Violet shakes her head. Tries to pull off her mask.

"No, Violet," Michelle commands. "Don't take it off. Honey, you need it."

Violet speaks through the mask. "No...hospital," she whispers. "I won't...go. They can't make me."

Michelle speaks pointedly to Mom. "I don't care if she doesn't want to go! Pull rank."

Violet shakes her head. "They can't take me...if I won't go."

"It doesn't matter..." Michelle speaks only to Mom. "There's a form for involuntary commitment. Explain when EMS arrives."

Mom's holding up the IV bag of solution but her hands are trembling. She's clearly not ready to pull rank on Violet.

"Fine. Where's my cell?" Michelle digs around the bag. "I'll do it."

"Michelle, wait!" Mom hands off the IV bag to Michelle and steps around her to stand directly in front of me. "I wanna know what God says."

"What?" I ask breathlessly.

"Mom..." Michelle's voice is strained, a mixture of sheer exhaustion and...disbelief, probably. "You want Violet to die on this bus out here in the middle of nowhere? Indigo is out of her damn mind. You can't continue to let her guide us into the abyss."

"I want to know what God says," Mom repeats. "So please tell me, Indigo. Tell *us*."

Michelle doesn't have to speak a word. Her expression says it all:

Stop with the voice in your head!

Do the right thing for Violet.

We need to get her to a hospital!

"Well?" Michelle breaks the silence. "What's it gonna be, Indigo?"

I close my eyes. *Please speak to me, Voice. Tell me what we need to do. Please don't leave me hanging this time.*

"Indigo…" The Voice whispers.

"I'm listening!" I cry. I don't even care if Mom and Michelle think it's weird I'm talking to myself. It's what they asked for, anyway. "Please. We need a word from you."

"Are you sure?"

"I'm sure."

The Voice sighs. **"Fine. Michelle's right. You need to get her to a hospital."**

I wipe my eyes before tears can fall.

"I'm sorry, Indi. I like giving a word. I only wish I had a better one."

"So what do I say to my family? Tell me exactly what you want me to say. Word for word."

"Word for word, say this: 'She needs to go to the hospital. It's the best place for her now. Michelle is right.'"

I nod. "Anything else?"

"Tell them you all can still get her to the Wave. Maybe not tomorrow. Maybe the next day when she recovers. Maybe next week. But for now, she needs

more medical help than Michelle can give. Get her to the hospital. Call for the ambulance."

I chew my bottom lip.

"Is God talking to you right now?" Mom asks.

I open my eyes and stare into Mom's, realizing that it might be the first time I've ever really looked deeply into my mom's eyes. They're brown. I don't know why I always thought Mom's eyes were black. And they're vibrant. And I can see the worry etched into the fine lines of the skin around them. Skin that crinkles with her pained expression. Her eyes don't seem cold and disengaged like I've thought for so many years, but rather, full, warm and… I study them closer. There's something else there. What's a good synonym for…*want*? It's *yearning*. That's what I'm seeing. Like decades of information are yearning and desperate to burst free. Stories I've never bothered asking her to share. Tales from her past. What was *her* childhood like? What were her dreams and why were they deferred? Surely she didn't plan to grow up and drive a bus. Surely she had something else in mind for her life besides all of us. Besides…this.

"Indigo…" Mom stresses. "We need a word. Is God talking to you or not?"

"The Voice is talking to me."

"And?"

"Yeah, Indigo." Michelle heaves the heaviest of sighs. "Violet's life depends on this. Enlighten us with the word of Almighty God."

"The Voice says—" I wipe tears as they slide down my cheeks "—that Violet needs to get to the Wave quicker than ever. He said to get the family back on the bus and drive."

208

CHAPTER FOURTEEN

The Voice has stopped communicating with me. No matter how many questions I ask...he won't respond. No matter how much I talk...he's not listening. Or maybe he is listening and *choosing* not to respond to screw around with me. Maybe he's mad at me for lying. Or maybe he was never real to begin with. It doesn't matter anymore. The mustard seed of faith has been planted, has rooted and is growing like a wild weed. We are getting to the Wave and Violet *will* live. That's all there is to it.

Speaking of people not talking to me. Add Michelle to the list. Though in truth she's not really talking to anybody but Pastor right now. Ever since the sun set and a blanket of darkness hijacked the sky, he's been passing stones behind his blanket cubicle. So even though it's late and clearly past everyone's bedtime, nobody can sleep through the scream- ing. With each whimper, shriek, grunt and howl, we all sink a bit farther into our seats. This trip has turned into our very own horror movie.

"Straight through," I explain to Mom as she listens to my fake instructions from The Voice. "We stop for nothing but gas and restroom breaks until we get to the Airbnb in Hodell. Tomorrow we arrive at the ranger station in Kanab, Utah, where we'll see if our numbers are called for the lottery."

"I can't drive for that many hours," Mom explains. "It's too much for me. I'm already exhausted."

"Then let Drew drive while you rest."

Mom shakes her head. "He'll kill us all."

"He can do it," I reply simply. "The Voice says he can." The lies just rush out of me like projectile vomit.

Mom nods. "What's this about a lottery, Indigo? Explain it to me."

"It's protected and preserved land. Only a few get to hike the Wave. Our numbers have to be called."

"And what if they're not called?"

"The Voice said not to worry about it. It's all taken care of. *Everything* is taken care of."

"Okay, Indigo. Anything else?"

"Have faith," I say like I am Moses incarnate. "Mustard seed faith, Mom. It's really all you need."

"Pastor, hold it for longer. I know you can hold it." Michelle's trying her hardest to speak softly to Jedidiah as we barrel down the highway with Drew at the wheel, driving like a cast member of *The Fast and the Furious*, but we can all still hear.

"I'm trying," Pastor cries.

"Try harder. The longer you can hold it, the easier it'll move down the canal."

I scoot out of my seat and head down the aisle to sit beside Violet, struggling to keep my balance as Drew switches lanes every two seconds to pass a new vehicle.

"Hey, Vee? Feeling better?" I ask.

"Hmm?" Violet is somewhat awake. I take her hand and hold it in mine.

To our right, Mom rests her head on Dad's shoulder. Her eyes are closed, but I know she's not asleep. It almost feels insensitive to even think about sleep when Pastor is suffering so.

"I'm sorry..." Violet whispers. "If I was mean." She pauses to take a deep breath. "Michelle says...it's a side effect. I... wasn't myself. I'm—"

"Violet, stop." I smile even though I feel like crying. "You don't have to apologize. It's okay."

"You need to squeeze the tip of the penis," Michelle instructs him.

Brandon and Nam howl with laughter near the back of the bus.

I cringe. Brandon and Nam's giggles, hoots, snorts, cackles (or any other synonym for being insensitive to another human's pain) are more than I can bear.

"Did she tell him to squeeze the tip of his *penis*?" Nam asks loud enough for the whole bus to hear.

I turn to Violet. "Sis?"

"Hmm?"

"I'll be right back, okay?"

She nods, eyes half-closed.

I walk down the aisle and slide in beside Nam and Brandon. They have to squish together to make room for me.

"Hey!" Brandon growls as he's forced up against the window. "Fall back, Auntie. Dang."

"Yeah, Auntie," Nam agrees. "Go sit somewhere else. What's your issue?"

I lean forward so no one else can hear me but them. "My issue is both of your big mouths."

Their eyes widen.

"Is the word *penis* funny to you, Brandon, because yours is so small?"

He shakes his head, the orange frames on his glasses sliding down his nose. "I—I dunno."

"What about *asshole*? Is that funny? Because that's what you and Nam are being right now. Little assholes. Laughing at a man who donated his wheelchair, his bus and his *time*. For adults who work nonstop like Pastor Jed, time is money. And you wanna know how much he's charging us for all of this?"

Brandon shakes his head so hard, his glasses fall onto his lap. He snatches them up.

"Zero dollars," I hiss. "He has done nothing but give to us and be good to us and all you monster brats have done is laugh at his pain and misfortune."

Brandon's literally shaking now. Good. Serves the little turd right.

"So here is how things are going to go for the rest of this trip. You two are going to behave like little angels instead of demon seeds from the depths of hell."

"Whatever." Nam folds his arms across his chest. "Mom says all they need is two signatures to have you committed. I heard her tell Dad that you belong in a straitjacket. You're not the boss of us."

"I may not be the boss of you." I drum my fingers on my cast. "But I am the boss of my collection of photographs. You guys know how I'm always taking pictures, right?"

Brandon and Nam exchange horrified looks.

"I have memory cards on board, *filled* with embarrassing photos of you two." I cock my head to the side. "Like, Nam… remember when you pooped your pants at the Georgetown Morgue haunted house a few Halloweens ago? I have photographs of your shit-stained sweatpants."

Nam hangs his head. Brandon cracks up.

"Oh, is that funny, Bran? Because I have a dozen frames to go along with my vivid memory of your mom testing out a YouTube makeup tutorial on you. I wonder how all of second grade would feel to see you wearing Plum Dandy eye shadow and Crème de la Crème lipstick?" I ruffle his mop of curls. "I actually liked the look on you. It made this Einstein hair-don't you got going on really pop."

"Hey!" Brandon's bottom lip quivers. "That's private."

"Is it?" A smile stretches across my face. "I'm monitoring your behavior from now on. Call each other booger monsters or call Pastor Farty-Mc-Fart-a-Saurus and I'll upload a pic onto the embarrassing family photos website and send a mass email to all the parents on your class email lists. Each disturbing thing you say and/or do." I hold up one finger. "One pic." I tap them gently on the cheeks. "Starting now."

"But, Auntie—"

I scratch my chin. "Perhaps I'll start with the photo of you, Nam. You know, when you came off the waterslide at Wild Waves without your swim trunks? And you had to run naked, snot-faced and crying to get a towel from your dad? Your ashy behind on display for all of Seattle to see? All footage captured by..." I tap my chest. "Yours truly."

"Auntie, you can't show those pics." Nam's voice is weak.

"I can do whatever I want." They both seem to cower in fear. I pinch their cheeks. "I'm watching." I lean forward and whisper, "I'm listening. Ready. Set. Go."

I scoot back down the aisle into the seat beside Violet. She's sitting up now, rubbing her legs vigorously. "Where'd you go?"

"Just chatting it up with Bran and Nam. Good times."

"Practicing being nicer?"

"You could say that. Are your legs cramping up? You cold? I can get more blankets."

"I'm not cold." She stretches out her neck to make sure no one is looking, then rolls up her pant leg. "Look."

I lean forward to examine her legs. Her calves are *swollen*. Abnormally so. It looks grotesque. It looks...deadly. A shiver rushes up my spine as I remember the words from The Voice:

Michelle is right. She needs to get to the hospital.

She pulls her pants back down and the bus rumbles on in the dark. I know that Violet's swollen legs are a clear sign she's taken a turn for the worse; somehow she knows it, too.

"You can't tell Michelle, Indigo. Okay?"

I look at Violet. It's the first time in years I've seen her appear a mess. Her hair is pretty much all over her head, her painted nails are chipped, her lips dry, eyes red and swollen. Dark circles are under her eyes.

"I'm serious, Indi. You can't tell her. When we get to the Airbnb, insist to sleep in my room. Insist to do… everything she normally does at night."

"But I don't know what to do. I'm not a nurse."

"I can talk you through it." She pulls her messy hair into a bun on top of her head, accentuating the dark circles under her eyes and her sunken cheeks. "Suggest she sleep in Pastor's room…because of his kidney stones or something. Tell her… Oh, I know. Tell her it's *God's* orders. Yeah. Blame it on the voice in your head."

"So you basically want me to lie?"

"Indigo, you lie all the time. And if I'm going to make this hike, I can't have her hovering, scaring the shit out of me with all the medical jargon. It's too much." She sips from a bottle of water. "What does God say, anyway? Is he…talking to you…now?"

Should I tell her? Tell her that I haven't actually heard from The Voice since I ignored his advice? Explain that The Voice has pulled a Troy Richmond and bailed faster than I can say *Hey, wait up*? Then I'd have to admit that The Voice suggested she be hospitalized. Admit he *warned* me this very thing was going to happen. I bite the skin around my thumb. "I…don't hear him. Right now, I mean."

Drew picks up the microphone. Clears his throat. "Good evening, family. Thanks to my *expert* driving, we made up some time from the few delays and are about fifteen minutes from the Airbnb in Hodell. Gather your things. Put on your shoes. You're not free to move about the cabin just yet. But get ready. Ten-four."

Michelle is now kneeling in front of Violet and me. "Vee, I hope you don't mind sleeping in Pastor's room. We'll pick one of the rooms with two beds. I can sleep on the floor. Doesn't really matter to me. I only wanna be able to keep an eye on you two. I don't imagine he'll pass another stone tonight. Might even be the last of 'em."

Violet kicks me.

"Ow!" I turn to Violet. "That hurt."

"Accident. Sorry. But…isn't there something you wanted to tell Michelle?"

"Um." I turn back to Michelle. She's glaring at me. "Uh, yeah. The Voice in my head…says I need to stay with Violet tonight. Just me and her. She and I. We. Sorry."

Michelle laughs. Not a *ha ha* laugh. The kind of laugh that says *This is some* bullshit. "Okay, well, I have to wash her incision. Help her take a bath. Give her her medicine and basically check on her every hour on the hour. Something you're not equipped nor qualified to do—"

"Indigo can do it. I'll talk her through it all. Plus, God's with her," Violet explains.

"And you'll be close. It's a house," I add. "If anything goes wrong, I'll walk four steps to the next room to find you."

"Fine." Michelle sighs. "I officially give up. You win, Indigo."

She moves down the aisle.

"Michelle's gonna murder me in my sleep."

"That was brave." Violet squeezes my hand. "Thank you, sis."

216

★ ★ ★

As we turn into the driveway of the Airbnb in Hodell, Utah, I'm a bit surprised to see how remote it is. It's basically the only house in sight. It's miles and miles of dirt and rocks on acres and acres of land. A vast nothingness. In the distance are mountains, but it's really too dark to see details, so they look more like ominous shadows, reaching high into the sky. Or maybe they look like monsters, lined up and ready to attack.

Drew turns off the ignition and all eyes turn to take in the Airbnb house that will be our home for the night. It's a nice-sized colonial, well lit, relatively new construction with concrete pavers that lead to the front door. Also worth noting: it's surrounded by about a hundred American flags.

There are two different flagpoles on opposite ends of the lawn, both with flags blowing in the wind, half-mast. I always thought a flag flying half-mast meant someone died. I really hope that's not the case for this place.

One monster-sized flag hangs from the side of the house, dangling from the roof to the ground.

There are a dozen tiny flags hanging from the porch railing.

Holiday lights in the shape of flags on the lawn.

Red, white and blue flowers line up to look like flags.

"This is creepy AF," Alfred whispers, leaning his head up against the window.

"It's not creepy." Dad sounds…well…creeped out, but he's trying to keep a positive spin on the weirdness. "It's patriotic."

"And I know my baby girl," Mom adds. "She probably

researched the best Airbnb with the best reviews. Right, Violet?"

Violet shrugs. "Actually, Mom, since it was short notice... I didn't have a ton of options that were wheelchair-accessible."

"Oh, shit," Alfred says.

"It was either this or a lodge and barbershop combo closer to the trailhead. But that one had a review that said it had bedbugs and sometimes roaches."

Hmm. Bedbug bites and roaches or...whatever the hell lies beyond this red, white and blue *striped* door. "I'm sure it's fine," I say. "The Voice says we got nothing to worry about."

That seems to relieve everyone's tensions.

Violet's situated in her chair and lowered on the lift. I rush outside to meet her.

"This is remote," Dad says as everyone else disembarks and takes in the splendor of the middle of nowhere. "I wonder if you get Wi-Fi out this far."

Nam approaches Mom. "Grandmother, can I help with your bag?"

Mom frowns. "Huh?"

"Your bag looks heavy and I'd like to assist you," Nam repeats.

"And I'll take your purse." Brandon steps up beside Nam, gripping his backpack with one hand, his other hand extended.

Mom rears back, eyes the boys suspiciously. I'm sure she's imagining them taking her bag and purse and setting them both on fire. "No. I got my purse *and* my bag, thank you very much."

"If you change your mind, Grandmother..." Brandon looks over at me for approval. I hold up my camera with one hand and smile. He swallows. "Please let us know."

I push Violet's wheelchair across the concrete pavers to the front door of the large colonial. As if the owners are peeking through the peephole watching and waiting, the front door swings open upon our approach. A cheery, white-haired husband and wife step onto the porch.

"We were beginning to think you guys weren't coming," the man says with a friendly chortle.

I'd say they are about Mom and Dad's age, give or take a few years. The two seem warm, kind and normal. That is, until they step into the light and get a nice good look at all of us. Their eyes bulge. They stop cold, panicked expressions creeping onto their faces.

Alfred and I exchange looks. We know this scene. It's played out before many times. That moment when a white person is surprised to see the people they've been communicating with over the phone or internet...are black. It's obvious that this sweet little country couple was *not* expecting a motley crew of African Americans to step off a bus covered with eyeballs.

Mom knows the look too, because she steps forward and presents her best newscaster voice. This is a thing in our family. When white people look at us crazy or get that judgmental *oh no, it's black people* look in their eyes, we overenunciate and overarticulate like we're in speech class.

"Good evening." Mom sounds like a new hire on *Date-*

line. "We apologize for the delay. Utterly thrilled we made it safely. Utterly."

The wife exhales. Mom's *Dateline* act seems to have relaxed her a bit. "Oh, yes. We're happy, too. I'm Sandi. And this is my husband, Bob."

"Sandi and Bob, it's a pleasure to meet ya." Dad's playing the game as well. Using his ultrawhite, Bryant Gumbel voice.

Alfred and I roll our eyes. I should ruin it all and declare, *What's crack a lackin'? How y'all be doing up in Hodell!!*

"Well, come on in," Bob finally says, as if he's got no other choice.

They usher us into the home.

Inside, it's much more disturbing than a few hundred American flags on the lawn. First off, the walls are all painted red. I'm sure it's in homage to the United States, but it mostly feels like we've stepped into the hell waiting room. Like, *Y'all have a seat, please. Satan will be riiiiight with you.*

Second. There are paintings hanging on the walls. So many that it looks more like a museum than a home anyone would want to live in. My eyes study those hanging in the foyer:

A Native American holds a human scalp in one hand, a tomahawk in the other.

A slave ship with hundreds of slaves lined up and *chained.*

A public hanging?

"Welcome to our home. You'll have full use of the place," Sandi explains. "When we have renters, Bob and I stay in the apartment above the garage so you all can have privacy."

"Now we would like to remind you," Bob starts, "we don't allow any sort of drug use or drug paraphernalia."

Mom's jaw tightens. "I am *sorry*? No one in our family participates in recreational drug use, if that is what you are insinuating." Uh-oh. Mom's stopped contracting verbs. This can't be good. She only does that when the black-girl-with-an-attitude is *struggling* to be tamed. Plus, I can see her left hand twitching. I know she wants to place that hand on her hip and add, *Say it again! Say you don't allow drug use again, Bob!*

"Oh, no, no. Not insinuating at all," Sandi exclaims as if Mom thinking that is absurd. "It's what we say to all the renters."

"Oh, I'm sure you do." Dad's got just the tiniest hint of sarcasm in his voice, but Bryant Gumbel seems to still have control of his vocal cords.

Drew drifts to the photograph of the American Indian holding the tomahawk and human scalp. "This painting." He shakes his head. "This is *terribly* offensive."

"But a nice companion to the slave ship." Alfred's still leaned up against the door like he's about to run out of the house and search for a Holiday Inn.

"Oh, the artwork on our walls is of course for sale, and also in tribute to American history. A local painter does them for us," Sandi explains nonchalantly.

"American history wasn't always pretty." Bob wraps an arm around Sandi.

"We're *very* patriotic," Sandi declares with a head nod.

"You don't say?" Michelle responds coolly.

Pastor Jedidiah clears his throat. I'll admit, it's nice to see him standing up straight. "It's a beautiful home. The paintings do a nice job of reminding us that our country has quite a story to tell."

"Thank you," the wife says warmly to Pastor. You can tell she's happy we have at least one white person with us.

"Is there somewhere nearby we can grab dinner?" Michelle asks. "My boys are hungry. We haven't eaten." Michelle isn't pretending for these people. Her head is cocked to the side with an expression on her face like… *I really want you people to try me. I double dog dare you.*

"The nearest convenience store is about a twenty-minute drive up the 99 North," Bob says cheerily.

"And if you go twenty minutes south, there's a Cracker Barrel."

"A *Cracker* Barrel?" Alfred repeats.

"They close at ten, honey," Bob says.

"Oh, you're right." Sandi snaps her fingers. "What about stew? We have some stew left over from dinner. You people are welcome to it."

"You people?" Mom repeats.

"Let it go," Dad whispers.

"I like stew." Alfred finally takes a step away from the door. "What kind of stew is it?"

"Rabbit," Sandi declares proudly. "With chestnut dumplings. Rabbits run wild, so we're lucky to be able to eat them fresh. We set traps. Then we boil them."

"You guys boil rabbits?" Brandon asks, his voice shaking.

Drew grabs his keys. "What's east and west? There's gotta be somewhere we can eat."

"Nothing east," Bob replies. "But west… Let me think

here." He rubs his chin. "Can't seem to think of anything west either."

"Now, we do have a freezer full of food," Sandi offers. "A few frozen pizzas left."

My mouth waters at the thought of a fresh slice of pizza.

"Is it rabbit pizza?" Alfred asks.

"Sausage, pepperoni and cheese, I believe." Sandi smiles.

Alfred raises his hand. "We'll take it. We'll take the whole lot."

"Help yourself." Sandi yawns. "Now we'll let you people hold down the fort so we can get some shut-eye."

"There is that *you people* again." Mom's *Dateline* exterior is beginning to crack.

"Hold down the fort?" Drew repeats. "Is that a dig because I'm Native?"

Bob's jaw drops. "You're Native *American*? Let me guess—Cherokee?"

Drew shakes his head. "No."

"Chickasaw? Choctaw? Ahh…" Bob grins. "I bet you're Navajo!"

"Oh, we *love* the Navajo!" Sandi exclaims. "Bob's grandfather was four percent Navajo on his Ancestry DNA test."

"I'm not Navajo," Drew replies.

Bob shrugs. "Well, whatever kind of Indian you are, we think it's fantastic. Our country honors our Natives." Bob and Sandi give Drew a synchronized salute.

Brandon reaches up to touch one of the paintings.

"Don't touch that, Brandon," Michelle scolds him.

"It's one of my absolute favorites." Sandi moves to Brandon

and kneels in front of him. "That's Christopher *Columbus.*" She talks like she's hosting an episode of *Sesame Street.* "Do you know who he is and why he's important to our nation's history, little one?"

"Yes, ma'am." Brandon nods. "My dad says Christopher Columbus was a murdering, lying piece of shit, who is probably burning in hell as we speak." Brandon looks over at me with eyes of panic. "I mean, piece of garbage."

Drew doesn't even bother scolding Brandon. In fact, he smiles.

For a brief moment, Sandi's speechless. Then she stands. "Oh, my." And slowly backs away to Bob.

"If you people need us, just give us a holler." Bob holds two thumbs up and he and Sandi rush toward the front door.

We watch them exit.

"You see that, Isaiah?" Mom snaps. "*You* people?"

"Hold down the fort?" Drew repeats. "And these paintings should be *criminal.*" I've never seen Drew look so upset.

"Sorry, everyone," Violet cries. "I didn't know. I feel terrible."

"Oh, honey." Mom's demeanor switches. "It's fine."

"Yeah, Violet," Drew says. "It's extremely offensive, but cozy."

Everyone chimes in to make Violet feel better about the American history horror shit show we just walked into.

"I kinda like it," Dad adds, dragging luggage down the hall. "The red walls make it warm."

"Yeah." Alfred flips his cap back. "Like hellfire."

Dad gently slaps Alfred on the shoulder. "Son. You're not helping."

"Where is the freezer and where are the pizzas?" Alfred replies. "I'll help by loading them up into the oven."

"I know that's right." Mom and Alfred move into the kitchen with the boys close behind. "Careful with the freezer, though. I am not in the mood to see a bunch of frozen bunnies."

"Think I'll hit the shower and the bed." Jedidiah pushes his palms together and bows. "It's been quite a long day. Namaste, Indigo, Violet. The two most beautiful colors of the rainbow."

"Namaste, namastah." I bow back. "Pastor, can I ask you a question?"

"Of course, Indigo."

"What does *namaste* mean?"

"Wonderful question indeed. It means the light in me recognizes and honors the light in you. In other words, no one is greater than the other. There is no true leader. We are one."

For some reason his words make me look over at Michelle. She looks away. "I like that, Pastor," I reply. "Namaste."

"Pastor." Michelle steps in front of me. "Take a downstairs room so I can be close to you and Violet." Michelle squeezes Violet's shoulder. "I know you're with Indigo, but I'll be in to give you your medication and check your O2 sat. Then I promise to leave you alone."

Michelle and Pastor move deeper into the house.

"Indigo?" Violet says.

"Yeah?"

"Can you push me into the bathroom? I'm about to throw up."

I push her as fast as I can and we move into a large bathroom at the end of the hall. When I shut the door, I jump back and gasp. Hanging on the wall: a five-foot crucifix with a bleeding Jesus surrounded by a string of blinking Christmas lights.

"Are you okay, Indi?"

"Uh, yeah. Sorry."

"Could you turn on the water?" she asks. "I don't like for anybody to hear."

I twist on the water in the sink and claw-foot bathtub, trying my hardest not to focus on the crucifix soaked in fake blood.

"And can you help me?"

I rush to assist her. Guiding her out of her chair so she can kneel beside the toilet. Once she's situated, she lets loose, heaving into the bowl. She throws up for so long she's finally just dry heaving. I flush the toilet, stand, grab a few paper towels, wet them with cool water from the sink and hand them off to Violet.

She accepts gratefully and wipes her mouth and face. "In the bag, hanging on my chair, is a toothbrush and toothpaste."

"On it." I search inside the neatly organized bag, grab her toothbrush and paste and stand beside her while she brushes her teeth. "Want me to take you to one of the rooms? So you can lay down?"

She places her toothbrush on the counter. "In the pictures

online, they had a beautiful backyard. Let's go to the back-yard. That okay?"

"Of course, Vee. Anything for you."

The back porch highlights a massive expanse of land. The night sky is blanketed with thousands of twinkling stars as far as the eye can see. Out here, there is no light pollution, so it's as if you're staring straight into space. Like you can reach out and gently glide your hand along the line of stars, the way you'd slide your hand across ivory piano keys. I imagine the stars would hum a tune just the same. The air is crisp and clear. The night comfortably still. The mountains in the distance are like giant armed guards protecting our well-earned moment together. Though I know the moment won't last for long. Someone is always checking on Violet. Tending to her needs. Not to mention, I can smell the scent of baking pizzas filtering outside. I'm sure it'll be only a moment before we're called to eat.

My camera is still slung around my neck, so I flip it on and point it toward the sky.

"I've never taken shots of stars before," Violet says. "How do you do it?"

"You start with as wide an f-stop as the lens will allow. I like a shutter speed of about twenty seconds. Manual mode—"

"But wouldn't they be blurry like that?"

I smile. "The secret—turn the white balance *off* and set the optical resolution to the highest setting. Bada bing. Bada boom."

Click-click-click.

"Here. Take a look." I pull my camera strap from around my neck and hand it to Violet.

She scrolls through the photos. "*So* gorgeous. How did you know that?"

I shrug. "I like to play around with different settings until something works."

"You're so brilliant. I wish I was as good as you."

"Huh? You're way better than me. *Your* photos are brilliant."

"My 'brilliance' comes from books…and memorizing what people tell me to do. You come up with everything on your own. You're…a natural." She continues scrolling through my photos. She laughs. "Omigosh! Look…at all these. You took all of these and I didn't…even realize."

"You like them?"

"It's me and Dad." She gets a faraway look in her eyes. "We look so happy. You captured that…so well." She pauses to adjust her sleeves. It's no longer the color of the day for us, since Michelle had to go and cut off her olive T-shirt, so now Violet wears a black-and-gold hooded *Hamilton* sweatshirt. "Oh, the marathon!" She grins. "Top five highlights of my life, for sure. I mean, afterward…wasn't so great. But crossing that finish line." She keeps scrolling. "Willy! You got shots of *Willy*? Gosh, he was so sweet." She lowers her head and begins to cry.

"What's wrong, Vee?"

"I'm just… I'm really sorry."

"Sorry? Why?"

"I feel…bad."

"Like you're gonna throw up again?"

"No." She cries. "Indigo, I've been...a terrible sister to you."

"Violet, you're the best sister ever. Please don't cry." I lean forward and grab her hand.

She shakes her head. "I pushed you away. I shouldn't...have shut you out the way I have these past few months. I..." She pauses to wipe her nose.

I dare not interrupt. I'm barely even breathing. I desperately need her to continue. She *has* shut me out. It's true. And for so long, I've wanted to know why. What did I do wrong? Why did I have to lose my best friend?

"I knew I was hurting you, Indi. I guess... I guess I didn't care." She sniffs. "Or maybe on some level... I wanted you to hurt, too."

"Violet. You don't mean that."

"See? I told you I was terrible. I *do* mean it. I didn't think it was fair that I was dying. I felt so cheated." She secures her cannula behind her ears. "I always thought that if I worked hard and did everything right... I thought life would bless me for it. I had it all figured out. And then this happens. And you..." She quiets for a moment. "Maybe I shouldn't admit it."

I sit in a stunned silence. All this time I've been thinking it's not fair that I get to live while Violet dies, and it turns out... she's been thinking the same thing. I heave a heavy sigh. Far off in the distance, I can see wild horses running at the base of the mountains. It's the closest thing to real-life magic I've ever seen. Aside from the sun, I suppose. If only every living thing could be so free.

"I get it," I start. "You don't have to say it. I'm basically a screwup, so why am I the one who gets to live?"

"Indigo—"

"It's cool. I'm not mad at you for thinking it. I think the same thing, too. It's why I was going to kill myself."

"Kill yourself?"

"It's why I was climbing the building."

"But Mom said you were trying to take a picture for me."

"Lies. I was planning to jump but then I chickened out and fell on accident. I wanted to die, too."

"*Indigo?* I don't understand."

"It was to even the playing field! To right this terrible wrong. You shouldn't be dying. It should be me. I know that's what you were going to say and it's okay. I'm not mad at you for thinking it."

"Indigo, that's *not* what I was going to say. Are you insane? You think I want you to die?"

"If there was a choice to be made. Yeah."

"Indigo?" She pauses to take a deep breath. "Why do you think I work so hard to be better than you?"

My eyes squint in confusion. "You don't. You're just better."

"You're wrong. I study all day and night. Take extra classes. Read massive amounts of books…and all you do is lift your camera, and click-click, it's perfect. You intuitively *know*. You don't have to work at being brilliant. *I* do."

"I'm not brilliant."

She laughs again. "Indigo. You are."

"But you get better grades than me."

"That's because I study. You never crack open a book. If this trip…were under different circumstances…and… I saw you capture the night sky so vividly the way you just did… wanna know what I would have done? I would…have found a class online or…somewhere. I would have learned how to take a better photo of the sky than you."

"I don't believe you."

"Believe it, Indigo. You always think I'm one step ahead of you. But the truth is… I…always worked hard to catch *up*. *You're* the leader. You always have been."

I hear the words she's saying. But they're not quite sinking in. Me? The leader? *Impossible*.

"If there was a choice, Indigo, I don't think either one of us should die."

"Then why were you going to kill *your*self?"

"Indigo, death with dignity isn't suicide. It's physician-assisted dying."

"I don't see the difference."

She takes another pained breath. "If you were in pain… and a doctor had medicine that could end your suffering… wouldn't you want to take it?"

I lean my head back on the patio chair and study the thousands of stars I can see lighting the night sky. All those suns in faraway galaxies. Suns whose light will someday dim. What a waste. "I do get what you're saying, Vee. I guess I just believe in waiting on miracles."

"Me too, Indigo. Why do you think I'm here? Because when you told me about the voice…suddenly living…seemed like the best idea ever."

"So you do want to live?"

"Of course I do." She starts to cry again. "It would've been so unfair. With so much space between us. I was gonna die."

She was gonna die. Without a proper goodbye. With us more disconnected than we've ever been. "I'm sorry I'm living and you're dying. Violet, I would give anything to switch places with you. You *know* I would."

Tears spill onto her lap. She pulls the sleeves of her sweatshirt over her hands in her delicate Violet way. "But would I do the same for you? You're so selfless. I have always envied you." She turns to me. "*That's* what I was going to say. Not that I wish you were the one dying. But that… I'd give anything to be just like you. It's all I've ever wanted."

Her words leave me speechless.

"Promise me something. If this doesn't work out and—"

I shake my head. "No. This will work out. You're going to live and we're going to have our whole lives together. We're gonna travel the world. Me and you, Vee."

"But…if something should ever happen to me, I want one thing from you. One promise."

"Anything," I whisper.

"Forgive me."

The door to the back patio slides open and Mom sticks her head out. "You girls come eat because Nam and Bran are snarfin' down pizza slices faster than I can blink. Better hurry before it's all gone and nothing's left but rabbit stew." Mom gasps. "Look at that." She points.

The herd of wild horses race back across the plain. Violet grabs my camera off her lap, fidgets with the settings and takes a few quick snapshots of the animals. She stops to scroll through the photos. "Ahh, it's too dark. And they're moving so fast. You can't really see the detail."

"Try setting the shutter speed to freeze motion."

Violet makes the adjustment.

"It's better if you're moving with the camera," I add. "But if you blur it, you might get something cool."

Click-click-click-click.

Violet reviews her photos. "Ahh, so nice." She hands the camera to Mom. "Look at these, Mom. Indigo was right."

Mom looks at the pictures over Violet's shoulder and nods. "Stunning, Violet. You're an amazing photographer." She squeezes her shoulder. "You two come eat. I'm heading back in. It's freezing out here. Violet, you'll catch pneumonia. You don't even have a coat on."

She moves back into the house, sliding the patio door shut with a soft click.

"See that?" I say, when I'm sure she's out of earshot. "She said that to get to me."

"Said what?"

"'Violet, you're an amazing photographer.' I mean, you are. But that was a dig. Trust me."

"Mom may be set in her ways, but she's not…diabolical. She doesn't want to hurt you."

"I think she does."

"Why don't you talk to her? Tell her how you feel."

"Right. How would that conversation go? 'Hey, Mom, I think you secretly hate me and wish I was the one dying.'"

"Indigo."

"You know it's true. If she could make a deal with the devil she would, and I'd be the one in that wheelchair."

"I disagree. I think Mom...is afraid of you."

"What does that mean?"

"She's...not equipped to be Lynsey Addario's mom. She doesn't think she's good enough. Your destiny...it scares her."

"She told you that?"

"No. I just...know."

"But we have the same destiny. Why doesn't your destiny scare her, too?"

"Because you're the leader, that's why." Violet shivers. "It's cold. I'd like to go in...if you don't mind. That okay, Indigo?"

"Don't mind at all, sis."

I stand, slide open the patio door and push her back inside.

CHAPTER FIFTEEN

Michelle was right. Night shift with Violet *is* rough. It's beyond rough. It's indescribable. To think this has been Michelle's life each and every night. How could I not have known?

If Violet's not throwing up, she's crying out in pain. If she's not crying in pain, she's shivering from chills. I massage her legs. I wipe her head. Rub her temples to ease her migraine. Sing to her. Read her books I download on my phone. In between tending to her, I try to sleep. But the sleep isn't deep and doesn't last for long. Violet is always in need.

"Doesn't seem fair," Violet whispers to me while I slather Chestix Rub on her frail back. "That so many people in the world are suffering. It's the same moon, but one man dances under it, another man dies. It's the same day, but one girl hugs her loved ones so tight. Another girl has no one to hold. She is all alone."

"Yeah," I say softly as she drifts back to sleep. "Doesn't seem fair at all."

In addition to the swelling in Violet's legs, her belly is swollen, too. She looks like she's as pregnant as Michelle. I know I should take the five steps to Michelle's room. Ask for help. But Violet is adamant:

"It's nothing a sweatshirt can't hide," Violet murmurs as the digital clock on the nightstand switches to 3:00 a.m.

A sweatshirt can cover up her swollen abdomen. Sweatpants can hide her swollen legs. But the little O2 sat monitor Michelle taught me to use won't lie. And thankfully the number hasn't dipped again.

I watch Violet's chest heave up and down as she drifts into a deep sleep for the first time all night. I decide to shower and get dressed for the hike. We need to be loaded up on the bus in an hour to make the long drive to the station in Kanab. I write a note and tape it to the wall across from the bed, telling Violet to text me if she wakes and needs anything. But I hope she doesn't wake soon. I hope she sleeps. She needs it.

I'm munching on cold pizza in the dark kitchen when the lights are flipped on and Mom enters. She's dressed in jeans, sneakers and a black sweater. Judging by how red her eyes are, she looks like she may have pulled an all-nighter as well.

"Good morning, Indigo," Mom says with a yawn as she peels off the lid from the canister of coffee on the counter and scoops it into a small coffeepot. "You want some coffee?"

"Sure. I'll take some."

"Did you sleep well?"

"Yes. I slept good," I lie.

"I'm glad somebody slept." She pours bottled water into the pot and presses a button on the base. "Your father and I are in a room dedicated to the Great Depression. Giant photo, right in front of the bed—a line of malnourished children waiting for food at a soup kitchen or...ration coupons. I don't know. It looks sad, though." Mom sits across the table from me as the machine starts to percolate and the strong scent of coffee warms the chill in the drafty kitchen. "Pastor says he's good to drive today. Think I'll have him take us through a drive-through for breakfast."

I take another bite of pizza. The cheese has almost solidified since it's been sitting in the fridge, so my jaw is throbbing from having to chew so hard.

"What's going on with your hair today, Indigo? I swear you make a point for it to look bad."

I zip up my dark blue Lucky Jeans hoodie. "It's pulled up into a bun. What's wrong with that?"

"Did you use gel? It's all fuzzy. The trick is to use hairpins. Wrap it around, hairpin, repeat. And then you need to slick down the baby hairs with that Eco styling gel I bought you so it doesn't look all nappy around the edges."

"Mom, nobody says *nappy* anymore. It's like calling Asian people *Oriental*. I know you slept in a Great Depression room but it's not the Great Depression. We've evolved. *Nappy* is dead."

Mom cocks her head to the side. "Are you getting smart with me, Indigo Phillips? I don't care if you *are* hearing the voice of God. Show *me* respect."

I extract a pepperoni from underneath hardened cheese. "Right. Sorry. I'll remember to gel my nappy edges. Thanks for those wise words. Namaste."

Mom leans across the table and says pointedly, "I feel like I can't win with you."

"Serious?"

"Yes, I'm serious. You *always* have an attitude."

"You told me my hair looked a mess and I need to gel my nappy edges and it's not even 4:00 a.m."

"So?"

"So, Mom, that's *rude*. I'm sorry but I do have an attitude when someone *insults* me."

"I'm not insulting you, Indi. I'm trying to help you. Don't you want to get a boyfriend?"

"Here? In Hodell?"

"At some point. You've never had one. Are you gay?"

I stuff the pepperoni in my mouth and swallow. Not only is it tasteless, it lands in my stomach like a stack of hot stones. Heartburn rushes up my chest. I try to swallow it away. "No, Mother. I'm not gay."

"'Cuz if you were, I'd be okay with it. Your father and I—"

"I'm not gay!" I stand.

"Jesus, Indigo. Calm down. You'll wake up the whole house."

"Considering we need to go soon, that's a good thing." I slam down into my seat.

Mom folds her arms across her chest. "Is there something bothering you, Indigo? Something you need to talk to me about?"

"Yeah. Now that you mention it. You could've turned off *Game of Thrones*."

"What on Earth?"

"That day I told you about the photography award. You could've read my article and looked at my photo."

"I read that article."

"You could've read it *then*." My eyes well with tears. "You could've hugged me, told me I did a good job. Why didn't you? Why *don't* you?"

"Why don't I what?"

"Hug me."

"Indigo, you have got to be kidding me." Mom rubs both temples, something she does when she's trying hard to ward off a screech-and-scream. "Is this a plea for help because you're not hugged enough?"

"No. I guess I sometimes feel like you don't like me."

Mom's silent. In fact, it's the first time I've actually observed her speechless.

"You like Violet. That's obvious. And I know you love all of us. But you act like you don't *like* me."

Another long moment of silence passes before she says, "You honestly feel that way?"

I nod.

"Indigo Phillips." Mom leans back in her chair. "Of course I like you."

I wipe my eyes with the sleeve of my shirt. "It doesn't show."

Mom nods in understanding and we sit in yet another

awkward silence. This one lasts for a minute or two. Finally she speaks.

"What can I do to be better, Indigo? What can I do so you know I like you?"

What can she do? She can hug me. Say nice things about me. Show more interest in the things I like. Look at me the way she looks at Violet—with adoration and respect. But I only shrug in response and mumble, "I dunno, Mom." Because for some reason I feel like it should come from her. Telling my mom ways she can show me love would be like going to see a comedy show and explaining to the comedian all the ways he or she can make you laugh. It wouldn't be the same.

Mom stands, moves to the counter and pours coffee into two mugs. Both are decorated with Jacqueline Kennedy's face. She takes a sip from one of the cups and sighs. "When I was eight years old," Mom starts, her back still to me, "my mom decided parenting was overrated, I suppose. She checked out and checked *in* to the local taverns around town. I was home alone. A lot. I slept in the hall closet because I'd be so afraid." She finally turns around. Her eyes are red and welling with tears. "In the mornings I'd dig in the dirty clothes hamper for clothes to wear to school. I wasn't clean. I smelled. The teachers at my school thought I was nothing. Just some wayward, dirty, smelly black kid who wasn't gonna amount to much of nothing. Hardly ever ate a good meal. If I was thirsty, there was water from the sink or a fridge full of beer. On the rare occasion Mama did come home, all she did was rage and hit me." Tears spill down her cheeks. Tears spill down mine as well. I wipe them away as she moves to take the seat across from me once again. She slides the other Jacqueline Kennedy cup across the table. I grip on to it like it's a security blanket, barely bothered that the heat from the porcelain is almost burning my fingertips.

"I hated being alone. But I wasn't sure which was worse. Being alone or being with her. I promised myself if I ever made it out of that house alive and had kids of my own I would be there. I would really *be* there." She pauses to take a sip of her coffee. Her hands visibly shaking. "I put a roof over your head. I keep you in nice clothes, eating good food. My *life* has been about nothing but *you*. About all my kids."

"But, Mom—"

She holds out a hand to silence me. "I'm trying my hardest to wrap my mind around Violet's illness. You say you're talking to God? I talk to him all the damn time. And every day I wake up to the same situation, so what does that tell you? Nothing ever changes. In fact, it gets worse. Every day she's lost more weight. Or something else has gone wrong. I hear her crying out in the night. I know she's in pain and there's nothing I can do to fix it." Mom sobs. "The reality is—" more tears spill down her cheeks "—I may have to bury my child. And that is the worst pain for a parent. So I'm sorry if I don't have the answers you seek right now. All I can say is that I do love you. I do *like* you. I care. God knows I care. You talk to him, right?"

I nod.

"Well then, ask him and he'll tell you." She stands, pushes her chair in, tries to steady her shaking hands as she holds on tight to the former first lady's face. "I'm here, aren't I, Indigo?"

Her cheeks are soaked with tears. Her eyes red and pained. Making your mom cry has got to make you eligible for some sort of corporal punishment. "Please don't cry, Mom. I'm sorry I even brought it up."

"Don't be sorry, Indigo. Just know that I'm here. I'm *here*. That's gotta count for something, doesn't it? Please, let it count for something."

"It counts, Mom."

"Glad to hear it." She exits the kitchen.

When I move back into the bedroom, Violet is sitting on the edge of the bed, her nightgown sticking to her skin from sweat.

"You okay, sis?"

"I'm good."

She doesn't sound good. Her voice is strained and groggy and she's coughing a lot. Somehow she looks frailer than the night before. Her sunken cheeks now present a ghastly shadow. If death had a face...it would be Violet's.

"Indi, can you help me to the bathroom?"

I help her up. When she stands, there are deep red blood-stains on the white bedsheets.

"Shit."

"What's wrong?" She turns and sees the blood. "Oh, no."

Our cycles have been synced our entire teenage life. It's not that time of the month for me. "Is it that time of the month for you?"

She shakes her head. "No."

"Um...okay...don't worry," I say even though I'm worried. I rush to her wheelchair and push it forward. "Have a seat. Maybe your cycle came early. That's all."

She struggles into the chair.

I tear the sheets off the bed and check the mattress. "All good. Didn't seep through. No worries."

I toss everything into a corner. "I'll throw these in the wash but let's get you in the bath."

"You're okay with seeing my naked body?"

"I see mine every day. It's the same body."

"Yeah, but I'm all pale and bloated and…covered in blood. Plus, I haven't shaved my legs in over a month."

"Same body. Same blood. Same hairy legs. And what's my excuse? We'll get you squeaky clean and then I'll French braid your hair."

"Indigo." She grabs both my hands. "I'm dying."

Her words send a shiver up my spine. "No. Don't say that. Today you'll live. The Voice promised. A little longer. Hold on a little longer, Violet. Please."

"Is it okay that I'm scared?"

"I'll be brave for you. I'll be brave for the both of us."

When the family moves outside to load up onto the bus, it's still dark outside. Pretty much everyone is half-asleep. But one thing that's certainly changed for the better—Pastor. He's back to his old, cheerful, enlightened self. Dressed in a Nike warm-up suit with Birkenstock sandals, holding his signature bottle of Trader Joe's olive oil.

"Goooood morning and what a glorious morning it is." He whispers so as not to wake Sandi and Bob or the rabbits or whatever other creatures live out here in no-man's-land. He greets us all with a dollop of oil. When he slathers it on my forehead, I don't even wipe it away.

"I'm *so* glad you're better, Pastor."

"Never push away an opportunity for growth, Indigo."

"Even if it's painful?" I ask.

He pats my back. "Especially if it's painful."

Violet's wheelchair is situated on the lift. I try to rush onto the bus to be the one to help her down the aisle, but Michelle steps in front of me.

"Hey," I say breathlessly.

"I overslept." Michelle yawns. "How was Violet's night?"

"Great," I lie. "She slept super good."

"Really?"

"Oh, yeah. Barely even moved." I reach into my bag and hand her the notepad she gave to me. "I wrote down all the O2 sat numbers like you told me to. It was all good."

"Wow." Michelle breathes a sigh of relief. "Gotta be honest. It was nice to get a good night's sleep. Thank you."

Thank *me*? Say what? "Oh. Um. Yeah. No doubt."

"I feel like I owe you guys an apology."

I tap my foot anxiously. What if Dad's helping Violet to her seat? What if he feels her body trembling? Sees how cold she is. Notices her swollen abdomen.

"So let me say it. I'm sorry, Indigo. I've been a pill this whole trip, haven't I?"

I want to reply by yelling, *You've been a pill my whole life, Michelle!* Instead I say, "I've probably been a pill this whole trip, too."

Michelle doesn't argue with that. She rubs her belly. Somehow it looks bigger than it did yesterday. "Maybe I have an issue with not leading."

Maybe?

"Can I explain something to you, Indigo?"

"I guess. Sure."

"Every family has a leader. It's just the way it is."

"And you're ours?"

"It's always felt that way." She sighs. "I was fifteen when you and Vee were born. Mom needed me. Relied on me. So after undergrad, when I got accepted into medical school and—"

"Wait. You got accepted into *medical* school?"

She nods. The light in her eyes dims. "At the time you and Vee were only seven. Alfred was five. The school was on the East Coast. I couldn't have imagined leaving my family. I wasn't ready."

Michelle passed up on medical school? For *us?* My stomach sours as guilt rushes in.

"But I've always wondered what if, you know. What if?" She forces her hands through her straightened strands of hair. "I went to see a psychic a few years back. Wanna know what she said?"

My brow furrows. "Uh…that psychics aren't real?"

"Indi, stop it." Michelle slaps me on my noninjured shoulder and laughs. "She said that *I* was the leader of my whole family. But—" she swallows "—that I had a little sister creeping up at my heels destined to take my place."

"Wait… What?" I look her dead in the eye. "A psychic told you that?"

"It made me so mad!" Michelle laughs again. "Mostly because I knew without a doubt she was talking about you." Michelle crosses her arms under her chest. "And you know what? I'm okay with it. I'm good with you leading. Finally. I guess." She shrugs. "Funny thing. I actually woke up this morning, and for the first time, I thought…" She leans forward and whispers, "What if this works? What if it *works*?" Her eyes are sparkling in the night with hope and anticipation.

It's not often I see this side of Michelle. So since I don't know what to say, I lurch forward and hug her. It's literally the first time I've *ever* hugged Michelle. "Namaste, Michelle." I pull away and run onto the bus before she can say another word. Dad is helping Violet stand.

"No, Dad!" I rush down the aisle and slide in front of him. "I got this."

Dad raises his hands and steps aside. "All right, then. You got it."

I allow her to rest her arm around my shoulder and we move down the aisle together. Once she's situated in her seat, I sit beside her. Like a guard. Like Gandalf, I will not let anyone pass. She's safe with me beside her. Once the rest of the family is loaded up, we take off into the dark morning.

After a quick stop for breakfast at a fast-food chain about a half hour outside of Hodell, the drive to the visitor's station is pretty quiet. Since we had to get up so early, everyone has fallen back to sleep, including Violet. Even as the sun begins to peek up over the mountains, no one really stirs. Pastor Jedidiah seems thrilled to be back at the wheel. He whistles a happy tune.

I stare up at the ceiling and whisper.

"Are you there?"

There's no response.

"Kinda rude, don't you think? To bail on me like this."

Nothing.

I peek out the window. On the horizon, the orange sun infuses light into the gray dawn. It's breathtaking.

"I'm a no-good loser," I say tauntingly. "See? I'm self-deprecating. Don't you wanna call me a name, like Selfina Depricioso or something? C'mon, Voice. Talk to me. *Please.*"

Nothing.

I lean my head back and stare up at the eye on the ceiling.

"How you feeling, Indigo?" Pastor asks, speaking softly so as not to wake anyone.

I lean forward. "I don't know. Tired. Scared. Crappy. How are you?"

"Feel amazing." He sings. "Glorious day to be alive."

"How come you're always so positive, Pastor? Do you ever get mad and scream or complain? Michelle said you passed *six* stones. I *saw* them. It looked crazy. That kinda thing would usually make a person complain."

"Oh, I used to be a big complainer, Indigo. Had my own business. Lived in New York City. Made *millions* of dollars. Complaining was a way of life. The only sort of life I knew."

"A millionaire? Get *out.* So did you lose your money in the stock market or something?"

"I was diagnosed with a very rare and aggressive form of

cancer when I was thirty-seven. Given six months to live. So I sold my business, sold my fancy penthouse apartment. Gave away almost everything I owned. And donated my money to various charities. All of it."

"*Wow.* Every penny?"

"Every cent."

"Why did you do it all? Because you were dying?"

"Not because I was dying. Because I wanted to try living. Indigo, I'd spent decades trying to outdo everybody. And with a word from the doctor, realized that in my efforts to win, I'd been losing in the worst way imaginable. Somehow that doctor telling me my life was about to be over made me realize that there's only one way to win in the game of life."

I lean forward, eager for the answer. "How do you win in the game of life?"

"You stop playing."

"But then what do you do?"

"Find out what makes you happy. Then do *that*. Experience that."

I frown. "That's impossible. There are so many things we have to do that don't make us happy. Like school or… I dunno…laundry. Healthy eating. Working. Nobody can spend all day doing what makes them happy."

"*Being* happy is vastly different from pursuing what *makes* you happy. You can pursue what makes you happy for the rest of your life."

I think of Violet and my heart aches. "But, Pastor, what happens when what makes you happy, you can't have it anymore. Like, I dunno, a professional ball player who gets a permanent injury and can't play the sport he or she loves. A singer who can no longer sing."

"Or a twin without her twin?"

A lump rises in my throat. "Yeah. What happens then?"

"I think…" He pauses. "In a true pursuit of happiness, you understand that there are infinite paths to happiness. Today, what makes me happy is driving down this deserted road, talking to you, Indigo. I'm intensely happy. But tomorrow, we won't have this moment. Next week you'll be back in school. I'll be back at work. You see? Just because the moment flees from us, doesn't take it away. We keep it forever. Think of life like a jar and happiness like pieces of candy. We're filling up the jar. To infinity and beyond."

"So a true pursuit of happiness…"

"Is ever changing. Ever expanding."

We turn off a main highway and start down a dirt road. It seems like we're heading even deeper into the middle of nowhere. As if that were possible. I wonder what made the settlers keep going. If I were traveling in a covered wagon and saw all this nothing, I woulda definitely turned to the family and been like, *We've reached the end of the road, guys. Let's go back.*

"Wanna know a secret I've been keeping from you, Indigo?"

"What's that, Pastor?"

"God talks to me, too."

"Wait… You actually hear the voice of God? Like, God speaks to you?"

"As clear as I can hear you."

"Does he sound like Dave Chappelle?"

"Ellen DeGeneres."

"Get *out*."

"I kid you not. You know, I think God sounds the way you need her to sound."

"What did the voice say to you? The first time you heard it, I mean."

"She asked me a simple question. 'What would make you happy, Jedidiah?'"

"And what did you say?"

"I said I didn't know. But I was desperate to find out. I did have a clear picture of what *didn't* make me happy. Which is why I got rid of most everything I owned. That first night, after the apartment was sold and the bank accounts were empty, I remember feeling scared. It was the first time I'd felt anything in so long. It was exhilarating. I decided I wanted to share what I was learning from the voice of God. So I borrowed a camera from a friend and started an online church. The Church of Love and Light. I talked and talked. I talked so much, I forgot I was supposed to be dying. And when I went back to the doctor, the cancer was gone. They couldn't explain it."

I'm enraptured with every word he speaks, sitting so far on the edge of my seat, I fear I might fall off and spill onto the floor, but the bus is so loud and rumbly and I don't want to miss a word.

"The *physical* church was born soon after. The New Faith International Church of Love and Light. We've since gone global. Opened churches in seven different countries."

"You're a megachurch."

"But we never ask for money. It's the New Faith way, and yet it still pours in. You know we get over twenty million dollars a year in donations."

"That means you're a millionaire again."

"My *cause* brings in millions, but I only take a small salary."

"How much?"

He keeps one hand on the wheel and makes a zero sign with the other. "I take nothing."

"You've gotta eat and have a place to live, right?" Although I imagine the megachurch has some rooms he and his wife could crash in.

"I work. In addition to my work as the church pastor, my wife and I have our own website. We make jewelry with crystals and stones. And we're both certified Reiki therapists. It's our family business and our only source of income. We own a one-bedroom houseboat right on the Fremont Canal. Take public transportation. We live a simple life. We like it that way."

"You're fascinating, Pastor Jed."

"That's what God's always telling me." He chuckles.

CHAPTER SIXTEEN

We're just outside of the station. The family starts waking one by one.

Mom looks out the window. "Well, isn't this beautiful."

"If you're into that sort of middle-of-nowhere beauty." Dad yawns.

Mom's phone rings. "I can't believe a call got through."

"Mom, it's Utah, not outer space," Michelle chides her.

"Tell that to Verizon, Michelle, because I have zero bars." Mom studies the screen on her phone. "Oh, Alfred, it's your school."

Holy *shitballs*. I twist around to look at Alfred sitting by himself. We exchange horrified looks.

Mom slides her finger across her screen. "Hello? Hello?" Mom says again. "Sorry? I can't hear you. Service isn't so good right now. Can I call you back when we—" Mom sighs. "I lost them. Isaiah, you called the school and told them Alfred would be out for a couple of days, right?"

"No. Alfred told me you did it."

Mom turns to Alfred. "Alfred, why did you tell your father that, when you told me *he* called them?"

"My bad," Alfred mumbles, scratching under his hat like he's got fleas. "I thought... I—I guess I got confused."

"You got confused?" Dad shakes his head. "What else is new? School probably thinks you're truant."

"Like I don't have enough on my plate," Mom mutters. "I'll call them as soon as I get service again."

Good God, I hope she never gets service.

Violet stirs. I turn to her as she's rubbing her eyes and sitting up. "How you feeling?" I ask it even though it's the question I'm constantly bombarded with. A question that if you answer it honestly, people run from you. A question I loathe.

She gives me a thumbs-up. Which is basically her nice way of saying, *I feel like shit, Indigo, but I don't wanna be negative.* I give her a thumbs-up in response, which is basically my nice way of saying, *Hey, I'm sorry you feel like shit, but we're almost at the Wave, so hold tight, sis.*

Pastor Jedidiah picks up the mic. "Ladies and gentle ladies. We are moments from the visitor center in Kanab, where we will enter a lottery to hike the Wave. It's been quite a journey to get this far. I've felt blessed every step of the way. I hope you all feel the same."

When he hangs up the mic, my stomach turns, churns, bubbles and all synonyms for: things your stomach does when you're in a *panic.* I know we have a hiking wheelchair but will there be hills to climb? Rough turns? Cliffs? Tight sections of the trail too narrow for a chair? Will it be snowy? Rainy?

I've always wondered what people mean when they say their life flashed before their eyes. How could years and years of information be observed in a second? But now I get it, because every possible thing that could maybe go wrong on or before this hike flashes before mine.

My and Violet's twin powers have been reactivated because she knows what I'm thinking. She squeezes my hand. "Don't worry," she whispers. "We'll win. Our number will be called. Everything will work out. I believe it."

Pastor turns the bus into a gravel parking lot already half filled up with cars, RVs, vans and trucks. *This* many people showed up on a random Wednesday, desperate for a chance to take a freakin' hike?

After we park, Dad and Mom look over at me. Do they want me to say a word? I don't have The Voice to guide me along the way. Although, now that I think about it, the last time he guided a word, it was a bit of a disaster.

I stand, facing the family.

Brandon and Nam are huddled together in a seat with Drew, staring up at me as if I don't belong in a straitjacket, but am a clever and magnificent soul who possesses all answers to making this work.

Alfred applies ChapStick.

Michelle looks…hopeful.

Mom and Dad hold hands.

Pastor scoots in beside Michelle and smiles.

Violet nods in support.

"I really want to thank you all for trusting me and taking this journey across the country with me. It means…" I clear my throat. "It means a lot. That you're here. That we're all here. For Violet." I look at Mom and smile. She smiles back. "That's all I wanted to say. I'm gonna run in ahead of everyone and put our name on the list."

"What does God say?" Brandon asks. "Like...will we win?"

I chew the dead skin around my thumbnail. The Voice *did* say he's super psychic. He said to get to the Wave and those permits to hike were as good as ours. In fact, *easy peasy lemon squeezy* were his exact words. "The Voice promised me Violet would live. I believe him. See you guys in a second."

Pastor Jedidiah opens the bus doors and I rush off.

The visitor center is pretty basic and bland as far as offices in the middle of nowhere go. When I walk through the door, people are crowded around, sipping on cups of coffee or chatting in corners. It's a small and cluttered space with lots of old posters tacked to particle board hammered to painted walls.

Wandering types, hippies, couples old and young, a few families with tween kids; all seem to be waiting patiently for the lottery to begin. Most are in groupings of two or three. There are no parties as large as ours. Not that I can see, anyway.

I step to the counter and present the online form I printed out. "Hi."

The employee barely looks up. She has short brown hair that rests on her shoulders. "Name?"

"Indigo Phillips." I slide the form across the counter. She quickly retrieves it.

"How many in your party?"

"Ten."

Both eyebrows rise as she looks up. "You do understand we only offer ten walk-in permits a day?"

I nod.

"So you'd have to be the first number called for everyone in your party to win."

I nod again.

She shrugs. "So long as you understand. We've had some of the same people in here day after day. It's a tough lottery to win."

"The rest of my party is on the bus. Should I go get them?"

"No rush." She hands the form I've filled out to another worker standing behind the counter. "Just so long as they're here before the lottery starts at eight."

"Cool. Thanks."

"And hey, listen," she says as I start to move off. "If numbers are called before yours, don't give up hope. If you're willing to break up your party, then you've still got a shot. People do it all the time. Yesterday a couple and their teenage kiddo agreed to take the two spots left when their number was called. Only the husband and the kid went." She leans forward and snickers. "Though I can't promise you if the couple is still married today."

I smile. "One of our guests has an all-terrain wheelchair. Are those okay on the trail?"

"Most of the trail is cross-country. Open and flat. A few hills but no crazy inclines. We certainly don't discriminate. But we also don't *assist*. So if you get stuck or need medical assistance, it takes hours to get EMS out on the trail. So long as you understand."

"I understand. Thanks."

"Phillips family party of ten, you're number forty-one. Good luck to you."

"Thank you."

Back in the parking lot, I'm chilled to the bone, so I zip my bomber jacket to the collar and pull my hoodie over my head. The sun *is* beaming bright but can't manage to take the nip out of the air. It will most certainly be a cold winter hike. Fluffy white clouds float across an otherwise clear blue sky. At least we can take rain and snow off the list of things that could go wrong today. More vehicles are pulling into the small parking lot. If we're number forty-one, that means there are forty people ahead of us. And judging by all the cars arriving, there will be quite a few after us as well. This *will* be a tough lottery to win.

As I move toward the bus, I hear a sound and freeze. It's a sound I know so well. One that's typically paired with bad choices I've made throughout my teenage years—Mom's classic screech-and-scream.

Gravel crunches beneath my boots as I race across the parking lot. Eye of the Tiger stands out like the worst eyesore against the red rocks and mountains in the distance. I bang on the doors. They swing open so I can rush on board.

Mom is standing over Alfred, screech-and-screaming at the top of her lungs. Dad is pacing up and down the aisle. Michelle is sitting with the boys looking like she'd seriously kill to get off this bus. Drew looks dazed, confused. Pastor is waving a lit Palo Santo stick back and forth. Then there's poor Alfred. Poor, misunderstood Alfred. Cowering in his seat. His Seattle Seahawks cap pulled so low I can see only his chin.

Dammit. They *know*.

"What are we supposed to do now, Alfred?" Mom screeches. "It's almost the end of the semester. You'll have to repeat the tenth grade!"

"Cheating?" Dad paces.

"What is your last name, Alfred?" Mom cries.

Alfred lifts his cap and stares bug-eyed at Mom.

"And what is my last name?" she screams.

Alfred's looking confused. Dear God, it's a nonrhetorical rhetorical. *For the love of everything good and pure, answer it, Alfred!*

"My last name is Phillips. Yours is, too?" Alfred finally offers.

I exhale. Whew.

"Exactly," Mom screeches. "Everywhere you go, you represent *me*! Everything you do reflects upon *me*."

"And me," Dad cuts in. "Not to mention everybody else on this bus."

"We raised you better than this, son. What would make you think it's okay to pay for answers to a test? Your whole life has now been affected for fifty dollars' worth of answers. Did you ever think studying would solve your problems?"

"Actually, it was forty-seven dollars," Alfred corrects Mom. "Not fifty."

"Boy, be quiet," Dad yells. "If we wanna hear you talk, we'll ask you a question."

I slump into the seat beside Violet.

"Mom listened to a message from Alfred's school," Violet whispers as Mom and Dad rage on.

"I know. He got expelled. He told me."

"You knew?" Violet shakes her head. "Poor Alfred."

"Indigo, you knew?" I turn. Michelle's across the aisle and somehow overheard us.

"Shh," I say.

"Oh, uh-uh." She shakes her head. "You knew! Mom and Dad? Indigo over here knew."

Mom spins around. "Knew what?"

"Indigo." Michelle points at me. "She knew Alfred was expelled."

"And you didn't think to tell anybody?" Mom shrieks.

"No, no, no." I stand. "We are *not* about to make this about me. This is Alfred's mess! All Alfred. I'm not the one expelled. He told me yesterday. What was I supposed to do? Ask you to pull over and drop a bomb like that?"

"Yes!" Mom screams. "That's exactly what you should've done."

Dad shakes his head. "Keeping something like this from us, Indigo? Unbelievable."

"I'll say it again. I am *not* taking the blame for this! Besides. The school can't expel Alfred anyway."

Alfred lifts his cap to look me in the eye. "They can't?"

"No! Not without a hearing. You have rights. You were supposed to get a written notice. A chance to call a hearing!"

How the hell do I even know this? I continue. "The school has a no-cheating rule. But Alfred got a D on the test he got the answers to. Which proves he didn't use them. Hire an attorney. Fight it."

Mom and Dad exchange hopeful looks.

"What about your friend Henry?" Mom asks. "He's a good attorney."

Dad shakes his head. "We need a student's rights attorney. I'll ask Henry, though. I'm sure he can refer us to someone good." He points at me. "If Indigo would've told us earlier, we could already be on top of things. Getting it all in motion."

"Yeah," Mom agrees. "If you knew all this, why *didn't* you tell us?"

"I don't run around telling people all the information that's crammed into my brain. I didn't tell you guys Michelle and Drew were getting a divorce—"

Mom's jaw drops.

Oh. My. God. I did not just say that.

Dad grabs the few strands of hair he has left and pulls on them like he's going mad.

"Come again?" Mom whispers as she moves down the aisle, her arms folded across her chest. "Michelle? Please tell me Indigo is talking nonsense."

Michelle bites her thumbnail.

"Go on," Mom urges. "Tell me it's not true."

Michelle groans. "Indigo, how did you even know this? Who told you?"

"So it's true?" Dad bellows. "Y'all are getting a divorce?"

"You're *divorcing*?" Nam wails.

"Yes," Michelle replies.

The bus erupts into utter chaos.

Brandon and Nam are hysterical.

Dad's still pacing, pulling on his tufts of hair, grunting and muttering under his breath.

Violet's coughing like she's about to have another attack.

Mom slumps down into a seat. "My children are cursed!" she wails. "Cursed!"

"So whose bright idea was it to get pregnant and file for a divorce?" Dad roars.

"Everyone." Pastor tries to interrupt the madness. "Please try to calm. Deep breaths in and out. Watch me."

Michelle climbs up on her seat and screams. "Everybody shut *up*!"

Michelle's scream is so loud, I cover my ears. I bet these gentle-soul, love and light hikers are wondering who let the riffraff eyeball bus into the visitor center parking lot. But at least Michelle's roaring voice gets everyone to quiet.

"Since Indigo went nosy and snooping around in my business," Michelle hisses.

"I wasn't snooping! You asked me to get your phone and it was on the screen. An email from your lawyer."

"You read it!" Michelle snaps. "That's *snooping*. Snooper."

"So then it's true?" Mom sniffs. "You're going to be a single mom with three kids? Oh my gentle Jesus, take the wheel."

"No! I mean, yes, we're divorcing, but it's not what you think."

"Everyone listen." Drew stands. "We didn't want to tell

anyone until after the New Year, when it was official." He looks at Michelle. "Should I tell them or you?"

"I'll do it." Michelle steps down off the seat. "I'm officially quitting my job and going to medical school after the baby is born."

Mom covers her mouth.

Dad gasps.

"We can't afford medical school," Michelle adds. "But I get a tax break and a few special grants if I'm a single mom. So we're…divorcing."

"But only on paper," Drew adds. "I would never desert my family."

"We're also selling the house to make it work." Michelle shrugs. "And…moving in with you guys."

Now it's my jaw that's dropping! Where exactly are they going to sleep? On the roof?

"That's why I've been on the phone so much this trip," Drew adds. "We're officially in escrow. All that's really left to do is put everything in storage."

Mom and Dad still stand in the aisle, speechless.

"I know what you're thinking," Michelle continues. "But don't look at it like we're cheating the system. We're trying to find a way to make this work. Over two hundred thousand dollars for medical school and with Drew's income being our only income. The baby coming. Divorce seemed like the best, most viable financial strategy to get us through this. We wanted to tell you guys in private but Indigo, the snoop—"

"Hey!" I point at Alfred. "Alfred getting *expelled* is not my fault." I point at Michelle. "And you and Drew cheating the

Internal Revenue Service and United States *government* is not my fault either!"

"After all these years?" Mom whispers. "My baby's gonna be a *doctor.*"

Dad's beaming. He's beaming so bright his bald head looks shinier than normal. "We'll make room in the house. We'll make it work. The boys can stay in Alfred's room."

"The hell they can," Alfred says.

Mom snaps her fingers at Alfred. "You be quiet, expelled person. You're not paying any bills. You own nothing. You don't get a say in anything."

Alfred sulks.

"So we're not gonna be bastards?" Brandon asks, glasses foggy, tears still streaming down his face.

Drew laughs. "Brandon, what do you even know about a bastard?"

Michelle wraps an arm around Brandon. "You're not bastards. That word is pretty antiquated anyway."

I wave my hand in the air. "I hate to break up this strange and confusing reveal. But we need to get inside before the lottery starts."

"Dr. Michelle Delacroix?" Mom squeals. "My baby is gonna be a doctor. Watch out, Seattle."

Watch out, Seattle, indeed. I can't help but smile watching Mom and Dad grin and bounce around like two little schoolkids. Michelle will at last be the ultimate, supreme boss. Leader extraordinaire. A doctor.

She'll make a good one.

CHAPTER SEVENTEEN

The lottery is held in a room directly off the main office. It's small, cluttered; old wooden chairs upholstered with green felt are lined up in rows. There is a long table situated at the front. Two visitor center employees are seated behind it in high-back office chairs. Written across a dry-erase board hammered to the wall behind them: Welcome to the Wave Daily Lottery.

Since it's standing room only, we all separate to find a spot to wait. Mom and Dad squeeze up against the wall. Alfred hovers near the door. Michelle's offered a seat by a kind gentleman carrying an oversize hiking pack, and Nam and Brandon pop a squat on the floor. Drew hovers over Michelle and Pastor walks around shaking people's hands.

The room seems filled to capacity. Over a hundred people at least, all vying for *ten* walk-in permits. Some excitedly film with their cameras or cell phones; many appear super stressed and tense; others act nonchalant, chatting as if they don't have a care in the world.

The employee at the front stands and waves his hand. He's probably in his fifties, wears tan pants with a uniform shirt tucked in. Salt-and-pepper hair. He's got an air about him like he lives for this lottery drama. Zeus complex for sure. He is the Lord of the Wave lottery and he knows it. Everyone quiets.

"Before we get started," he drones, "please acknowledge that you hear your name and number so that I can make sure everyone is accounted for. Once the lottery begins, if you do so happen to be one of the lucky winners, remain here in the room and I will have your permits issued to you promptly. If you don't win—" he shrugs "—have a good day, I guess. Or don't."

There's polite laughter.

"All right, here we go. When you do hear your name, please raise your hand high and say 'here,' just like you did in elementary school. I will, in turn, hold up your number so you can watch me drop it into the cage. Everything is fair. Numbers fall at random. Anybody can win but most of you will lose."

I lean over Violet's wheelchair and whisper, "Feeling lucky?"

She squeezes my hand. "Lucky number forty-one, sis."

I glance over at Mom and Dad huddled together against the wall, looking like two fish out of water among all these hikers and nature types. Mom with her silver bun and Dad standing so tall and bald and...brown.

As the worker starts calling out the names of those entered into the lottery and confirming their number and present status, I think of The Voice. His sarcasm was becoming like comfort food, like a hot plate at Ezell's. Without The Voice, I've lost my security blanket. Can we make this hike without him? Should I admit I kinda miss the guy?

"Indigo Phillips."

"Present!" I almost scream. A few people laugh.

"That you are." The visitor center employee nods. "You are number forty-one." He holds up the ball marked forty-one and drops it into a small wire contraption that looks like the thing they use at bingo nights at the neighborhood rec center in Seattle.

He continues up to number fifty-three.

"Fifty-three names have been called." He leans back in his chair. "A total of 111 hopeful hikers. Good luck to everybody."

I kneel beside Violet and take her hand in mine, watching intently as the man behind the table spins the black wire wheel that holds all the number balls. If Phillips isn't called first, we will have to break up our party. That's okay. We can start by eliminating Michelle. She's pregnant and shouldn't be hiking anyway. Nam and Brandon—they're next off the island. If push comes to shove, Mom and Dad can go after them. Then Pastor. The most important people are Drew, Alfred, Violet and me. Drew and Alfred will be able to carry Violet if the trail elevates. Dad could too, but with his bad rotator cuff, he's not to be trusted with twists and turns. Pastor could assist, but he'd selflessly give his spot to one of the family members. That's the Jedidiah way. I can pretty much count him out altogether if we're not the first name called.

At the table, a ball has at last fallen. The visitor center employee stops spinning the wheel to snatch it from its resting spot underneath the cage. "First lucky winner of the day."

I swallow.

"Number twenty-eight."

A group of participants by the door clap and cheer.

The employee reads from a sheet of paper. "This is a party of three."

I deflate. It's official. The entire Phillips family will not be making this hike together. That's bye-bye to Pastor, Michelle and…maybe Brandon. Only seven permits are left. My heart aches at the thought of more family members being pushed off the island.

"Seven permits left to give away." The man spins the wire contraption. Plastic balls tumble around like socks in a hot dryer until one falls through a small opening. The employee swoops it up. "Next lucky winner of the day is number forty-nine."

A couple directly in front of us raise their hands. "That's us!"

The man nods. "Congratulations. There are two in the party, leaving us with five permits."

I rub my temples the way Mom does to ward off a screech-and-scream as he spins the wheel. Five permits. Adios to Nam. Arrivederci to Mom. So now it could be Violet, me, Drew, Alfred…maybe Pastor? Mom and Dad won't want to be separated. So Dad would give up his spot for sure.

Another ball falls. "Lucky number thirteen."

A man raises his hand. "That's me and my wife."

"Party of two," the employee says as the couple hugs and kisses. "That leaves us with three permits left."

Now we're down to *three*? Violet and I exchange panicked looks. Even if our number *is* called, three...isn't enough. Drew wouldn't be able to carry Violet by himself. I could stay back. Drew and Alfred could take Violet. Yeah. That's it. I'll give up my spot for the cause. Sayonara to Indigo. I'm the next off the island.

The man spins the wheel and I bite the skin around my thumb, watching apprehensively as a ball falls through the opening. "Our next lucky winner of the day. Number one."

A woman raises one hand. She has children with her. I deflate. It's over. Our number wasn't called. My head slumps forward. Someone is going to have to peel me off this floor. My family trusted me. I trusted The Voice.

"There are three spots left and four people in your party," the employee states. "Do you want to take the permits and have one person sit out?"

I study the family. There's a teenage boy. Maybe fifteen years old. The two younger children look a little older than Bran and Nam. The woman shakes her head.

"I can't separate the family," she states sadly. The two younger children look like they're about to cry. "Unfortunately, we have to pass, sir."

A murmur erupts from the crowd. My head shoots up. Another shot? I turn to Violet. "Did she say what I think she said?"

Violet whispers, "We can still win."

"Tough call to make but I do understand." The man spins the wheel again as the dejected family exits the room together. "Lucky number nine."

A woman with an oversize backpack stuffed to the brim raises her hand. "Nine here!" She smiles. "Yes! Yes!"

"Party of one," the employee states.

I exhale. Only two permits left. Not sure how Violet and I could make this hike by ourselves. We'd need help. Maybe we could pair up with one of the other hiking groups? But... like they'd want to be dragged down by all of Violet's needs? It would be kind if someone agreed to help us, but it's not fair to even ask.

I glance over at Mom and Dad. Mom's head is bowed. I imagine she's praying. Dad's cracking his knuckles one by one like Alfred does. Speaking of Alfred, I scope him out leaning beside the door. Our eyes meet and he gives me a thumbs-up. He still has hope. He still believes in this mission.

The man spins the wheel. He spins and spins and spins until, finally, a ball falls through the opening.

The Voice promised. He *promised*.

"Number forty-one," the man says.

I scream. "That's us!" I cry. "That's us!"

Violet and I cheer and embrace.

The man picks up the form I filled out. "Ten? Whew. Only two permits left. I imagine you're willing to break up the party?"

I look over at Mom and Dad. Mom shrugs.

"Yes, sir! Absolutely. We'll take them."

The man leans back in his chair. "That's the last two and that concludes today's lottery. Congratulations to the winners, and to the losers...try again tomorrow if you can. We'll see you then."

People start filing out of the room as the happy winners linger. Mom and Dad move toward us.

"Indigo, how exactly is this gonna work?" Mom asks. "You and Violet can't take this hike alone."

"Maybe one of the men go with her?" Dad asks.

"They need at least three," Mom insists. "Two people to carry Violet when the trail gets steep. Now, I've been reading about this hike, and not only is it dangerous, people online say it's confusing. There aren't a ton of markers to guide you to the Wave. You can get lost. You can die. I'm not sending two teenagers out on a dangerous hike by themselves." Mom shakes her head. "Indigo, this isn't feasible."

"Then let Violet go with Drew," I suggest.

Dad shakes his head. "Your mom's right. It's too big a task for Drew alone. He'll be exhausted. I talked with one of the employees here. There's a portion of the hike where you have to cross over a river basin. It's winter and it's rained a lot this past month. What if there's water? Ice? I'm exhausted after carrying Violet for a few steps. How's Drew gonna manage five miles?"

"So what are you guys saying?" My voice is rising, hysterics building.

Mom and Dad exchange disheartened looks.

"We think..." Mom starts. "You should give the permits away."

"I won't do that!" I scream.

"Indigo." Dad sighs. "We don't see another option. You have no choice."

"But we came all this way," I wail.

I watch number twenty-eight, the party of three, getting their permits stamped and approved by the employee. They look downright jubilant. Two men and a woman. All in their twenties, it seems. Rucksacks strapped to their backs. Messy hair and wrinkled clothes that seem to suggest they've been living in one of the RVs parked outside to make this hike to the Wave a reality.

Alfred and Drew approach with Pastor at their side as the room empties, leaving only the winners and the visitor center employees.

"What's wrong?" Pastor Jedidiah asks kindly.

"We think it best Indigo give the permits away. They can't make the hike alone," Dad explains.

"Oh, dear." Jedidiah's happy expression turns sour. "That's heartbreaking, though I do understand. Parents know best."

"I have to agree." Michelle steps forward. "Indigo, we tried. We got here. And your number got called. I think that's miraculous in itself."

"Yeah, Indigo," Drew adds. "This has been a wonderful trip."

"Plus, there are a lot of hikes we can take today instead," Dad offers. "Amazing views of the Southwest to take in."

"Very good point." Pastor pushes his hands together and places them over his heart. "Zion National Park has hikes you don't need lottery permits to enjoy."

"Can we go, too?" Brandon asks.

"See?" Dad's trying to sound optimistic. "All the family can go. This will be better."

I look over Dad's shoulder. Watching as lucky number nine approaches. The party of one. She looks like she's in college. Twenty-one maybe. She's got her whole life ahead of her. She doesn't need to take this hike. At least not today. I scoot around Mom and Dad and rush up to her.

"Excuse me, miss?"

She spins around. "Yes? Can I help you?"

She's got a heavy German accent.

"My name is Indigo Phillips and that girl over there in the wheelchair—" I turn and point. Violet waves. "That's my sister."

The German girl smiles. "I can tell. Matching faces."

"She's terminally ill," I explain.

"Oh?" The German girl seems a bit thrown off. "I'm... so sorry."

"But God...or a voice that says it's God...started talking to me when I was up on a roof about to kill myself."

"Indigo, you said you were taking a photo!" Mom steps forward. "Kill yourself? You actually *were* trying to kill yourself?"

"I wasn't..." I pause.

Now we've got everybody's attention. The employees. The lotto winners. The room is silent. All eyes on us.

I could deny it. I *should* deny it. But instead I let my head fall forward, my shoulders slump and say so softly I wonder if anybody can even hear me, "I was thinking about it. Yeah."

But at least Mom hears me. Because she steps forward, places a hand on my shoulder and with the other hand lifts my chin so that I'm staring into her eyes...which are red and welling with tears.

"I'm sorry," I whisper. "Are you mad at me?"

She doesn't really respond. She simply pulls me close and wraps her arms around me tight. It takes me a few seconds before I realize that my mom is hugging me. Like...we're hugging. She lays her head on my shoulder and holds me tighter than she's ever held me before. So I lay my head on her shoulder, too.

I'm not sure how long we stand this way. Hugging in the middle of the park ranger station, but we're finally interrupted by a kind and sweet voice with a heavy German accent.

"You were saying? Sorry. But you were about to kill yourself and then God or a voice started to talk to you?"

I look up. That's right. I was trying to convince this girl to give us her permit so we can hike the Wave. So Violet can live. I look at Mom, who seems to be reading my mind. She wipes her eyes and nods her approval. I take a deep breath and turn back toward the girl.

"Right." I wring my hands together nervously. "So this voice starts talking to me and tells me that if I could get my sister to the Wave, she'd live. So my whole family—" I point to everyone. They all wave timidly. "We came cross-country. And that man." I turn and point to Pastor. He bows.

"Hello. Call me Jed."

"That's our pastor. He's a former millionaire turned shaman. He drove us on a bus covered in eyeballs. If you don't believe me, look out in the parking lot."

"That's your bus?" the woman from lucky number one asks. "We saw that coming in. We took pictures. Fascinating."

"That's us. Yeah." I fall to my knees and fold my hands under my chin, looking pleadingly up at the girl. "You're hiking alone. Maybe you can have mercy? Please, girl. I don't even know your name."

"Erika."

"Please, Erika? If you give us your permit, one of the men in our party can come with us and help carry my sister when the trail elevates. She has a hiking chair but it can't make the whole hike. She'll have to be carried over some parts. I know we won too, but if we don't get another permit, we can't go. Since you're going alone—"

"I'm not going alone." The girl slides her backpack off her shoulders and sets it at her feet. She unzips the front section and removes a beautiful metal case with a star imprinted on the top. She kisses the case. "Inside this case is my mother."

"Whoa," Alfred says. "Did not see that one comin'."

Erika continues. "It was her dream to hike the Wave. This was a planned trip, but I'm sorry to say, she did not make it in the flesh. I make the flight from Hildesheim alone. Been sleeping in Kanab for *seven* days. I enter the lottery every day since I arrive. Sleeping in cold RV. The heat breaks down. Tire breaks near Flagstaff. A homeless man steals my wallet, so I have to eat beef jerky for two days while I wait for money transfer to come through from my father in Osnabrück. I also get email message from landlord. My flatmate, she did not pay her half of rent, so we are evicted. I will have no home to return to and I have not showered since Sunday because the water is too damn cold on my rented RV. I come a long way to bring my mom here. I'm sorry about your sister. But I cannot give you my permit. It means too much to me."

"And I thought we had it bad." Alfred flips his cap backward.

Erika turns back to the table to retrieve her permit from the employee. I scope out the rest of the winners. They certainly look like they feel sorry for us, but nobody's making a move to offer us their permits. Most are even avoiding eye contact. I can't help but wonder what their stories are. How many of them went through similar hell to have their lucky number called? How many of them have the ashes of their dead parents stuffed in their backpacks?

I pick myself up off the floor and turn back to face my family. Violet's got tears streaming down her face. "I'm sorry, sis. I tried."

"It's okay," she whispers. "We all tried."

The employee who facilitated the lottery looks at me. "Miss? Does this mean you're giving up the two permits?"

I wipe away my tears. "Am I, Mom?"

"Indigo, I'm sorry." Mom's still crying. She wipes tears with the back of her hand. "I really am."

"Then yes, sir." I sob.

"You know," he says. "Sometimes we have a lottery and there's only one spot left. In that case, when the final number is called and it's a party of two, we allow one additional hiker a permit, as we don't like to encourage people to hike

alone, though hiking alone certainly isn't against the rules."
He nods in Erika's direction. She smiles and nods back.

I seriously stop breathing. Why is he saying this? What is
happening here?

He continues. "Looks like you got a serious case on your
hands. Seeing as how you got a special situation with a dis-
abled hiker, I'm gonna allow for one more permit."

I take a breath at last. "No. You're lying!"

"Telling the truth." He smiles.

The winners in the room start cheering. Erika claps the
loudest.

I rush to Violet and hold her tight. "We're gonna make the
hike, Vee. We're gonna do it! You're gonna *live*."

"I'm…gonna live," she cries.

"In addition," the man continues, "I'm requesting one of
the rangers to accompany you on the trail. When we get
special guests, the Bureau of Land Management likes to treat
them as such."

My jaw drops. We are about to hike the Wave.

The Voice was *right*.

CHAPTER EIGHTEEN

Barreling down the remote dirt road that leads to the Wave trailhead, I think back to the lecture on safety, rules and regulations given by the visitor center employee. It was actually quite brief and we were dismissed and sent on our way pretty quickly. But one thing stood out—a reminder that it's winter. Which means there will be an early sunset. This means we can't loiter at the Wave the way hikers do in the summer. We get there and we get back ASAP. I hope whatever sort of miracle we're walking into doesn't require us to linger.

Two rangers will meet us at the trailhead, where we'll hand off our permits. And one will guide our hike to the Wave. I'm nearly jumping out of my jeans and hoodie. This is *happening*.

The drive to the Wire Pass Trailhead is supposed to be a little under an hour, but with Drew at the wheel, we're minutes away. I'm gonna wager this is the first time this old dirt road has been raced across by a paratransit bus driving way over the speed limit.

Speaking of Drew. He's taking the hike with Violet and me. He and Alfred played a rousing game of best two out of three paper-rock-scissors. They both wanted it bad. But rules are rules. Drew won fair and square. There was a bit of chatter at the visitor center about Drew and Alfred going, and maybe me staying behind. But Mom and Dad quickly agreed it would be absurd:

"Violet and Indigo are supposed to do this together," Mom expressed vehemently. "Any other way would be unfair to the both of them. I don't wanna hear another word about it."

It made my chest swell with pride to have Mom vouch for me in such a way.

Glancing out the window, I'm surprised to see the billowy white clouds have taken a dark turn. I'm no meteorologist, but it looks as though they're ready to burst forth some sort of precipitation.

"Can somebody check the forecast?" I ask as Drew speeds along the bumpy dirt road. The weather app on my phone is taking forever and a day to load. It's searching and searching for service. There is nothing out this way. I don't even see the critters they warned us about at the visitor center. This takes remote to a whole new level.

"No service on my phone," Alfred calls out. "But if I were to make an educated guess, I'd say there was one hundred percent chance of snow."

I look out the window. Sure enough, flurries of snow have started to fall. "Geez luss!"

Violet squeezes my hand. "We've come this far. Snow can't stop us. Nothing can stop us now."

I watch as a light dusting of snow begins to top the bushes in this remote desert. It's beautiful, sure. Like the way you'd sprinkle powdered sugar over a holiday cookie at the end of a baking show on the Food Network. But doesn't this mean it's literally freezing outside? I start to shiver. The memories of being up on that icy scaffolding chill me to the bone.

The dirt road is forking—you can keep straight and I guess...drive over a cliff at some point? Or you can pull off into a parking lot. So thankfully that's what Drew does. Though the parking lot is basically a random splattering of cars scattered on dirt and gravel. Two park rangers are climbing down from a dusty brown Jeep Wrangler as Drew pulls the bus up beside them.

"I can come with you guys," Alfred offers. "They won't mind. We'll tell them they said it was okay at the visitor center. It's not like they can call and check. There's no service out this way."

"These people have been good to us. *We* follow rules," Dad states sternly. "Following rules keeps the world balanced."

"Following rules also keeps you enrolled in school," Mom adds. "You should try it."

Alfred slumps down into his seat. "Fine. Never mind, then."

Michelle's standing over me. "Excuse me, Indigo. I need to switch out Vee's oxygen and check her O2 sat."

I happily stand, strapping on a hydration pack stocked with three liters of water, the amount recommended by the rangers.

"How you feeling?" Pastor Jedidiah asks, leaning up against his seat as I pull a wool headband over my ears.

"Piqued, overwrought, beside myself, in a tizzy."

"Synonyms?"

"For *excited*. Yeah." I slide on my gloves.

"I'm excited, too." Pastor looks out the window. "My favorite thing about snowfall. The quiet. No other precipitation can fall so soundlessly."

"You think it'll be slick on the rocks?"

"Perhaps. But you're wearing hiking boots and the all-terrain wheelchair's got wheels for any weather condition."

"Jesus." Michelle gasps.

I spin around.

Michelle has rolled up Violet's sweatpants. Her swollen legs are on display for all to see. Michelle's eyes are wide with disbelief. "Violet, your *legs*."

"It's nothing, Michelle." Violet yanks her pants back down. "Don't make a big deal."

"What's going on?" Mom scoots down the aisle. "What's the problem?"

Michelle stands. She's trembling as we exchange terrified looks. My eyes plead:

You said I was stepping into my destiny.

You said it was my turn to lead.

Let me lead.

Michelle plasters a fake smile on her face. I recognize the smile. It's the one she uses when people think she's my mom. "I'm being difficult. She's fine. O2 sat seemed a bit low but it's fine. She's good to hike."

"You sure?" Mom looks and sounds pretty concerned.

Michelle fiddles with the zipper on her hoodie. "I'm sure."

Mom exhales, relieved. "Oh, good."

"Indigo?" Michelle says as Mom and Dad start chatting with Pastor. "Can I talk to you outside? Privately?"

Michelle and I are standing a few feet away from the bus, watching as Violet is lowered down the lift in the all-terrain wheelchair.

"When did it start?" Michelle speaks in a low, hushed voice.

I shrug.

"Indigo, please. Now is not the time."

"Last night. On the bus."

"So you lied? She didn't have a good night at all, did she?"

I focus my eyes on the snow as it melds with the parking lot gravel, pulling tightly on my hiking pack. "No. It was a rough night. Like you said it would be. And she was bleeding this morning."

"Bleeding?"

"I Googled it. I think it's her liver. Acute liver failure is probably what we're dealing with here. But it doesn't matter. I think she needs to take this hike anyway."

"Acute liver failure?" Michelle laughs. "Indigo, can you please stop Googling random symptoms and thinking you're a doctor."

"You don't think she has acute liver failure?"

"Girl, please. First of all, a person's liver doesn't just shut down and turn off like a heart can. Second, she'd be jaundiced. Yellowing eyes. Her skin color would be off. Her liver is not failing."

"Oh. Then why are her legs swollen?"

Michelle shrugs. "I can't run labs out here in the desert, so I don't know. My guess is she's been sitting too long and needs to move around. But that's just a guess. It could be a number of things."

"But her belly is swollen, too."

"Was she throwing up a lot last night?"

I nod.

"Normal. Her belly gets like that sometimes."

I breathe a sigh of relief. "And the blood?"

"Side effect of the Nathaxopril. It affects your cycles."

"We thought she was dying."

"Indigo, she is dying."

"You know what I mean." I glance over Michelle's shoulder. Violet's coughing pretty badly again. "When we get her to the Wave everything will be fixed."

Michelle stuffs her hands into the pockets of her coat. Flurries of snow land in her eyelashes. She blinks them away. Something's definitely changed about Michelle since this morning. Boarding the bus at the Airbnb she looked hopeful, and there was a twinkle in her eye. Now her eyes are ominous. As dark as the sky.

"What's wrong, Michelle?"

"Indigo, Violet's O2 sat was low when I checked it just now."

"What? No. *That* I didn't lie about. The numbers were good all night. I swear it."

"I believe you." Michelle blinks away more flurries of snow. "But I checked it a few minutes ago. It's dipped again."

"Can she make the hike?"

Michelle shakes her head. "She shouldn't."

"*What?* Michelle, please don't say this. Don't *do* this."

I glance over her shoulder again. Mom and Dad are loading Violet's hydration pack onto the wheelchair while the rangers and Violet chat away like they're new best friends.

"Indigo." Michelle looks deeply into my eyes. "I have a tough time with the voice of God being all...yeah, take this sick and dying girl on a dangerous hike."

"The Voice said to do it initially." I kick gravel with my hiking boots. "But then after the attack on the bus, he told me not to. He said to get her to the hospital. He said you were right." I brace myself for an explosion from Michelle but instead she turns to look back at the family. Violet, Mom and Dad continue to chat with the rangers. With the flurries falling on them like slow-motion raindrops, it looks like they're all stuffed inside a snow globe. "Are you gonna tell Mom and Dad?"

"Of course I am. Her blood's not getting enough oxygen. They need to know. She could become hypoxic again. This is the second day of low O2 sat and her oxygen is cranked up as high as it can go."

"Does that mean she dies?"

"Not necessarily. She needs more help. I'm no doctor..."

"Yet."

"Yet. Right. But if I were her doctor, I'd place her on a

ventilator. I feel like it's her only option at this point. The ventilator can keep her alive."

A shiver rushes up my spine. I know my sister. A ventilator wouldn't be an option for her. "But what if we get to the Wave and then she's healed and all is well?"

"In case we're not next in line for a miracle like that of the parting of the Red Sea, I'm calling for emergency services."

"No. Michelle, *no*."

"But…" She lays a hand on my shoulder. "I'm gonna give you guys a running head start."

I look up, blinking away snowflakes and tears.

"Somehow, Indigo. This faith you got. It's contagious or something. Most of me thinks this is insane. But there is this tiny part of me. Like…" She presses her thumb and forefinger together. "This small. Says what if? What if this could work, you know? What if this is real?" She takes off her gloves and wipes her eyes.

"How long will you wait before calling for emergency?"

"I'm gonna ride back with the other ranger and call from the closest station. However long it takes to get there."

"I should've told you. I'm sorry, Michelle."

"Don't be sorry. Keep the faith. Take it with you. See how far it carries you. I love you, Indigo." She leans forward and hugs me tight. "I love you both."

When I peek over Michelle's shoulder, Mom is moving toward us.

"Hey, you two," Mom says breathlessly, an air of excitement in her voice as she reaches our side, rubbing her hands together to keep them warm. "Mind if I talk to Indigo alone, Michelle?"

"Don't mind at all, Mom. I'll go and say goodbye to my sister."

Of course Mom doesn't notice, but I can hear in Michelle's voice that she thinks she could be saying goodbye to Violet forever. Michelle and I exchange troubled looks and she moves off.

"This is really amazing, Indigo. Violet seems so...alive. It's been too long since I've seen her this way."

I nod and kick a few pebbles of gravel around with my hiking boot. I know Mom's not here to talk to me about Violet. Somehow I know it's about me this time.

"I never thought I'd say this," Mom goes on. "But Alfred is right."

I push more gravel around with my boot. "Alfred is right about a lot of things."

"I wouldn't go that far." She chuckles. "But..." She pauses, seemingly gathering her thoughts. "At the hospital he said you might need to be assessed. That second attempts at...suicide are common."

"Oh. That." I stuff my hands into my pockets. "I'm okay with being assessed. But I can assure you. I don't want to die. I just..."

"Don't want to live without Violet?" Mom offers, a kindness to her voice I'm not used to hearing.

I nod. "Or maybe I feel like I don't deserve to live. Or... I dunno. Maybe I feel like the family would be better off if it was me dying instead of her."

Flurries of silent snowflakes continue to fall. It's cold outside. But I feel warm in this moment of truth. Finally free to tell my mom exactly how I feel.

"I don't want to see any of my children die, Indigo. One is not better than the other."

"I find that hard to believe. Violet seems like the clear favorite."

"Violet is easygoing. She agrees just to make peace. Smiles to put people at ease. Lets others lead. You challenge your father and me. You disagree often. You *always* want to lead. You resist authority and seem hell-bent on taking the road less traveled. Even though that road may lead you off a cliff someday. Or a building."

"Maybe it seems like we prefer Violet because perhaps our relationship—yours and mine—has been the least tended to. I take responsibility for that. I *will* learn your love language and try to speak it more often. I promise I will. But if I'm being honest… I like feeling like I have control over my children. And I am fully aware that I don't know how to guide you to where you're going."

"But Violet and I have the same dreams and aspirations. We're going the same place."

"But it's different with Vee." Mom shakes her head. "Violet's following the leader. And that's you. You've always guided her. Ever since you both started crawling. She only wants to do what you do. That's her path. That's her destiny. But I feel terrified when it comes to the path you've chosen. That day you told me about the award and the winning photo, I got scared. That's why I didn't want to look at it right away.

I didn't want you to see fear in my eyes. I don't ever want to discourage your dreams. But I was scared. I *am* scared. When you went upstairs, I Googled Lynsey Addario and I—"

"Wait. You Googled her?"

Mom nods. "I looked at some of her photos online and I thought of all she has seen and experienced to take those beautiful photos…and…" She swallows. "You're on a path to touch the world. But do you know how many great minds like yours have touched the world and seen nothing but darkness? I can't guide you past Seattle, Indigo. Learning I might lose Violet has been hard. Because I never imagined losing her. But you… Indigo, I have always known that I would lose you someday. I knew you would seek out great adventure and purpose. Your destiny…" She sighs. "Jesus, Indigo. It terrifies me."

For some reason Mom's admission doesn't surprise me. Perhaps having Violet by my side has given me a false sense of security. Perhaps I really wanted to die…because *I'm* afraid of my destiny, too. "I could stay close to home. I don't have to travel the world."

"You'd be a caged bird." The frown lines on Mom's forehead become more prominent as she shakes her head vehemently. "I don't want that. I'm okay with you spreading your wings to fly, Indigo. But *you* have to be, too. You have to want to live."

I stare off toward the path of the hike. "Do you think we'll find a miracle out there at the Wave, Mom?"

Mom pulls me close and holds me tight. "I think you already have."

★ ★ ★

Our ranger's name is Clint West. Like…that's his real name. Anyway, Clint is doing a wonderful job. Not only do we not have to worry about which direction is the right direction to the Wave, he gives us details and information about the history of the land and fun stories about weird and wacky hikers.

"Okay, quick." He spins around and walks backward. Despite having a name that sounds like he should be a member of a cowboy gang, Clint is a younger, nerdy type. I'd say early twenties. "Found a hiker passed out cold on this exact spot. Dehydration fifteen minutes in. Scariest thing. When I got here, I thought he'd dropped dead."

"What happened after you found him?" Violet asks, gliding up the incline in her all-terrain wheelchair. A wheelchair which, simply put, is badass. All Violet has to do is essentially twiddle her thumbs to move the giant wheels over the desert terrain of the trail and she's good to go. But her *coughing.* I groan. It's echoing across the open plain.

"After a bottle of water he was fine." Clint turns to walk forward again. "Out of shape and drank a Monster energy drink before hitting the trail. Just because you win the lottery doesn't mean you're sane. Or any other synonym for *competent.*"

Drew laughs. "You sound like my sister-in-law."

I study our surroundings. This stretch of land is like the employee in Kanab described it: cross-country, slight incline, unassuming—like you would never guess this road leads to some otherworldly beauty. Though the bursts of falling snow do seem like fairy dust is being sprinkled over the trail, directing us to some sort of enchantment. I lift my camera for the first time since the hike began.

Click-click.

"How do I sound like your sis-in-law?" Clint asks as we all trudge along.

"She reads the thesaurus for fun," Drew explains. "Synonyms are sort of her thing."

"I do that, too!" Clint exclaims.

"Well, birds of a feather. She's right behind you." Drew turns and winks at me.

My brow furrows. Why is Drew *winking* at me?

Clint spins back around so that he's walking backward once again. He points at me. "Is it you? Are you the one who reads the thesaurus?"

"Guilty," I say, more than slightly out of breath. Clint might be in shape and able to walk backward and talk. But the one word I've uttered has left me *winded*. It's not that it's a tough hike, it's just…well…a hike. And since Violet's been sick I haven't done any form of exercise. Unless you count climbing a building in the dead of night. I'm exhausted. But at least the winter chill is no longer to be feared. In fact, I'm sweating.

"Sweetness." Clint turns back around, moving across the slightly elevating terrain as if it's a hike for kids. He's practically skipping. "We should get together and exchange synonyms and antonyms."

Did he just ask me out on a date? A very weird…literary

date? Drew twists his head and winks at me again. What the hell?

"Fun fact time," Clint sings. "The Wave started forming over one hundred ninety million years ago. During the Jurassic period. Not to be confused with *Jurassic World*. Those movies started forming in the 1990s."

I rush up alongside Violet's chair as Clint rambles about the Wave.

"How you feeling, sis?" I whisper.

She waves me off. "Shh. I wanna hear this."

"It's said," Clint continues, "that the swirling rock formations were formed by high winds and rain erosion. So the winds pushed the sand dunes, and the dunes, over time, compacted and solidified."

"And what…about the colors?" Violet asks. "How did the colors form?"

"Ahh, good question." Clint seems more than happy to talk Wave talk. "Swirled bands of color is how we like to refer to them here at the Utah-Arizona border. Created by deposited minerals from the water runoff. Try saying that five times fast."

"Fascinating." Violet coughs. "I can't…wait to see it."

"I know, right?" Drew adds. "This is a once-in-a-lifetime experience. Glad I get to accompany you, sis." He lifts the hose from his hydration pack to take a sip of water.

Water. Good idea. I take a giant gulp of mine as well.

We're over an hour into the hike when the terrain changes. It's no longer crumbles of sienna brown desert dirt. We're now walking across slabs of hard red sandstone. Far off in the distance are splatterings of rocks that look like tiny mountain ranges.

Click-click.

The ruddy sandstone makes the flurries of falling snow glimmer so bright white it appears unreal. It's as if we're on another planet.

Click-click.

Clint points. "That's our destination way over there. On the other side of those rocks."

"Seems so close." Violet's wheelchair expertly rolls across the snow-covered sandstone.

"And yet so far away," Clint replies. "In about twenty minutes we'll have to move through somewhat of a narrow passage. Not claustrophobia narrow, but the wheelchair won't be able to fit. But after we cross between the dunes it's the home stretch."

"That's why I'm here," Drew says. "It'll be fine. We'll make it work."

"And it's okay...to...leave the chair?" I ask, sounding more out of breath than Violet.

"Sure," Clint replies. "The wildlife out here are usually pretty good about not taking things that don't belong to them."

"Ground squirrels have shifty eyes." I adjust the zoom on my camera. "I wouldn't put it past a gang of them."

Clint laughs. "Nothing worse than a gang of ground squirrels."

Click-click-click.

★ ★ ★

We've made it to the point where we have to ditch Violet's wheelchair. As we approach the dunes, Clint stops and turns. Up close, I notice he has blue-gray eyes, natural blond hair and a splattering of freckles on his nose. His appearance is timeless. Like a Nordic king from twelfth-century Sweden.

"You guys wanna take a break? Have some water? A snack? Violet, you need anything?" Clint asks.

Violet and I exchange determined looks. We both want to get to the Wave as soon as possible.

"No," Violet answers. "Drew, do you mind? Can we keep moving?"

Drew sips water from his hydration pack. "I'm good with that."

As Drew assists Violet, helping her out of the wheelchair, I swallow nervously. If Violet's blood's not getting enough oxygen, any sort of movement could send her over the edge.

"I can help," I offer. "We can do the six-legged thing you guys did at the marathon."

Drew shakes his head. "The basin slopes down but doesn't seem too difficult. I think the six-legged thing would make it more complicated at this point."

"I wish I could help," Clint offers. "But we're not allowed to assist hikers unless they're in some sort of peril. Though *peril* is a relative term. I tell my boss that all the time."

Drew kneels and Violet carefully climbs up onto his back. "Grab her water, Indigo."

I rush forward to take her hydration pack but Clint snatches it before I can.

"Why don't we pretend this hydration pack is in peril? I got it." Clint winks as he moves down a narrow path that leads to the passageway through the dunes.

Drew follows with Violet on his back. I'm last so my eyes can stay focused on my sister. I listen carefully to her cough and watch the rise and fall of her back as she breathes.

Almost there, Violet. Hold on for just a little while longer. Almost there.

It's quiet. Magically so. I could drink in the sound of the silence. Every once in a while, Violet lifts her head to catch a few flurries of snow on her tongue. It makes me smile.

Click-click.

I guess there are *some* sounds: Violet's coughing, Drew's heavy breathing and our hiking boots sloshing in the small pools of water between the dunes. Up ahead, through an opening, I can see the terrain is about to change again—it's *sand*.

"Sand?" I say more to myself than anybody.

"They don't call it a desert for nothing," Clint replies.

When we push through the opening, the sand is not a welcome addition to the hike. It makes each step that much more difficult. Poor Drew. It's tough to watch his labored stride with Violet on his back.

"It's the final push." Clint's trying to be optimistic though he can probably tell both Drew and I are *struggling*. "Bit of an incline, though. We should rest."

Clint doesn't need to say that twice. Drew nods in agreement and slowly kneels. Violet slides off his back and the two sit in the sand. Drew guzzles water so fast I wonder if he's gonna blow through his three liters before we even make it to the Wave.

"Here." Clint sets Violet's hydration pack beside her. "You drink, too."

She sips water.

Clint makes his way toward me. "Holdin' up okay?"

"I'm good. Thanks, Clint."

"Mind if I ask where you guys are from?"

I'm watching Violet intently. Searching for any of the signs I saw at the race. I think the hypoxia started with her being angry and uncharacteristically...mean, followed by confusion and slurred speech.

"Violet?" I call out. "How you holdin' up?"

"I'm fine." She continues to sip water in between her deep, guttural coughing.

Okay. Good. No slurred speech. "Uh, we're from Seattle."

"Nice," Clint replies. "I'm transferring to the University of British Columbia in the fall."

I turn to him. With the snow falling and the vast expanse of nothing stretching out to the horizon, his blue-gray eyes seem like an extension of the sky. "Vancouver? Why so far from home?"

"Majoring in agricultural science, and it's one of the best global universities for that. Plus, Canada is beautiful. I live for the outdoors. I think I'll be very happy there. At least until I graduate and work takes me across the globe. What college do you plan to go to?" Clint asks. "Or are you already in college?"

"I'm a senior in high school. Violet and I applied to a few. But I think I like the idea of staying close to home. For just a little while longer, anyway. So probably the University of Washington. If I get in, I mean. I don't see why I wouldn't."

Clint holds up his hand. "High five."

"Um, okay." We high-five. "Why are we high-fiving?"

"Because we'll be close. We can visit each other."

Heat rushes to my cheeks, warming me from the inside. "I, uh, think I'm gonna go check on my sister." I rush to Violet and kneel beside her. "Almost there," I say. "So cool, huh? We're doing this. We're making it."

"I think..." She pauses to take a deep breath and whispers, "Clint likes you."

"What?" I look up at Clint. He's checking some sort of device he's been holding in his hands the whole hike. A GPS maybe? "No. He's the ranger. He's being nice. That's what rangers do."

Drew leans forward and whispers, "Trust me. I'm not a ranger but I am a guy. I see the signs. He likes you."

I bite my bottom lip, still swollen from my fall. "Whatever. I'm not here for a date. I'm here for a miracle." I pop a squat beside Violet as her coughing starts up again.

She reaches to rub her chest. "I feel...like I'm suffocating in all these clothes. Can I take off my coat at least?"

"It's cold, Violet," Drew says seriously. "I don't want you to catch a chill. Michelle would kill me if you got sick."

Violet unzips her coat. "Just...for a second." She reaches under her layers and rubs her chest. Her breathing seems more of a struggle as each second passes.

"Violet? You should probably take slow breaths. Not so fast."

"Let's just *go*. Geez."

She sounds a bit agitated. Shit. Agitation is how the hypoxia started last time.

I look over at Drew. Even though it's snowing pretty heavily, he's still out of breath and sweaty. Having to carry Violet for so long seems to be taking a toll on him.

"Drew?" I call out. "You okay to get up this incline? It's sand. I'm having a tough time myself and I'm not carrying another person on my back."

Clint makes his way back over to us. "The hill is the last stretch. That's the Wave around those rocks. Once we're about two hundred yards from the finish line, the incline becomes a bit tricky. I wouldn't call it steep, but it'll be challenging for you, Drew."

"Okay, Indigo." Drew stands. "I'll take you up on the six-legged racer offer."

As I help Violet stand, her body starts trembling and her knees buckle.

"Don't...worry." She steadies herself by gripping on to my shoulder. "A little weak but I...can make it."

A little weak. A lot winded. Slightly agitated and a massive amount of coughing. The Wave is so close, but dammit, not close enough. If only I had The Voice here to offer me some sarcastic wisdom. What would he say? Probably something like, *Y'all are almost there. She gonna make it. I'm super psychic 'cuz I'm God!*

Drew and I get situated the way he and Alfred were for the race to the finish line and we trudge up the sandy incline.

It's a tough climb. I'm glad Drew and I are working together as I don't see how he could've managed it without help. My hiking boots sink into the sand. I'm laboring with each step, shoulder throbbing, casted arm feeling like an anchor intent on pulling me to the ground. It's as if I'm dragging my feet through quicksand.

Take one step.

Sink into the terrain.

Extract feet from the sand.

Repeat.

In between the simple struggle of walking, I'm trying to remember to breathe. Everything's a blur. Time. The snow. The sand. The bushes. The ruddy rocks. The cliffs of sandstone in the distance underneath a gray sky.

I think we're approaching the final ascent. The part that Clint said would be tough. And it *would* be a tough climb if you had nothing to carry. But with a hydration pack strapped to my back, an injured shoulder and a broken arm, and holding one half of Violet's weight, the climb seems insurmountable. My body is screaming with pain.

"We can do this," Drew says through clenched teeth. "Let's try to keep our steps synchronized. You okay, sis?"

"Yeah, I'm good!" I declare.

"I meant the other sis."

"I'm…good, too," Violet replies.

She doesn't sound good. She's wheezing and coughing violently.

I focus on my pacing, trying to get my steps in sync with Drew, convincing myself that if we're in sync, we're energetically aligned like Pastor's always preaching about. I watch his boots and count.

One-two-three.

Step, step, step.

Four-five-six.

Step, step, step.

Seven-eight-nine.

Step, step, step.

And suddenly our boots are gliding across curves of colored sandstone. We've *made* it. Somehow we've accomplished the impossible. We're here. We're at the Wave.

"Behold the awesome power of the Wave." Clint extends his arms dramatically.

It is a sight to behold, a wonderland of swirling sandstone, a magnificent display of artwork. It's as if Van Gogh himself were the one responsible for this masterpiece.

We carefully lower Violet so she's standing between us.

"Amazing," Drew exclaims.

"It…really is…beautiful." Violet falls to her knees and lands violently on the rocks.

"Violet!" I kneel beside her.

"I…can't feel…my legs." She's kneeling on all fours.

"What do we do, Drew?" I'm panicking. "I don't know what to do."

"I don't either!" Drew sounds more panicked than me.

Now Violet's eyes are clenched shut. She pounds her fists on the stone. It's happening again. It's happening!

I look over at Clint. "She needs help!"

"I can't radio this far out," Clint explains.

"Then *run*," Drew begs. "Please run! Tell them we need emergency services. Hurry."

"At some point on the trail, I'll get close enough to radio. It shouldn't be long." Clint races off.

I turn my attention back to Violet.

"Breathe, Violet. Slow. Watch me." I have no idea what I'm doing or if it can even help. I take dramatically slow breaths, imitating Pastor Jedidiah. Violet mimics me. It's helping. She's breathing.

"I..." She stutters. "I c–can't..."

"Shhh." I'm kneeling beside her, my hand lying across her back in an attempt to comfort her. "Violet, it's okay."

Drew is freaking out. Pacing back and forth on the curving, sloping sandstone. Pulling at his long hair. "It'll be forever before Clint can get help!"

"No." I shake my head. "Michelle already called for help."

"What do you mean?" Drew narrows his eyes at me.

"I mean Michelle called for help. We knew this might happen. Her O2 sat was low before we started."

"What? Jesus, Indigo!" Drew throws his hands in the air. It's the first time Drew's ever been angry with me. "You had *no* right to keep this from me. Or from Violet. This is fucked!"

I stand. "You think I care about your rights, Drew! I *don't*. This was fucked from the moment Violet was diagnosed. It's an idiopathy!"

"Idiopathy? What the hell does that mean?"

"Crack open a dictionary, big brother. It means this isn't my fault. Idiopathic means you're right. It means *fucked*!"

The sound of helicopter blades far off in the distance interrupts our argument. Helicopter blades that seem to be approaching fast.

"Oh, thank God!" Drew shouts. "They won't be able to see us. I'm gonna run back down the hill so they'll know our location. So they know where we are."

He takes off, leaving Violet and me alone.

She's breathing. They're shallow, difficult breaths, and she's clutching her chest as if she's in great pain. But she's breathing. At least she's breathing.

"I…won't…go…with them."

"Maybe you won't have to, Vee. I mean, we're *here*." I look up at the sky. "We're here!" I scream. "You hear me? You said to get her to the Wave. You said she would live!" I cry, my voice echoing across the desert plain. "So now what, huh? It's time to make good on your word. You promised! Let her live!" I'm sobbing. I'm hysterical. I can hardly see through the snow, through my tears, through my pain.

"Indigo…" Violet's frail voice calls out to me.

I turn to her.

"It's…okay."

"No!" I sob. "It's not okay. The Voice promised me. He promised. I believed him. We're here. You're supposed to *live*."

"But you see…"

The helicopter is growing closer.

"The Voice…was right. I lived. I did."

300

She reaches into her coat pocket and extracts the bottle of medicine that can end her life. I freeze.

"Violet. Wh-what are you doing with that?"

"I can't...get on that helicopter. They'll put me...on a ventilator. I'll be in a...hospital bed. I won't... I...can't."

I know my sister. She *won't* be placed on a ventilator. She will refuse. I can't say I blame her. What would life be like for her then? Unable to eat or speak. Connected to a machine for the few days she'll have left to live. Tears spill down my cheeks. I drop to my knees beside her. It's taking all my strength not to take that bottle out of her hand and toss it as far as I can throw. But it's not my right to do such a thing. I understand that now.

"This was the plan," she whispers.

It feels like my blood freezes solid.

"Indi...this was the *plan*."

"You can't mean that." I shake my head. "You couldn't have meant to come all this way and die."

"Not...here. Not...this way. But...it was always meant... to be a one-way trip. Indigo... I knew."

My chest aches. My throat burns. My eyes sting. The dots are connecting. No wonder there was no resistance from Mom and Dad. They would never have taken their terminal daughter on a trek across the country if Violet hadn't explained that it was to be her final farewell. "They knew too, didn't they? Mom and Dad?"

"They knew. I was supposed to take it...tonight. *After...* the hike."

I swallow to hold back the sobs. "And Michelle?"

"Only Mom and Dad knew. I…made them promise to… keep my secret. Only…them."

"Fuck!" I slam my fist onto the stone. Pain shoots up my arm and snakes around to my injured shoulder. My thoughts race back to when Violet gave me the schedule. "Yesterday morning. In the kitchen." My chest heaves. "You mentioned flights. Are there plane tickets home?"

"For Mom…and Dad…and you. And me… I guess. Everyone else will…ride back with Pastor."

My shoulders shake as the sobs erupt from deep within. The sound of the helicopter is so close now. I'm sure they can see Drew. I'm sure they're going to be landing soon.

She twists the cap off the bottle. "Indigo. It is my right to die."

"I know." I hang my head in defeat, tears spilling onto the stones of the Wave.

"Indigo, look…at me."

Somehow I find the strength to meet her eyes. They're red and pained, but she still manages to look beautiful. With the snow falling. With the swirls of sandstone surrounding her like a halo.

"It is my right to die. But…" She pauses to catch her breath. "It is your right…to live."

"But, Violet. I want *you* to live." I cry. "This whole trip was so you could live."

"Don't you see? The Voice…was right. Indigo…" She's struggling to get the words out. "I…lived. This trip. It was…" She extends her arm. Snowflakes instantly melt when they land on her trembling fingertips. "So beautiful. So perfect.

302

So…amazing. I lived, Indigo. I live now." She reaches out and wipes my tears. "Don't cry. I will see you again. On the other side."

"I will miss you till then," I whisper.

She takes my hand. "Forgive me? For dying this way."

"Forgive me for living."

Her chest heaves as the sound of the helicopter blares louder than ever. I know it's landing. Only moments before they reach us now.

"Look…" She points. "It's us…in the sky."

There is a small opening in the clouds. A tiny tuft of blue sky. There is also a small glimmer of a rainbow, barely visible. It's not arching across the desert or anything. But the colors are there. I see it. Violet does, too.

"Stay with me," she says. "And don't…let them take me… until I sleep." Violet downs the medicine from the bottle. Swallows painfully. "This isn't suicide," she whispers.

"This isn't suicide," I repeat, almost blinded by my tears.

"I'm dying with dignity."

"You're dying with dignity. It's your right."

She lies on the rocks.

I pull off my gloves and lie beside her.

"Any…good riddles?" she says so softly I almost don't hear.

I squeeze her hand, trying to transfer all the warmth and life I have left. "What's invisible…" Tears continue to blur my vision. I wipe them away. "And makes people…suffer." I intertwine my fingers with hers. "You get symptoms like sweating…and nausea…and just a general feeling of discomfort." I sniff. "It makes you feel pain." I rub my chest, hoping that will somehow take away the ache. "And yet…no one can live without it. No one."

Her eyes start to close. "Hmm," she whispers. "I…give…up. What…is it?"

I scoot closer so that my body is curled up beside hers. Her cheek feels surprisingly warm. "It's love."

She smiles.

CHAPTER NINETEEN

When the paramedics rush up the hill, Violet is asleep in my arms. I stuff the empty bottle into the pocket of my coat, hiding it from the EMTs before they whisk her away. Drew is hysterical. He's screaming and wailing in agony as they load her into the helicopter. Clint tries to calm him to no avail. I won't watch the helicopter go. I can't watch them take my sister away.

Instead, I walk across the sloping rocks of the Wave. The snow still falls in peaceful flurries. The roaring blades of the helicopter meld with the beating of my broken heart. Drew's anguish echoes in the tranquil space.

These dunes began forming one hundred ninety million years ago. Shaped by wind and water erosion. What a life these rocks have lived. What stories they must have to tell. I move down an incline until I find myself beside a pool of water collected near the base. The shade from the shelter the rocks provide gives me a chill as I pause to stare into the water. It acts like a mirror, reflecting the landscape around me. Reflecting the face that belongs to us both. It's almost as if she's on the other side, staring back at me. Her skin no longer pale. Her cheeks full. Light sprung back into her brown eyes. Hope restored. A lifetime of endless possibilities awaiting.

I can hear someone calling my name. Screaming for me. Maybe it's Drew. Perhaps it's Clint. I wave goodbye to my reflection and somehow it seems as if Violet waves back, urging me along. Blessing my simple sojourn. I shuffle past the water, traveling through the crevices, deeper and deeper into the twists and turns of the Wave.

"Indigo..."

"Yes..." I reply softly.

"They're looking for you."

"I know." My fingertips slide across swirling rings of color. There are so many working together to create this miraculous masterpiece: red, brown, orange, white, yellow...even a little violet. Yes. I can see violet, too. "You said if I brought her here she would live."

"I said that. Yeah."

"You were right. She lived. She really did." I stop walking and close my eyes. And suddenly I'm transported. Back to Seattle. Back to the top of the old industrial warehouse. Holding on to the rusted scaffolding in the dead of night. The icy rain beating down on me. The wind roaring. My fingertips burning from cold as I hold on. The anguish. The hurt. The complete desperation. Tears slide down my cheeks. Being up on that building never really was about dying for me. I can see that now.

"Then what *was* it about?"

I open my eyes. The details of that nearly fateful night seem to float away like dandelion seeds blowing in the wind. Impossible to hold on to while the brilliant Wave spirals and coils around, as if welcoming me into a new dimension—or I'm falling deep down into the rabbit hole at last. "Didn't I tell you not to read my thoughts?"

"I can't help it."

"Right. Because you're God?"

"Right. Because I am God. I am."

"Not just the voice in my head?"

"Well..." The Voice pauses. **"Maybe they're one and the same."**

"Yeah." I glide my hand along the striped sandstone as I continue on. "Maybe they are."

"It's your turn now."

"My turn?"

"To live."

I think back to what Violet said last night at the Airbnb. *Doesn't seem fair. It's the same moon, but one man dances under it, another man dies.*

She's right. It doesn't seem fair. And yet the fact remains. For every one who dies...there is another who lives on.

"My turn, huh?"

"But you have to want it. You have to *want* to live."

"Well, I'm here, aren't I?"

"Yes. You're here."

"That's gotta count for something. Please, let it count for something."

"It counts, Indigo."

"Glad to hear it." I round a corner. The rocks bend with me, beckoning me even farther. I raise my arms and point my face toward the sky as if I am a bird, ready to catch a passing breeze...spread her wings...and fly.

★ ★ ★ ★ ★

ACKNOWLEDGMENTS

Before I give my sincere thanks to all the amazing people who deserve it, I'd like to point out a few things.

Nathaxopril is not a real drug.
Hodell is not a real city.
Neither is Urlington.

In addition, I took some creative liberties with the Wave lottery process. In real life, should you be lucky enough to win walk-in lottery permits, you have to wait until the *following* day to use them.

Okay. Now that we've got all that technical stuff out of the way.

This book is about family. So I'd like to start my acknowledgments by thanking mine.

Mom. I have so many stories inside of me, and you have

always encouraged me to pursue my passions and follow my dreams. And when those dreams seemed impossible...you encouraged me to dream even bigger. Thank you.

Thank you, Dad—my fellow Libra and kindred Spirit. My siblings. James, Shona, Adaryl, Tammy and Jaden. My nephew and niece, Michael and Kiara. And of course my daughter/best friend, Cameron. Thank you ALL for believing in my writing and loving me unconditionally.

I'd like to thank my oh so amazing team of editors: T. S. Ferguson, Natashya Wilson, Libby Sternberg and Jennifer Stimson. Thank you for believing in this story and for all the hard work you put in to make it sparkle and shine. Extra special thanks to T. S. Ferguson and Natashya Wilson for guidance I've grown to depend on.

My awesome agents at Triada US. Dr. Uwe Stender, Brent Taylor, Lauren Spieller and Laura Crockett. Extra special thanks to Dr. Uwe Stender, who works harder than anyone I know. And never gives up fighting for what he believes in.

Thank you Laura Gianino and Linette Kim for all the hard work you do. I appreciate you both. And Carmen Price, nurse extraordinaire, for offering your guidance and medical expertise. The early drafts depended on you. All mistakes my own.

My beautiful beta readers: Kevyn Richmond, Sarah Skilton, Ravyn not Raven Willuweit and Michael Willuweit. Additional thanks to Michael Willuweit—for your beautiful additions to the discussion questions

Also big thanks to my cover design team, Erin Craig and Elita Sidiropoulou. In addition, big thanks to Tiffany Jackson, Adi Alsaid and Nancy Richardson Fischer. I admire and respect your work so very much. So to have you endorse mine? It brings tears to my eyes. Thank you so much.

A heartfelt thanks to the family of Brittany Maynard and to her widow, Dan Diaz. Thank you all for being so passionate and generous in sharing *her* story, which inspired this novel.

Last, thanks to my readers. You guys are the reason I spend hour after hour, month after month, year after year dedicated to words. I hope they inspire you the way you all inspire me.

Until next time!

Dana L. Davis

QUESTIONS FOR DISCUSSION

1. For many of us, our first experience with euthanasia is when a family pet is "put to sleep" to end pain and suffering. In the novel, Violet defends her decision for medically assisted suicide by stating, "I'm only assisting the plan that's been laid out for me. It's dying with dignity. It's the law. And it's my right." (Page 147) Euthanasia and "death with dignity" laws have been controversial. When might doctor-assisted death be permissible and when do you think it's not permissible? Should the decision be solely that of the individual, or should other people be involved?

2. The novel begins with Indigo attempting suicide. What are her reasons for attempting suicide? Do you think her reasons are valid? Is there ever a valid reason to end one's life? While we don't know too much about Indigo's life beforehand, what are some things she could have done before attempting to take her own life? What are some

things we can do when friends or family members are in emotional distress and contemplating suicide?

3. Violet is diagnosed with a terminal illness. While some people may think finding out they will die relatively soon is terrible, it does allow an individual to put their life in order and do things that they've always wanted to do before they die. For children with a terminal illness, the Make-A-Wish Foundation pays for an individual and their family to make a dream come true. What are some things you'd like to do or see before dying? What prevents us from doing what we most want to do?

4. Though Violet admits envy drove her away from her sister, she also admits it was envy that pushed her to work hard to achieve her goals. What are some examples where envy positively affected your life? What are some examples where envy negatively affected your life? What is the difference between envy and jealousy? Or is there a difference?

5. In the novel, Michelle and Drew are making some sacrifices in order for Michelle to pursue her dreams of going to medical school and becoming a doctor. In our country, some families can afford expensive schooling for their children while others cannot, leaving some students to have to take on large amounts of debt to earn a higher education degree. Should the price of college be free or reduced at public universities? What benefits or problems might arise from free college?

6. We have become a society that demands justice. But "right" and "wrong" can be relative terms. After the Phillips family is almost robbed, Pastor Jedidiah not only insists on letting the young man who attempted to rob them go, but also gives him money and offers him help and counseling at his church. Should we have alternative punishments for certain crimes? Should mental health and life circumstance be a determining factor when implementing appropriate punishments for criminal offenses?

7. In the novel, Indigo hears a voice that is not hers. Do you think it's possible for us to receive messages through a voice in our head? Have you ever felt intuition or guidance from an outside source that you couldn't see or identify?

8. While thinking about life without her sister, Indigo tells a classmate, "Imagine being the sun. But pretend it's four billion years from now and you're all outta fuel. A sun with no hydrogen—*cooling*. Your sun days are almost over. Do you bow out gracefully and simply explode? Or should you search for another thing to be?" (Page 41) What do you think Indigo is attempting to convey with this statement?

9. Indigo wonders if she really hears the voice of God or whether it's just the voice in her head that we all tend to hear. "'**Well...**' The Voice pauses. '**Maybe they're one and the same.**'" (Page 307) Do you think Indigo was actually hearing the voice of a higher power? Or do you think Indigo was being guided by nothing more than her own intuition? What about the story made you feel one way or the other?

RESOURCES

It is your right to live.

If you or someone you know is in emotional distress, crisis centers across the country can offer assistance 24/7 via call or live chat.

Suicide Prevention Lifeline:
(800) 273-8255
https://suicidepreventionlifeline.org/

Society for the Prevention of Teen Suicide:
http://www.sptsusa.org/you-are-not-alone/

American Foundation for Suicide Prevention:
https://afsp.org